A HISTORY OF THE POLISH REVOLUTION OF 1830

BY

JOSEPH HORDYNSKI

MAJOR OF THE LATE TENTH REGIMENT
OF LITHUANIAN LANCERS

Cover Design by Dr. George F. Nafziger

Originally Published Copyright (C) 2007
Winged Hussar Edition © 2017

Printed in the United States of America

ISBN 978-1-9454303-2-9
LOC 2017952469

We are interested in hearing from authors with book ideas.

Published by The Nafziger Collection, Inc.
PO Box 1522, West Chester, OH 45069-1522

in conjunction with

Winged Hussar Publishing, LLC
1525 Hulse Road, Unit 1, Pt. Pleasant, NJ 08742

Cover art: Painting by Kossak Wojciech; *Battle of Grokow, 25 February 1831.*

Notes on this Edition.

The original title of the work is *History of the Late Polish Revolution and the Events of the Campaign.* It was published in 1832, one year after the end of the Polish Revolution and was part of the common practice of this period where military officers wrote books of the wars to supplement the newspapers of the day. The author, Joseph Hordynski, was a participant in the war and had a first-hand view of its events. However, as he was not present at every battle and every event he discusses, he was obliged to consult both newspapers of the day and other participants. It is subject to the errors that result from the absence of access to archival materials, but it is an important eyewitness account.

This work has had its spellings updated and some grammatical errors corrected. Otherwise, it is an intact transcription of the original work. The quality of the maps in that manuscript was not particularly high and what could be done to salvage or improve them has been done.

UNITED STATES OF AMERICA.

LIBERATED from prison, and from the prospect of a gloomier future by some of your fellow citizens, I have been so fortunate as to reach these happy shores. Providence has granted me to behold that fair country, and that nation, which every lover of freedom desires to see with his own eyes, and every freeman of Poland is wont to think of with love and esteem. Your land, long since the asylum of the persecuted, has welcomed me with hearty benevolence. From the first moment of my arrival to the present time, I have received daily proofs of your sympathy. Full of gratitude, and in the hope of doing you an acceptable service, I cannot better employ the moments allowed me during my stay among you, then by giving you a faithful account of our revolution, and of its true causes and motives, as well as of the events of war by which it was followed. By a brief statement of the circumstances which brought about that revolution, I wish to inform you of the injustice and outrages, which my nation was compelled to endure, during fourteen years, in which both its natural rights, and the constitution solemnly guarantied to it, were trampled underfoot. By a true account of the events of the ensuing war, you will be enabled to convince yourselves of the means by which small forces became victorious over a colossal power, as well as of the causes of the final catastrophe to which Poland has been doomed.

I am convinced that in many respects my narrative will be entirely opposed to the representations given in public papers; for our land, like most countries struggling for liberty, was surrounded by enemies rather than friends. The sources from which these accounts, have been drawn, are, first, my own recollections of events of which I was an eyewitness; secondly, the reports of my friends and comrades who were present; and lastly, (particularly as to the operations of the detached corps) the official reports of the army, which have not yet escaped my memory. The same course I have followed in the design of the plans, which have been traced partly from my own recollections of positions and scenes at which I was present, partly from the accurate reports of friends, and partly from public reports, assisted by my personal knowledge of localities.

Americans, - I am neither an author nor a scholar by profession, but a simple republican and soldier. In such and one you will forgive faults in the form and style of writing. Do not then judge me as a writer, but see in me an unhappy Pole, who presents to your sympathies the picture of the fatal disasters of his unfortunate country, and of the manner in which it strove to regain its liberty, that first and greatest of national blessings. In this hope of your indulgence, I beg you to accept this work as a token of my gratitude and as a memorial of my short stay among you, as well as an expression of the great esteem, with which I shall always remain,

Americans, your devoted servant,

JOSEPH HORDYNSKI.

To the gentlemen who have aided me by the translation, the execution of the plates, and the publication of the work, I offer the only recompense which they will permit me to make—my heartfelt thanks; and I assure them that in the feelings which prompt this acknowledgement, all my comrades will participate.

CONTENTS

correspondence between the ministers Grabowski and Lubecki. - The march of the army delayed. - Answer of the Emperor Nicholas to the Deputies. - His proclamation. - Its effect on the nation. - The Diet demand of the Dictator an account of his trust. - The result of their investigations. - Chlopicki deprived of the Dictatorial power. - The civil administration entrusted to Prince Adam Csartoryaki, and the command of the army to Prince Michael Radzivil, each subordinate to the Diet.

CHAPTER V.......67

Remarks on the policy of the late Dictator. - System of operations adopted. - The army leaves Warsaw. - Statement of the existing forces. - Of the forces proposed to be raised. - Unfortunate consequences of the delay in the preparation of the forces. - Statement of the voices with which the war was actually commenced.

CHAPTER VI.......75

Entrance of the Russian forces into the Kingdom. - Proclamation of Marshal Diebitsch. - Their effect. - Disposition of the Russian and Polish forces. —Plan of operations of the Poles.

CHAPTER VII.......85

The opening fire - Affairs of the 10th and 11th February. - Combat of Stoczek. - Disposition in consequence of that battle. - Battle of Bourne. - Retrograde movement to Dobre. - Combat of Makowiec. - Passage of the Orsyca. - Combat of Dobre. - Attack on the right wing at Minsk.

CHAPTER VIII.......95

Retrograde movement of the 18th of February.—Details of this movement, and of the actions which took place.—The army reaches the field of Praga –Its reception at Warsaw.—Position of the army.—Battle of Wawr and Bialolenka.—Operations of General Dwernicki against the corps of Prince Württemberg.-Defeat of that corps by General Dwernicki at Swiena.—Renewal of the enemy's attack on the main army on the 20th.—Its successful resistance.—-Review of the events of the preceding days.—-Examination of the plan of operations of the Polish Army.

CHAPTER IX.......105

Renewal of the enemy's attack on the 20th. - Its result. – Review of the events of the preceding day. – The enemy's loss. – Examination of the plan of operations of the Polish Army. – Neglect of fortifications. – Want of concert in the different operations. – Advantageous offensive operations neglected. – Acts of the National Government. – Provision in lands for the soldiers. – Abolition of the Corvee, &c.. – Marshal Diebitsch remains in a state of inactivity. – Negotiations are opened by him. – His propositions are declined. – Position of the 24th, and battle of Bailolenka.

CHAPTER X.......113

Position of the armies of the 25th. – Great battle of Grokow. – Details. – State of the Russian army after its defeat. – Examination of the plan of the battle of Grokow. –

CHAPTER XIV.......157

The insurrection in Lithuania. - Dispositions of the Lithuanians at the breaking out of our revolution. - Their offers of co-operation were rejected by the Dictator. - View of the condition of Lithuania under the Russian sway. - Scheme of the Russian Government to destroy all Polish national feeling in that province. - The insurrection is brought about by the massacre of the patriots at Osmiany. - Capture of numerous towns by the insurgents, and dispersion of their garrisons. - Storm of Wilna, and delivery of prisoners. - Several partisan corps are formed. - Their destination and successes.

CHAPTER XV.......163

Plan of operation against the two corps of Rosen and Kreutz. - Battle of Tgani. - Reflections on the state of the Polish cause after the victory of Igam. - Review of the course of the campaign. - Condition of the Russian army. - Discontents in Russia. - Representations of the Senate at St Petersburg to the Emperor. - Comparative view of the forces of the two armies at the present stage of the conflict.

CHAPTER XVI.......173

Position of the two armies after the battle of Igam. - Plan of a simultaneous attack upon the Russian forces upon opposite sides. - Instruction to the different corps. - Operations on the enemy's front -Unfortunate operations of General Sierawski, and the first defeat. - Details of those operations. - Operations of General Dwemicki. He defeats Rudiger; but by a false operation exposes himself to be attacked disadvantageous. by two Russian corps. - In the course of the action the Austrian frontier is passed by the combatants. - An Austrian force interposes, and General Dwernicki consents to go into camp. - His arms and prisoners are taken from him, while the enemy is permitted to leave the territory freely. - Reflections on the conduct of Austria. - Consequences of the loss of Dwernicki's corps - The cholera makes its appearance in the two armies.

CHAPTER XVII.......183

The Russian commander resumes offensive operations. - Object of the attack of the 25th of April. - Combat of Kuflew. - General Dembinski evacuates the position of Kuflew and awaits the enemy at Bady. - Battle of Minsk. - The enemy suddenly evacuates his position. - Reflections on this stage of the conflict - Positions of the two armies.

CHAPTER XVIII.......191

General Skrzynecki resumes the offensive. - He decides to adopt an enlarged plan of operations, and to make the revolutionized provinces supply the place of a corps d'armée. - The corps of Chrzsnowski is sent to occupy the Russian corps of Witt and Kreuta. - Admirable execution of this enterprise. - Attack on Kock. - Attack of Rudiger's camp. - Plan of operations by the main army against the Russian Guards - Forced march from Kaluszyn by Praga to Serock. - Advanced post of the Guard attacked and defeated. - The corps of Sacken is cutoff. - The 2nd Division under Gielgud sent into Lithuania. - The Imperial Guard are driven with great loss beyond the frontier. - Retrograde movement.

the small force left there. - Skirmish at Willcomien. - The opportunity of concentrating all the forces at Keydany, and repassing the Niemen, is neglected - The enemy presses his pursuit - Battle of Rosseyny. - Attack on Schawla. - Loss of the ammunition and baggage of the corps. - The corps retreats in order to Kurszany, protected by a rearguard of cavalry and light artillery. At Kurszany the corps is subdivided into three parts. - Destination and strength of each. - Examination of this plan.

CHAPTER XXIV.......245

The three subdivisions of the Lithuanian Corps take their respective destinations - Details of the operations of that of General Rohland. - He meets alone the attack of the whole Russian force. - Battle of Powendnny and Worna. - General Rohland, on his way to Polonga, learns that General Chlapowski had marched towards the Prussian frontier. - He presses his march to overtake and form a junction with him. - The greater part of the corps of Gielgud and Chlapowski were found to have passed the frontier, when that of Rohland came in sight - Indignation of the soldiery. - Death of General Gielgud. - General Rohland, joined by a portion of the corps of Gielgud which had not yet passed the frontier, continues his inarch to Nowe-Miasto. - He declines a proposition from General Kreutz, to surrender. - Successful skirmish with the enemy's cavalry. - General Rohland takes a position at Nowo-Miasto, and awaits the enemy. - The Russian forces, however, do not continue their pursuit, but go into camp. - Propositions to pass the frontier are sent to General Rohland by the Prussian authorities. - They are submitted to the corps, and accepted.

CHAPTER XXV.......255

Effect of the news of the Lithuanian disasters on the minds of the people. - Distrust of the National Government - The Russian army resumes the offensive under general Paskewicz. - He decides to pass the Vistula. - Examination of the merits of this plan. - Plan of General Skrzynecki to act on the different detached corps of the enemy. - Advantages of General Chrzanowski over the corps of Rudiger. - The Russian forces execute the passage of the Vistula. - General Skrzynecki crosses the Vistula at Warsaw to operate against the enemy on the left bank. - An inquiry into the conduct of General Skrzynecki, and the appointment of a Council of War is demanded by the nation. - Arrival of the corps of General Dembinski at Warsaw.

CHAPTER XXVI.......261

Operations of General Dembinski's corps. - He traverses the country between Schavla and the Niemen without being observed by the enemy. - Attacks and disperses a brigade of Russian infantry. - Passes the Niemen and throws himself into the forest of Bialostok. After clearing that forest, is joined by the corps of General Rozychiw - Reaches Warsaw. - His reception at Warsaw. - View of the exposed situation of Peskewics after his passage of the Vistula. - Examination of the plan of operations of the Polish commander - Morbid state of the public mind at Warsaw. - Sknynecki and Czartoriski deprived of their trust - Capture of the city. - Documents showing the influence exercised by the cabinets in discouraging active operations. - Conclusion.

APPENDIX.......271

Jozeph Baron Chlopicki

INTRODUCTION

Geographical extent, population, and political importance of Poland, as anciently constituted. - Conduct of Napoleon in 1812. - Congress of Vienna. - Grand Duchy of Warsaw erected into a kingdom. - Dispositions of Alexander. - Zajaczek appointed Viceroy, and Constantine commander of the army. - Constantine encroaches upon the civil administration. - Acts of tyranny. - Meeting of the Diet - Public debates suppressed. - The Polish Conspiracy of 1821. - The Russian Conspiracy of 1824. - Union of the Patriotic Associations. - Death of Alexander. - The Revolt of St. Petersburg) - Punishment of the Patriots. - Coronation of Nicholas. - Constantine appointed Viceroy of Poland. - Oppressions of the Government - Patriotic Club. - Influence of the French and Belgic Revolutions - The Quartering-tax - Excitement in Warsaw. - Arrest of the Students at Praga. - Day of the Revolution fixed upon,

IN the early part of July 1812, when the victorious armies of Napoleon had occupied Wilna, and threatened to annihilate the throne of the Czars, the Polish nation cherished the hope of recovering its former grandeur. The destiny of Poland was then in the hands of Napoleon, and it may be said with truth that on the destiny of Poland depended the security and peace of Europe.

Poland, as is well known to the reader, viewed in regard to its geographical situation and extent, as formerly constituted, forms a strong outwork against the Russian colossus. Its territories extend to the eastward as far as the Dneiper, and westward as far as the Oder. Toward the north, they reach the Baltic and the government of Skoff, and their southern frontiers are the Carpathian Mountains and the Black Sea. This vast region, composed of the present Kingdom of Poland, the Grand Duchy of Posen, of Samogitia, Lithuania, Livonia, White Russia and Black Russia, Volhynia, Podolia, Ukraine, and Gallicia, is inhabited by twenty-two million. Poles of the same descent, the same manners and customs, and the same language and religion. According to its ancient limits, the Kingdom of Poland is among the first in Europe with regard to population and geographical extent.

The deputies, who, at the period above named, were sent from Warsaw to the Emperor Napoleon, laid before him the most earnest solicitations for the restoration of this state, and endeavored to direct his views to the future, in order to convince him of its necessity. They concluded with the following words; -"Dites, Sire, que le royaume de Pologne existé, et ce decret sera pour le monde l'equivalent de la réalité." To this he answered; -" Dans ma situation, j'ai beaucoup d'interêts à concilier, beaucoup de devoirs à remplir. Si j'avais regné pendant le premier, le second, ou le troisieme

13

partage de la Pologne, j'aurais arme mes peuples pour la defendre. J'aime votre nation, j'autorise les efforts que vous voulez faire. C'est entièrment dans l'unanimité de sa population, que vous pourez trouver l'espoir de succes. Je dois ajouter que j'ai guaranti a l'empereur d'Autriche integrité de ses domaines."[1]

Such a reply from Napoleon, the Poles could never have expected. For, who accompanied him so faithfully in all his expeditions as the sons of Poland? Thousands of Poles lie buried in Italy, Egypt, St. Domingo, Spain, and Russia, who had fought for the integrity of the French Republic and for the aggrandizement of Napoleon. His cold reception of the deputies of Poland filled all patriots with sadness. They were now convinced, that the good wishes of Napoleon for Poland were not sincere, and that, through his marriage with Maria Louisa, he had come under Austrian influence. Thus, the hope of territorial enlargement and national existence vanished away, and Napoleon, by his indifference to the interests of Poland, accelerated his own fall. The burning of Moscow, which was a chance that did not enter into his calculations, became the turning point of his fate. The Poles, who had contributed to his greatness, did not desert him in his distress; they were his companions to the very last. Half a squadron of them followed him to Elba, at his own request. The disasters of France decided the fate of Poland. By the Congress of Vienna, the Grand Duchy of Warsaw was made into a kingdom, and subjected to the iron scepter of Russia.

At the first moment of entering upon the government of the Kingdom, the Emperor Alexander seemed disposed to load Poland with benefits. On his return from Paris he was received by the inhabitants of Warsaw with the most unfeigned goodwill, and his stay in that city was marked by acts of beneficence. The words with which he then addressed the representatives of the nation, are still in the memory of every Pole. - *"Gentlemen, I respect and love your nation. To these feelings on my part, in which all Europe partakes, you are entitled by your continual and disinterested sacrifices for the prosperity of other nations. I swear to maintain your constitution with all the privileges guarantied by it; and this same constitution I promise to grant to your brethren in the provinces, which are to be united with you in one kingdom."* The nation believed in these promises the more readily as the affectionate deportment of the monarch seemed to confirm them. During his stay in Warsaw, he paid visits to several of the most popular and patriotic families and individuals, and everywhere express-ed himself in terms of the highest esteem for the Polish nation.

This show of benevolence, and the dreams of happiness with which it inspired the people, were not, however, of long duration. Before his departure from Warsaw, the Emperor named as Viceroy of Poland the old General Zajaczek[2], raising him to the dignity of a Prince, and his own brother, the Grand Duke Constantine, as Commander-in-Chief of the Polish Army. The appointment of these persons to the supreme power was already in direct opposition to all the promises he had made. For Zajaczek, through the infirmities of his advanced age, was unfit for the post of viceroy, and could be but an instrument in Russian hands; while in Constantine, the Commander-in-Chief of their army, the Poles received a tyrant.

Not long after the departure of Alexander, the encroachments of the Russian cabinet began to be felt. Removals of officers took place in all the branches of government, in particular of those known as patriots, who were supplanted by minions of Russia, men full of ambition and intrigue. In the first year of the Russian Government, the bureau of Police was enlarged, and filled with persons whom the nation despised. The Polish Army, which had gathered laurels in so many countries of the three continents, and which was held in such high estimation by the first monarch and general in Europe, was exposed, on the very first days of the new government, to the insults of Constantine. There was not an officer, but was grossly offended by the Grand Duke, and more than all, those who wore military decorations for their merits. No past services were valued; they only exposed those who were distinguished by them to greater persecution. In the first six months, many officers, among whom was the renowned General Sokolnicki, committed suicide; and nearly one half the officers and generals asked their dismission, among whom was General, the late Dictator, Chlopicki, who preferred poverty and want to such an ignominious service. The Polish Army, those soldiers animated by feelings of honor and the love of distinction, were to be transformed into the machines of despotism. They who had faced death in so many battles, who were covered with wounds, and who had been called "brethren" by the greatest leader of his age, were now to be beaten with the Russian knout. In the first year, few days passed in which some of the soldiers did not commit suicide.

This Prince, who appeared not to find victims enough for his cruelty in the army, began to meddle with all the branches of administration, and to control them. Soon the liberty of the press was prohibited, freemasonry was interdicted, and a Bureau of. Spies was established. The chief in this Bureau of Spies were Rozniecki, the vice-president of the city of Warsaw, Lubowidzki, a man of the name of Macrot, and Schlee. From the documents found upon Schlee and Macrot, it was ascertained that there were in Warsaw alone 900 spies. In the provinces, their number amounted to 2000. The expenses and salaries of these spies, according to accounts found among their papers, drew from the public treasury $1,000,000, or 6,000,000 Polish gilders. Thus, our poor country, instead of employing her resources for the happiness of her children, was forced to pay the mercenaries hired to distress them. Soon Warsaw and the whole kingdom became one vast prison. These spies endeavored to steal into every company, and were present in all public places. They tried to catch every conversation, and distorted every word spoken, with however innocent an intention, in regard to the policy and administration of the country. In order to extort money, they accused some of the most respected and honest persons, who were thrown into prison, and many of whom were never again seen by their families, from the midst of whom they had been dragged in the night-time, in order to conceal the crime from the eyes of the world. Persons who did not take off their hats in the streets before the Grand Duke, were compelled to draw barrows of mud upon the public places. There passed hardly a month in which some students were not arrested, and, without any trial, at the mere denunciation of a hireling spy, thrown into prison, where they lingered for years. Thus, faded away in dungeons many fair and hopeful youths, the flower of our nation. In Warsaw, besides the public gaols, there were, beneath almost all of the barracks, prisons, where the victims of tyranny were tortured. The very orangery of the Grand Duke was transformed into a prison, from which some persons were liberated during the revolution, who had been confined there for years. It was in

15

this prison that Lukasinski had been kept for a long time, though subsequently bound to a cannon and carried into Russia. In the gaols below the barracks of the artillery many dead bodies were found.

At the first meeting of the Diet, when the Grand Duke Constantine was among the deputies from the city of Praga, and debates commenced on various subjects which concerned the welfare of the country, - such as, the liberty of the press, the abolition of the central police and the spies, and the deposition of several of the higher officers, for which petitions had been sent to the monarch, - a decision was promulgated that the Diet should act in subordination to the will of the Grand Duke, and, in order to add force to this decision, the palace and its galleries were surrounded and filled by guards. All public debates during the session were prohibited, and a ticket from the police was required for admission. These tickets were distributed among Russian generals, officers of government and their families, and creatures of the court. Before such an auditory, discussions of the most sacred interest to the nation were to take place. No patriot could behold, without tears, the senators and fathers of the nations, descendants of Tarnowski, Zamoyski, Chodkiewicz, and Kosciuzko, sitting with sad and drooping countenances, exposed to the scoffing and laughter of those minions of the court. The sacred halls were transformed into a theatre for Russian spectators.

In all the different bureaus, spies held important offices, and thus those bureaus became scenes of the most detestable intrigues. Law and right were trampled underfoot, and the constitution itself was derided. They used to express themselves in the following and similar terms: - "What is the constitution? It is an impediment to the administration of the government, and the course of justice. The Grand Duke is the best constitution."

A few years had passed away in this wretched state of the nation, when, towards 1821, our noble patriots, Krzyzanowski, Jablonowski, Plichta, Debek, and Soltyk, conceived the idea of emancipating their country by a revolution. Whilst occupied with their noble scheme, they were most agreeably surprised by receiving information, in 1824, of a similar patriotic union in Russia for throwing off the yoke of despotism. Their joy was increased when they received a summons from this patriotic union in Russia, at the head of which were Pestel, Releiew, Bestuzew, Kichelbeker, Murawiew, and Kachowski, to join hands with them. This junction was effected in Kiev, on the day of the great fair, when Prince Jablonowski became acquainted with some of their members, and was initiated into their plans. The invitation was received by the Poles with delight. Accustomed to combat for liberty, they offered with their whole hearts their aid in the redemption of the Sarmatic nation from the chains by which they bad been so long bound down.

Soon after this, it was agreed to meet in the town of Orla, in the province of Little Russia, where solemn oaths were sworn to sacrifice life and property in the cause. Resolutions were taken, and the means of their execution were devised. The Russians promised to the Poles, in case of success, the surrender of all the provinces as far as the frontiers which Boleslaw-Chrobry had established. This promise, as well as that of eternal friendship between the two brother-nations, was sanctioned by the solemnity of oaths. The day fixed upon for the breaking out of the revolution, was the 25th anniversary of the accession of Alexander, in the month of May 1826 and Biala-Cerkiew in Volhynia was the place selected for the first blow. The reason for choosing this place, was, that the whole imperial family and the greater part of the army were to assemble there, on the great plain of the Dneiper, to celebrate the anniversary of the coronation. This occasion was to be improved, to gain over all the well-disposed generals, and at the same time to secure the imperial family. In the meeting at Orla, it was required of the Poles, that, at the moment of the breaking out of the revolution, they should take the life of the Grand Duke Constantine. To this proposition, however, Prince Jablonowski answered in these well known words: *"Russians, brother Sarmatians, you have summoned us to co-operate in the holy work of breaking the bonds of slavery under which our Sarmatic race has so long pined. We come to you with sincere hearts, willing to sacrifice our fortunes and lives. Rely, my dear friends, on this our promise. The many struggles in which we have already fought for the sake of liberty, may warrant our assertions. Brethren, you demand of us to murder the Grand Duke. This we can never do. The Poles have never stained their hands with the blood of their Princes. We promise you to secure his person in the moment of the revolution, and, as he belongs to you, we shall deliver him into your hands."*

The patriotic associations on both sides endeavored to increase their party, by the initiation of many brave men in the army and in civil life. In Lithuania, the respectable president of the nobles, Downarowicz, and the noble Rukiewicz of the Lithuanian Corps, with many other officers, were admitted into the conspiracy, among others Jgelstrom, Wigielin, Hoffman, and Wielkaniec. All the plans for the approaching revolution were arranged with the utmost circumspection, and every circumstance seemed to promise success, when the sudden death of the Emperor Alexander, at Taganrog, in the early part of December, 1825, darkened our bright hopes.

The news of his death had, at first, a stunning effect upon the Patriotic Club in Petersburg. Nevertheless, they resolved to act. They hoped to profit by the troubles between Constantine and Nicholas, about the succession. On the 18th of December of the same year, the "signal for revolt" was given in Petersburg. Some regiments of the guard were on the side of the patriots, and with them assembled great numbers of the people ready to fight for liberty. Yet all this was done without sufficient energy, and without good leaders. It was unfortunate, that at the time, Colonel Pestel, acknowledged by all to be a man of great talents and energy, happened to be absent in Moscow. The people assembled in their holy cause, but, being without leaders, began to fall into disorder, and a few discharges of cannon were sufficient to disperse them.

As the Grand Duke Constantine, on account of his marriage with a noble Polish lady, Grudzinska, in 1823, was obliged to renounce the throne of Russia, the imperial power was, by a written document, given to the Grand Duke Nicholas, as the eldest in succession after him.

Some days after the proclamation of Nicholas, all the prisons of the realm were prepared to receive their new inmates. Petersburg, Moscow, Wilna, Kiev, Bialystok, and Warsaw, were appointed for the places of trial. Over the whole of Poland and Russia the sword of cruel revenge was suspended. In Petersburg, the martyrs of liberty, Pestel, Muraview, Releiew, Bestuzew, Kachowski, were hung on the gallows, and more than two hundred persons of the noblest families were sent to Siberia. In Wilna, Eiow, and Moscow, an immense number were thrown into prison, or transported to Siberia. In Bialystok, the Russian general, Wiliaminow, was appointed an inquisitor. This infamous character treated the wretched prisoners with the utmost cruelty, Rukiewicz[3], Jgelstrom, and Wigelin, were exiled to Siberia for life,

In Warsaw, the Grand Duke himself undertook the business of establishing an inquisition over the unhappy prisoners. This court was composed of persons in the Russian interest, a circumstance, the melancholy consequences of which soon became manifest. Senator Soltyk, an old man seventy years of age, was flogged with the knout. Krzyzanowski, unable to endure the tortures inflicted upon him, committed suicide. General Procurator Wyezechowski, that unworthy son of Poland, sentenced all who were condemned to death, to be hung on gallows, and their bodies to be exposed upon the wheel. This horrid sentence, however, was, notwithstanding all the Grand Duke's influence, mitigated by the Supreme Court of the Senate, which still contained many worthy men under the presidency of the venerable woye-wode, Bilinski. The infamous Wyezechowski was unable to oppose this virtuous old man, whose powerful eloquence was a mirror of his noble heart. President Bilinski, fearless of the threats of the Russians, whose briberies he was accustomed to treat with disdain, guided by the articles of the criminal code, altered the sentence of death to a few years imprisonment. This mitigation of the sentence was signed by all the senators, with one exception.[4]

After Nicholas had ascended the throne over steps of blood, he was crowned, in 1826, Emperor of Russia. Two years after this, in 1828, he was again crowned in Warsaw as King of Poland. This monarch at first intended not to go through with the ceremony of the coronation in Warsaw, in order to avoid the Oath of the Constitution. Yet, from fear of revolutionary scenes, he suffered himself to be persuaded to do it, and took the oath, like his predecessor and brother, Alexander, to maintain the constitution and the privileges guarantied by it.

Poland may have suffered under Alexander; yet be loved the nation like a friend, as everyone of my countrymen will allow. When he was mistaken in his measures, it was, that, surrounded by bad men and enemies of our nation, he was prevented from knowing the truth. He was himself too much engrossed in pleasures, to visit the hut of the poor in order to obtain information of his condition. Poland forgave him all his faults, in the grateful recollection that he had restored her to a separate existence, and respected the constitution. Far different in our eyes appeared the present Emperor, Nicholas. Partaking of the errors of his predecessor, he exhibited none of his virtues. Alexander, with a benignant countenance, permitted everyone to approach him freely, and his features were never distorted by passion. Nicholas, on the contrary, seemed to terrify by his very look. His lowering and overbearing eye was the true mirror of Asiatic despotism. Every movement was that of command; and his imperious air was in true harmony with the ruling passion of his mind. Such a sovereign, acting through the instrumentality of a brother like himself, the Grand Duke Constantine, must needs bring distress upon our country. Whole volumes might be filled with the relation of the atrocities of this government. The daily increasing host of spies in its employ, among whom even females were. found, regarded nothing as sacred, and mocked at the most holy institutions. They lavished away millions of the public funds. Everything was permitted to them. In short, the intention of this government seemed to be to plunge our country into the deepest distress, in order to force us to the abandonment of every national feeling, and to make us slaves of the Russians. Yet in this hope they were deceived. The more the nation was oppressed[5], the more its energy of character was steeled, and the more the love of country developed itself.

Two worthy sons of Poland, Wysocki and Schlegel, mourning over the martyrdom of Krzyzanowoski, Soltyk, Dembek, and Plichta, and meditating on the distresses of their country, resolved to attempt its deliverance. By these two young champions of Poland, the first idea of the revolution was conceived. They communicated their hopes to several other patriots, and thus was formed the Patriotic Club. This association, nourishing in their secret breasts the holy spark of liberty, increased it soon to a flaming light, by which the whole nation was led to honor and glory. These heroic men fearlessly persevered in their endeavors, during five years, exposed to the greatest dangers and amidst thousands of spies. Witnesses of the continually aggravated oppression of their country, they became more and more animated to risk everything for their holy object.

While this tyrannical government was exulting in the success of its measures, and the honor and morals of our country were fast declining, the revolution of France occurred, and it instantly roused every mind to a comparison of our state with that of the French, who had thrown off the yoke of a Machiavellian dynasty. The three days of July were days of joy, not only to every brave son of France, but to every patriotic heart in Poland.

How much were they enraptured, who hitherto in secret had been laboring for the redemption of their country! The happy result of those glorious days was a peal of terror to the Grand Duke Constantine, and to the whole swarm of agents in his tyrannical sway. It gave them a presage of their approaching retribution. Yet, instead of adopting milder measures, and endeavoring to propitiate the nation, their cruelties went on as before. The government had, indeed, advanced too far in its barbarous system to draw back. The activity of the spies was redoubled. From the first reception of the news of the French revolution, there did not pass a day on which some persons were not imprisoned in Warsaw or the provinces. On the night of the 7th of September, forty students were seized in their beds and carried to prison.

Again, the new revolutionary eruption of Belgium cheered and encouraged the heart of every patriotic Pole. The hour for throwing off the yoke of tyranny was fast approaching. The leaders of the revolution succeeded in communicating their sentiments to continually increasing numbers. Many officers of the 4th Regiment of the Line and of the sappers were initiated. Yet at this very time, when the revolution was every moment expected to break out, the Russian despot, in concert with Prussia and Austria, commenced his preparations for a war against France and Belgium. The Polish Army was destined to serve as the vanguard of this expedition, and Modlin and

Warsaw were stored with large quantities of arms and ammunition from Russia. All the regiments were completed, and the order for marching was momentarily expected.

These circumstances attracted the notice of our patriots, and they decided to accelerate the revolution, in order to anticipate the march of the army. The eruption was hastened by the following event. The citizens of Warsaw were obliged to furnish quarters for the officers of the army. To lighten this burden, and to avoid various inconveniences, as well as to accommodate the officers, - by an understanding with the inhabitants, it was determined, that instead of furnishing quarters, a quartering tax should be paid. It was intended in this regulation to proportion the tax to the size of the houses, and consequently to the profit which the proprietors would derive from letting them. The tax would in this way be equalized, because, wherever levied, it would be attended by a proportionate compensa-tion, and it was satisfactory to the inhabitants. This regulation, however, was executed in an entirely different manner. In many cases the heavier taxes were paid by the poorer inhabitants, and indeed they had sometimes to provide quarters in addition to the payment of the tax. All the persons employed by the police as spies, and who had by vile means acquired immense fortunes and kept the finest houses in Warsaw, were exempt both from the tax and the providing of quarters. The money collected for the tax was purloined by the commissioners for quartering, who thus amassed millions of gilders.[6]

A short time before the revolution, the gross impositions of this commission were discovered. The inhabitants of Warsaw began to murmur against it, and addressed the government for the removal of the persons employed, and the substitution of others in their places, who should be deserving of the confidence of the citizens. Among others, the de-position of the president of the city, Woyda, was demanded; and when the government refused to comply with the request, he was publicly insulted and flogged in the streets. The discontent of the citizens, in particular of the poorer classes, continued to increase, and of this discontent the patriots made use in endeavoring to propagate their views of the necessity of a revolution. Public opinion was from day to day expressed more boldly. Papers were pasted up in the streets, with inscriptions such as these: - "The dwelling of the Grand Duke will be let from next New Year's Day." - "Away with the tyrants! Away with the barbarians to Asia!" A great concourse of citizens assem-bled one evening before the city hall, and demanded the punishment of the quartering commissioner, Czarnccki, who, in his desperation, committed suicide.

The holy moment was now fast approaching, and Warsaw was in anxious expectation. Fear and terror was painted in the faces of the spies, while, on the other hand, all true patriots were in raptures of joy, and waited impatiently for the moment to strike the blow. For several nights, the whole garrison of the city had been under arms, by the orders of the Grand Duke, who, tortured with the consciousness of so many crimes, had no rest, and surrounded himself with large bodies of guards. A hundred gens d'armes were on horseback for many nights, constantly bringing in their victims. Strong patrols of Russian soldiers traversed the streets. All was in vain. His mercenaries could not protect the tyrant. The word was given, the oath was sworn, to fight for our sacred rights and the freedom of our country.

An event which served to irritate all minds, and hasten the revolution, was the arrest and imprisonment of eighty students. These brave young men were assembled in a private house, in order to pray to God in secret for the souls of their murdered ancestors, on the anniversary of the storming of Praga, by the bloody Suvaròv, in 1796, when none were spared, and Praga swam with blood, and was strewed with the corpses of 30,000 of its inhabitants. Neither old men, women, children, nor pregnant mothers, were spared by the barbarous Russian soldiers. In memory of this event, the patriots had every year met for secret prayer, since public devotions on the occasion had been forbidden by the Grand Duke. The above-mentioned students, with some priests, were in the act of worship, praying to the Almighty, and honoring the memory of their forefathers, when the doors were broken open with great violence, and a number of gens d'armes, under their captain, Jurgaszko, with a company of Russian soldiers behind them, entered the apartment. Our brave youths continued their prayers upon their knees about the altar, and in that position suffered themselves to be bound, and dragged away to prison. But this was the last act of cruelty the Russian Government was permitted to perpetrate, for it exhausted the patience of the nation. The measure was full, and the hour of retribution was at hand. The news of this outrage was spread through Warsaw with the quickness of lightning, and it thrilled every heart. This was the occasion for fixing upon the 29th of November, as the day for commencing the revolution, on which day the 4th Polish Regiment, many of the officers of which were among the initiated, were to mount guard in Warsaw.

21

NOTES

1. "Say, Sir, that the Kingdom of Poland exists and that declaration will be, in the eyes of the world, the equivalent of the reality." To this he answered: - "In my situation I have many interests to conciliate, many duties to fulfill. If I had reigned during the first, the second, or the third partition of Poland, I would have armed my people to defend her. I love your nation; I authorize the efforts which you wish to make. It is alone in the unanimity of your population that you will find the hope of suc¬cess. I ought to add that I have guarantied to the Emperor of Austria the integrity of his dominions."

2. Zajaczek commenced his military career in the time of Koscusko, continued it among the Polish legions, and accompanied Napoleon to Egypt, where he served with distinction. He was present in all the later campaigns of Napoleon, till 1809, when he returned, on account of his advanced age and the loss of one of his legs.

3. This nobleman (Rukiewicz) had two beautiful sisters, Cornelia and Theresa, whose heroic behavior deserves to be recorded. He was secretary of the Patriotic Club in Lithuania, and kept the records and papers of the society in the village where he lived, near Bialystok; and in order to do this business without disturb¬ance, he had prepared a little summer-house in the garden near his mansion. He happened to be from home when arrested, and immediately after his arrest, the police sent a Russian officer with gens d'armes to his village, in order to take possession of his papers. His sisters, who were ignorant of the event, were quietly at home when they beheld the officer with his suite riding into the courtyard. A presaging fear of the truth seized them, but gave place immediately to a heroic resolution. The younger remained in the room in border to receive and detain these agents of tyranny, whilst the elder, Cornelia, carried in haste some combustibles to the summer-house, which was soon on fire, and more than two hundred persons, whose names were contained in the register, were thus saved by the presence of mind of that heroic lady. She returned to the parlor with the noblest and most delighted men, and, on the officer's inquiring as to the cause of the fire, she answered with a smile, "Gentlemen, I only wanted to save you the trouble of some further brutalities. I have burnt the papers and documents of my brother. You may be sure not to find any-thing left; and now I am your prisoner. Drag me along with you, to increase the number of your victims." Both the ladies were carried to prison, and treated in the most unworthy manner during three years. When these noble sisters were dismissed from prison, they found themselves bereft of every consolation. They had no parents left. Their only brother, who had been both parent and brother to them, was now gone. They could not endure the thought of leaving him to pine away so far from them in chains, and they resolved to partake and thus to relieve his sufferings. Regardless of the remonstrances of their friends, they left everything, and traveling in the humblest manner, mostly on foot or upon the wagons of the peasantry, they under took the journey to Siberia. It is not known whether Providence granted them to reach their beloved brother or not.

4. To this court, which was called the Supreme Court of the Diet, and which was established in order to try these prisoners of state, was appointed General Count Vincenti Krasinski, a man of great merit, a brave soldier as well as a good citizen, and on this account very much beloved by the nation. The soldiers, indeed, regarded him as a father. Yet this man could so far forget him¬self as to take up the bloody pen to sign the death of his fellow citizens—the only one of his nation. It is with painful feelings that I name him in this narrative as the enemy of his country, after having been faithful to it for fifty years, and after having made for it the greatest sacrifices. Vincenti Krasinski, whom his country has erased, as a lost son, from the register of her children, is a strong example of the great power of Russian seduction.

5. As already remarked, it would be impossible to describe the various kinds of cruelty exercised by the Russian Government. Yet, in order to make the reader acquainted with some of them, I shall here state a few facts. - In our country, the distilling and brewing of spirituous liquors, and the planting of tobacco, as well as the sale of these articles, was a privilege of the landed propri¬etors. Warsaw, as the capital and the most populous city, was the best market for these productions, and all the noblemen en¬deavored to bring their produce to Warsaw for sale. In this manner, they supplied themselves with money and enhanced the value of their grain, while their liquors, as well as tobacco, could be sold at very low prices, to the pecuniary benefit of all the labor¬ing classes and the soldiery. These advantages, however, soon became an object of attention to the government agents. One of their number, the Jew, Nowachow-iez, who, by the greatest impo¬sitions, had acquired an immense fortune, devised a plan for mo¬nopolizing the production and sale of every kind of liquor and of tobacco. He obtained the exclusive right of selling them, and all the noblemen were forbidden to dispose of these articles without his permission, for which a duty was to be paid. For the monopoly, he paid to the government 2,000,000 of Polish gilders ($333,833.13) for which he more than doubly indemnified himself by the enormous taxes levied upon the consumers of these articles. This innovation, so oppressive to the poorer classes, and invented merely to enrich this Jew and his partners, irritated all the land proprietors, and still more the laboring classes, who were suffer¬ing by it. For two years in succession petitions were made for the reformation of these abuses, but the government only insisted upon the prohibition with the greater severity. Nowachowiez, indeed, employed a guard, who wore uniforms. All the environs of Warsaw were filled with these guards, and the greatest exces¬ses were committed bv them. A poor day-laborer, after having purchased at some distance from the city, some brandy and tobacco, carried these articles at evening to Warsaw. On his way he was stopped by these men. They took all from him, and demanded a heavier fine than the articles were worth. . As the poor man was unable to pay the fine, they abused him, and were about to carry him to prison. He succeeded, however, in making his escape, and, as it was in the vicinity of the residence of a nobleman by the name of Biernacki, he sought shelter on his estate. The guards in pursuit entered the mansion of this nobleman. Bier¬nacki heard the tumult of the guard seizing and roughly handling the poor man, and, ascertaining the cause of the disturbance, he censured them for their inhumanity about such a trifle. In order, however, to save the man from fur-ther insults, he retained him, with the intention of sending him the next day with a note to Nowachowiez for his exculpation. The very moment that Bier¬nacki was occupied in writing the letter, an officer of the gens d'armes, with four privates, stepped in. Biernacki inquired the cause of this visit, and was told in answer, that he was arrested for having protected a defrauder. Thus, surrounded by four sol-diers, this man was publicy carried through Warsaw to the prison of the Carmelites. Not satisfied with this, Nowachowiez suc¬ceeded in obtaining from the Grand Duke, who hated Biernacki as a patriotic Pole, a squadron of Russian Uhlans, consisting of 200 horse, to quarter for a whole week on his estate, in execution, as it is termed. The Russian soldiers took possession of all the buildings on the estate. In the apartments which they used for barracks, they broke all the furniture, lustres, pianos, etc. and carried in their straw for sleeping. In the courtyard they made a fire, for which they used the pieces of furniture for fuel. They took the wheat from the barns to feed their horses, and butchered the cattle. In short, the most shameful depredations and excesses were committed by officers and soldiers, regardless of the situation of the lady of this nobleman, who was confined in childbed, and who for a whole year was in danger of her life from the conse¬quences of her terror.   This barbarous order of the Grand Duke ruined the fortune of that unhappy man and the amount of his property destroyed may be estimated at least at from 70,000 to 80,000 gilders. Biernacki was imprisoned for a whole year, after which he was dismissed to weep over the sufferings of his wife, and his ruined fortune. The poor offender was punished with 800 blows of the knout, of which he died in a few days.

The second story perhaps surpasses the former in cruelty, and would suit the times of Nero. General Rozniecki, and the vice president of the city of Warsaw, Lubowiecki, had their agents, who traveled through the country in order to superintend the services of the secret police. Among them wa3 a Jew, named Birnbaum, whose crimes surpass conception. He traveled through the whole country, and everywhere found pretexts for accusa¬tions against the noblemen, who had to pay him fines to secure themselves from prison. He took up vast sums, that were never accounted for to his superiors. They were divided with Roz¬niecki, Lubowiecki, Macrot, and Schlee, with some Russian gene¬rals, and the servants of the Grand Duke, Kochanowski and Trize, all of whom, like this Jew, made immense fortunes, some of them to the amount of hundreds of thousands. When, in order to encourage the manufactures of the country, the importation of all broadcloths, cotton and linen goods were forbidden, Birnbaum, in secret understanding with his superiors, found out the way of drawing to himself the greatest advantages from this decree. He persuaded two other Jews, by the promise of a part of the gain, and of his protection, to smuggle these articles and to sell them among the gentry of the country. A place on the frontiers was selected for a depot of these contraband wares, which the country noblemen purchased in ignorance of their unlawful importation, and induced by their low prices. On a sudden, Birnbaum visited these districts, examined the warehouses of the noblemen, found the contraband goods, and forced them to the alternative of either paying him a large sum of money or going to prison. Many, for the sake of peace, paid the fines imposed; others, who refused, were imprisoned. By such means, this Jew, as was found afterwards by the records and documents of the police, brought to prison more than a hundred persons, who were treated in the most barbarous manner. They had no food given them but her¬rings without water, and many of these unfortunate persons died in consequence. At last Birnbaum fell out with his accomplices, on occasion of the division of profits. He had them, likewise, thrown into prison to perish there. Their families, however, accused him at their Kahal, or Council of the Jews, and by means of money contrived to have him arrested. He was poi¬soned in his prison, as many persons of consequence were found to be implicated in his impositions

(The Kahal is a Jewish court of administration composed of the elders, who are responsible to the government for their nation and are of great authority.)

6. One man of the name Czarnecki, a commissioner of the Quartering Bureau, in a short time made by these means two million guilders; and this robber of the poor carried his luxury so far as to make use of bathing tubs lined with silver.

CHAPTER I

Principles of the Revolution. The First Night. - Attack on the Barracks of the Russian Cavalry. - Their Dispersion. - Attempt to secure the person of the Grand Duke. - Capture of Russian General officers and spies. - Actions with detached borders of Russian cavalry. - Two companies of Polish light- infantry join the patriots. - Death of Potocki and Trembici. - The Russian infantry attacked and dispersed. - Armament and assembling of the people. - Detachments sent to Praga.

IT is undeniable that the history of our nation abounds in heroic acts and glorious passages. Need we instance the times of Boleslaw, Casimir, Jagiello, Augustus of Warna, and Sobieski; or the deeds of our renowned generals Czarnecki, Chodkiewicz, Tarnowski, Sapieha, Kosciuzko, and Poniatowski? Yet, in our whole history, nothing transcends this last revolution; and indeed, *few* more memorable events have ever occurred. Its plan was based on the purest motives, and this constitutes its peculiar character. Those true sons of Poland, Wysocki and Schlegel, had no other design than to regenerate public morals and the national character, which had already begun to deteriorate under Russian in-fluence; though, perhaps, there may have mingled with these another impulse - that of vengeance for the ignominy to which we were subjected. These feelings were shared by the whole nation - certainly a rare instance in history. Inspired by the example of the brave, even the wavering joined in upholding the good cause to support for which the sword was drawn. It was this unanimity which emboldened us, small as our numbers were, to meet that colossal power dreaded by all Europe. We were not animated to this unequal struggle by any vain desire of conquest, but by a resolution to shake off a yoke so disgraceful, and by the wish to preserve our civilization, and to extend it even to Russia. In drawing the sword, every Pole had in view not only the freedom of his own country, but that of his Sarmatian brethren also. The Poles believed that Russia still remembered those martyrs of liberty, Pestel, Bestuzew, Morawiew, Kachowski, and Releiew, who suffered an ignominious death, and more than five hundred others who were sent in chains to Siberia. We believed they would bear in mind, that, in 1824, they themselves summoned us to fight, side by side, with them against despotism. Their words were still in our memory - "Poles, help us in our holy cause! Unite your hearts with ours! Are we not brethren?" Unworthy nation - soothed by the momentary blandishments of the autocrat, who scattered his decorations with a lavish hand, they forgot their own past sufferings and the future that awaits them. They suffered themselves to be led against those who were in arms for the liberty of both nations. At the very time when the funeral rites of those who had died in battle, Russians as well as Poles, were being celebrated in Warsaw and all the provinces, they burned our villages, and murdered our fathers and brothers. Russians! You have covered yourselves with eternal shame, in the eyes of the whole world. Even the nations you consider your friends and allies condemn you!

THE FIRST NIGHT

The patriots assembled early in the morning of the 29th of November, to renew their oaths and ask the blessing of the Almighty on their great undertaking. The moment approached. Seven in the evening was the hour appointed for the commencement of the revolution. The signal agreed upon was, that a wooden house should be set on fire in Szulec Street, near the Vistula. The patriots were scattered over the city, ready to stir up the people on the appearance of the signal. Most of them were young men and students. Some hundred and twenty students, who were to make the beginning, were assembled in the southern part of Warsaw. All was ready. At the stroke of seven, as soon as the flame of the house was seen reflected on the sky, many brave students, and some officers, rode through the streets of that part of the city called The Old Town, shouting "Poles! Brethren! The hour of vengeance has struck! The time to revenge the tortures and cruelties of fifteen years is come! Down with the tyrants! To arms, brethren; to arms! Our country forever!"

The excitement spread through this part of the city with incredible rapidity. The citizens flocked together from all quarters, shouting, "Down with the tyrants! Poland forever!" At the same time a hundred and twenty students left their barrack (which is called the Hotel of the Cadets, and is situated in the Lazienki Royal Gardens) under their gallant leaders, Wysocki and Schlegel, and marched to the quarters of the Russian cavalry, cuirassiers, uhlans and hussars. It was resolved to take immediate possession of all the chief gates. The issuing out of the Russian troops was thereby rendered very difficult and bloody, as the barracks were surrounded by a wide and deep moat, over which there were few bridges. On their arrival, the cadets found the soldiers in the utmost confusion. Some were saddling their horses, some were leading them out, and others were occupied in securing the magazines, &c. In short, panic and disorder pervaded officers and men; each sought his own safety only. Our young heroes took advantage of this confusion, and after firing a few rounds, rushed with the *hurrah* through the gates. This charge sufficed: a hundred and twenty of these young Poles, after having killed forty or fifty men with ball and bayonet, dispersed some eighteen hundred Russian cavalry. Cuirassiers, uhlans and hussars mingled together, joined in the cry of terror, and began to seek concealment in garrets, stables, cellars, &c. A great number were drowned in attempting to cross the canal in order to escape into the adjoining gardens. As the barracks were closely connected with wooden buildings filled with hay, straw, and other combustible articles, not a man would have escaped had they been fired. The young Poles refrained from this, in mercy. The Russians might all have been made prisoners; for so great was their panic that they were not ashamed to beg for quarter on their knees. But these advantages were, for the time, neglected. The cadets abandoned the attack, and hastened into the city, where their presence was more necessary.

While their comrades were attacking the barracks, some ten or twelve students traversed the gardens towards the palace of the Grand Duke (called the Belvedere) in order to secure his person.[7] Some of them guarded the passages on the side of the gardens, while others penetrated to the tyrant's apartment. But he had escaped through a secret door.

On the failure of the party of cadets sent to secure the person of the Grand Duke, they left his apartments without in the least disturbing the repose of his lady. As they reached the foot of the stairs they met Lubowicki, the vice-president of the city, coming to the Grand Duke for instructions. As soon as he saw them, he began to cry for aid, but the next moment fell on his knees and begged for his life. They took him with them, intending to extract from him all the information he was able to give. In the courtyard they met the Russian general, Gendre,[8] aide-de-camp of the Grand Duke, with some ten or twelve armed men. They resolutely attacked him. Gendre fell under their bayonets, and his followers fled. The party meeting with no further obstacles, returned to their friends, whom they found at the Sohieski Bridge. The company of cadets, after having finished their attack upon the barracks of the Russian cavalry, marched along the high road which traverses the Park, over the Sobiesk Bridge, towards the main avenue between the terraces of the hospital Ujasdow on one side, and those of the Botanical Garden on the other. After having arrived at this bridge, they heard the noise of horses in front, as of cavalry advancing. It was in fact a company of Russian cuirassiers, who were on guard in this part of the park, and who were now hastening to save the barracks. Immediately a plan was formed to receive them. The cadets, forming in a line, concealed themselves in the Park near the street. The cuirassiers came up; they were permitted to advance, and were then received with a brisk fire. The heavy cavalry, who could not turn in this narrow road, suffered severely. Sixty bodies were found on the spot. The rest fled in the greatest disorder. From this bridge, that handful of brave young men passed the street of Wieyska, and, after arriving at the barracks of Radziwil, they met a squadron of Russian hussars returning from a patrol. At the same time, they heard the Russian cavalry in pursuit, who had gained time to mount at their barracks. This was a critical moment, but it was met with resolution. One half threw themselves into the ditch in order to receive the hussars; and the others formed a platoon, and with hurrahs and the shout of "Poland forever!" discharged their pieces and attacked the cuirassiers in their rear, at the point of the bayonet. The Russians were thrown into disorder, and fled with the greatest precipitation, leaving many dead behind them.

The cadets, not having lost a single man in all these skirmishes, arrived at the part of the city called the Nowy-Swiat, (or the New World), and the Trzy Zlote Krzyze, (the Three Golden Crosses.) Here they found two companies of Polish light infantry, and with them the two Polish generals, Stanislaus Potocki and Trembicki, who were giving commands for restoring order by force, and for arresting the assembled inhabitants. The company of cadets arrived, and hailed the light infantry with the following words: - *"Brothers! Are you here to shed the blood of your brethren? Have you forgotten the Russian tyranny? Come to our embrace, and hand to hand let us attack the tyrants. Poland forever!"* This address was enough. They disobeyed the commands of their unworthy generals, and joined the cadets and the populace. When the two generals had the madness to reproach the soldiers, some of the cadets went to them and told them in a few words the state of affairs, and on their knees and with tears entreated them not to forsake the cause of their country. To Stanislaus Potocki the command of the army was offered. At the same time, they were both warned of the fatal consequences of their refusal. It was of no avail. These infatuated men could not see the justice of the cause, and began to insult the students. Upon this the cadets left them, and they fell victims to the indignation of the populace.[9] In this place some gens d'armes, who undertook to disperse the citizens, were killed. After the union with the two companies of light infantry, it was decided they should both march to the street of Szulec, on the left bank of the Vistula, endeavor there to assemble the citizens, and establish a degree of order, and after that to take possession of the bridge, for the purpose of maintaining the necessary communications between Praga and Warsaw during the night, and to defend it to the last against any attack of the enemy.

The cadets marched directly into the city through the Nowy-Swiat, singing patriotic songs and shouting "Poland forever!" Everywhere the citizens answered their shouts with the greatest enthusiasm, and joined the ranks of those brave youths. Both old and young men, and even women, left their dwellings in order to increase the numbers of the liberators of their country. In their passage through that street this company made prisoners of many Russian generals, officers, &c. who were on their flight. After advancing as far as the palace of the Viceroy they met with Polish General Hauke, and Colonel Mieciszewski. These worthless men, accompanied by some gens d'armes, were on their way to the Grand Duke in the Belvedere. Some cadets stepped in their way, and exhorted them to dismount and surrender themselves. Instead of answering, general Hauke drew a pistol and wounded one of them, which act cost him and his companion their lives.[10]

In the same manner, General Siemiontkowski, with some gens d'armes and soldiers, endeavored to disperse and arrest the citizens assembled in the Saxon-platz. He likewise was a Russian instrument, and was hated by the nation.

Whilst this company of cadets was engaged in the south part of the city, the 4th Regiment, a battalion of which had mounted guard, were active in another quarter. This regiment, as soon as the signals were given, revolted. The battalion on guard beat the alarm-drum at every guardhouse, and the two other battalions formed for the attack of the Russian infantry in their barracks called the barracks of Sapieha. The shouts of the soldiers and citizens advancing to the attack mingled with the noise of the drums on every side. A great number of Russian general officers and spies were taken in their flight, in the Little Theatre Street, and Napoleon Street.

As soon as the numbers assembled would admit of it, divisions were detached to liberate the prisoners, especially those in the Franciscan and Carmelite prisons. These prisons, always guarded by Russian troops, were stormed. The Russian soldiers were driven in, and a massacre commenced in the corridors, where a great number of them fell by the bayonet, together with many police officers and turnkeys. The doors were broken down and an indescribable scene took place, when the victims, already sentenced, perhaps, to death, or reserved for tortures, were set at liberty. With tears in their eyes, they fell into the arms of their deliverers. Here, a father found a son—there, a son a father. Many of the emaciated captives could only creep to meet the embraces of their brethren. But what was most shocking, was the appearance of four ladies who had been incarcerated for having resisted the brutal advances of certain Russian generals. They were reduced to mere skeletons. There was not one of the spectators who did not shudder and weep at the sight, and swear to avenge them. A hundred and seventy students, and from forty to fifty older persons, Polish soldiers and citizens, all innocent victims of the system of espionage, were rescued from these two prisons.

The above-mentioned battalions of the 4th and the Sapper Battalion marched to attack the Russian infantry in the barracks of Alexander and Stanislaw. On their arrival there, they found some companies under arms, and summoned them to surrender. Instead of complying, they began to fire, and our soldiers fell instantly upon them with the "Hurrah." They were dispersed in a moment, and many officers and soldiers were made prisoners. So, panic struck were many of the officers of the Russian Guard that they did not hesitate to creep head-foremost into the cellars, whence they were dragged out by the legs. The Russians fled from the barracks and the city in the utmost disorder, and took refuge beyond the Powonzki barrier.

After all these successes, the northern, eastern, and western parts of the city were occupied, at about noon, by divisions of patriot soldiers and citizens.

A small part of the south side of the city only was now in possession of the enemy's cavalry, who had at last left their barracks. A few houses opposite the Lottery Buildings were set on fire, as a signal for assembling. Strong patrols were sent to the western part of the city, and by them all the public treasures and the bank were secured. One of these parties, composed of sappers, met the Russian colonel, Sass,[11] in his flight. As he did not stop at their challenge, he was shot.

When the city had been nearly freed of the Russians, great multitudes hastened to the arsenal for arms and ammunition. Here they found the Polish general Blummer, who was rash enough to resist. He ordered his soldiers to fire on the people, bat they refused to obey, and joined their brethren. This general was slain, - a just punishment for his murderous intentions. All the apartments were immediately opened, and more than 80,000 muskets, pistols, sabers, and carbines were obtained. They were distributed with admirable good order.

The people, being now, armed, were arrayed in divisions, under different commanders, and sent to various parts of the city. Parties were appointed to patrol the streets and arrest all spies[12] and Russian officers who might attempt to fly. They arrested upwards of three hundred. One of these patrols went to the Office of the Secretary of Spies, Macrot, to seize his person and papers. This man hid himself in the cellar, with some of his satellites, and fired upon the patrol. The consequence was that Macrot and his people were massacred.

Toward two in the morning, the quiet of the city was restored. Most of the patriots assembled in the Ulica Dluga, (or Long Street), to consult on the measures to be adopted on the following day, and the manner in which the nation should be addressed by the patriotic party. They called to memory the cruelties of the Russian Government, and urged the necessity of a revolution to prevent the decay of all moral and national feeling. They implored the people to aid in this holy cause, yet at the same time besought them never to violate the dictates of humanity. "Dear brethren," they said, "let no one have a right to accuse us of cruelty. May the sanctity of our cause never be polluted by barbarous passions. Having a single end in view, national freedom, and justice, may we prove lions in battle, mild and indulgent to defenseless foes and repentant apostates. Brethren, let unity, love and friendship be ours! Let us forget private rancor and selfish interest! Children of one mother, our dear Poland - let us save her from ruin!"

These addresses were received by the people with the most fervent enthusiasm, and with cries of "Poland forever!" They swore to fight for her while a drop flowed in their hearts, and never to forsake the field of valor or the path of virtue.

The assembled multitude then knelt down before the Almighty, to thank him for a deliverance accomplished with so little bloodshed, and to implore a continuation of his mercies. It was a scene which no description can equal. In the depth of the night the immense crowds of people kneeling, their figures illuminated by the glare of the fires lighted in the streets, praying to God their deliverer, presented a sight to have touched even tyrants, could they have witnessed it.

When prayers were over, plans were adopted for the defense of the city. Some of the barriers were barricaded, and fortified with cannon. Officers were sent to Praga with detachments to reinforce the garrison at the bridge. Wagons were also sent to Praga for ammunition.

As the detachments approached the bridge, they perceived that their way was obstructed by a body of Russian cavalry. This cavalry were not aware of the presence of the two companies of light infantry who had been sent thither by the patriots. As the cavalry advanced upon the bridge the light infantry gave them a volley and charged. At the same time the detachments fell on from the Border Street, and compelled them to retire with severe loss. Some companies formed by the populace, had already taken possession of Praga, and all was quiet. Many wagonloads of cartridges, balls, and barrels of powder, were taken from the magazine to Warsaw before morning.

These are the details of the first night of our revolution. The order which prevailed in all these tumults and during the fight, was truly admirable. The foreigners then in Warsaw declared that they could not enough praise the behavior of the troops and populace in the very height of a revolution. The utmost forbearance was evinced toward persons and property. No individual was slain or abused without provocation, nor was any house or store entered without the consent of the owner. From the open windows of many houses even ladies witnessed our deeds, and waved their handkerchiefs, without fear of danger or insult. They were quiet and delighted spectators of the crowds, who, after expelling the Russians, moved through the streets in perfect order, shouting songs of joy. These were moments in which the heart of every good patriot rejoiced, and traitors alone hid their heads.

NOTES

7. The enemies of our country have endeavored to persuade the world that this party was sent to take the Grand Duke's life. It is an infamous calumny. The order to seize the Grand Duke, was given with the noblest intention; - to secure him from the dangers attendant on a revolution, and to prevent further bloodshed by his captivity. The Poles magnanimously intended to requite his long-continued cruelty with the kindest treatment. He would have been placed in safety, and supplied with all the comforts of life in the Bruhl Palace, which was expressly named for the place of his abode. The persons sent to seize him were selected for their habitual moderation and self-restraint. By his flight, Constantine accused himself. The just man fears nothing; the guilty con¬science anticipates danger. The Grand Duke injured himself as well as our cause by his flight. His melancholy end is well known.

8. Gendre was one of the Russian generals, who was among the chief spies. He was dismissed by the deceased Emperor, Alexan¬der, on account of impositions and even accusations of theft, nor was he allowed to show himself in Petersburg during the life¬time of Alexander. He arrived, in 1829, in Warsaw, when it was the pleasure of Constantine to associate and surround himself with the outcasts of society; and he made him his master of horse, and afterwards general and aide-de-camp. The swindling of this gen¬eral and his wife, in Warsaw, surpassed all imagination. They cheated and robbed the noblemen, the merchants, the Jews, and their own master, the Grand Duke. According to the accounts found during the revolution, their debts, in gaming and otherwise, amounted to more than a million of Polish gilders.

9. Every Pole lamented the melancholy fate of Stanisław Potocki. He was one of the most honest of men, and beloved by the army and the whole nation. 'He always kept aloof from all familiar intercourse with the Russians, and his house was a true Polish dwelling. He had always scorned Russian protection; and, to every patriot, the end of this man, who had become gray in the service of his country, is a sad recollection. • Yet everyone must confess his death was just, and cannot be a reproach to his countrymen, since he listened neither to the advice nor the entreaties of his brethren, and thus publicly avowed his adherence to the cause of despotism. - As to General Trembizki, he had always been a creature of the Russians, and a proud and mischie¬vous man.

10. The early part of the career of General Hauck was not without merit, but it was tarnished by his later conduct in Germany, and came to Poland, under the reign of Stanislaus, as a poor mechanic. After leaving his trade he was enrolled in the army, and advanced rapidly in the revolutionary war under Kosciuzko, in which he distinguished himself by military skill. In the wars under Napoleon he defended the fortress of Zamosc with great valor. But, from the beginning of the Russian sway and the arrival of the Grand Duke at Warsaw, this man became one of his chief minions, and by fawning and intrigue obtained the post of Minister of War. In the same year, he was raised to the nobility, and was made count, senator, and waye-wode. In the whole history of Poland, the rapidity of this advancement is unexampled: Hauke received these dignities as a reward for his oppression of his inferiors, and for acts of injustice of every kind. As for Mieciszewski, he had always been a villain.

11. This bad man was one of the principal instruments of our oppressors. He was one of the chiefs of the spies and his particular business was to observe all foreigners coming to Warsaw. He invited them to his house to ascertain their characters, and was assisted at his soirees in his base designs, by the female spies. Under the show of the utmost cordiality, by presents, and by means of love affairs, he was wont to endeavor to draw them to the Russian interest, in order to use them as spies in their own countries. He often succeeded, and several foreigners might be named, who came to Warsaw on the most innocent business or to gratify their curiosity,

but who, after having frequented the parties of Sass, and handled Russian gold, returned to their own country to betray it. Such are the means by which Russia steals deeper and deeper into the heart of Europe.

12. The Chief of Spies, General Rozniecki, escaped. He was one of the most vicious characters imaginable: his crimes surpass ex¬pression. He was the oldest general in the Polish Army, in which he had served forty years. He entered the service under king Stanislaus. Under Napoleon he commanded a brigade, and sub-sequently a division of cavalry. Of his character, while in the service of Napoleon, not much is known. Under the Government of Russia, this man, already sixty years old, degraded himself irredeemably by becoming one of the most atrocious and detest¬able tools of tyranny. A volume might be filled with the history of his intrigues, swindlings, and other crimes. As chief of the secret police, he had under him many agents whom he sent through¬out the land to extort money for him on unjust pretences. Woe to the unhappy man who refused compliance with any of his de¬mands! He was sure to find his fate in a prison. In the army, those who bribed him were promoted. Rozniccki was the inti¬mate friend of the Grand Duke. The following anecdote may serve to give the reader some idea of his consummate art in fraud: It was a part of Rozniecki's business to pay the spies, and they received their salaries at his house. He divided the delators into several classes, and rewarded them according to (the quickness and importance of their information. By his arrangement of this busi¬ness he cheated the very spies! In the room where he received their denunciations he had a chest of drawers placed, behind which a clerk was concealed. This clerk wrote down their reports as he heard them, taking care to date them somewhat earlier. When the spy had ended his story and applied for his reward, Rozniecki would declare that he recollected having heard the whole affair the day before. He would then leave the room and return with the forged record. Thus would he defraud the spy of his shame¬ful earnings. Accounts of immense sums received by him were found in his house during the revolution. He was more than once accused of murder by poison, and other enormous crimes, but the proceedings against him were suppressed. On the first evening of the revolution this man happened to be in an assembly of spies in the City Hall. He was there to give his instructions. On hearing the tumult, his conscience smote him, and he stole away without saying a word. Finding a coach at hand, he offered the coachman money to permit him to drive himself whither he pleased. He made his escape in the coachman's cloak. His effigy was exhibited on the gallows seven days, decorated with a dozen Russian orders.

CHAPTER II

The First Day. - Expulsion of the Russians from Warsaw. - Choice of Chlopicki as Commander-in-Chief. - Provisional Government, under the Presidency of Prince Adam Csartoryski. - Deputation sent to the Grand Duke - Propositions and answers-Abolition of the Bureau of Police. - Establishment of the National Guard - Proclamations addressed to the inhabitants of the provinces and the distant troops. - Provision for the Russian prisoners. - The Academical Legions formed. - Arrival of detachments from the provinces. - The Grand Duke consents to leave the kingdom, and addresses a proclamation to the Poles.

THE FIRST DAY of freedom, after so many years of oppression, was hailed with shouts of "Our country! Poland forever!" At about six in the morning the drums beat for the assembly of the troops in all the parts of the city in our possession. Crowds flocked from all sides to the public places. It was a scene never equaled. The whole people assembled, without distinction of rank, age, or sex. Old men who were past the use of swords, brandished their sticks and crutches, and recalled the times of Kosciusko. Clergymen, civil officers, foreigners, Jews, even women and children armed with pistols, mingled in the ranks.

The multitude, thus assembled, marched to the northern and southern parts of the city, to drive the Russians out. The 4th Regiment and a body of the inhabitants marched into the northern quarter of Warsaw, to attack two regiments of infantry who occupied the *Champ de Mars* and the whole district thence to the Powazko barrier. This division had with them two small pieces of cannon. As soon as they reached the point of attack they fired a few rounds, raised the "hurrah," and threw themselves upon the Russians, who made no resistance, but fled in disorder beyond the barrier above mentioned, where the pursuit ceased.

In the meanwhile, the Sapper Battalion had marched through the suburb of Cracow and the street of Wirzbwa to the southern part of the city.

They met the enemy's cavalry, at the Place of Saxony, a short distance from the Church of the Cross. The Russians discharged their carbines, and a brisk fire was kept up until the cry to cease firing and attack with the bayonet was heard on all sides. They gave way before the charge, and fled in the greatest confusion, as the infantry had done before them. They were pursued beyond the barriers of Mokotow. The whole city was, cleared of the Russians before nine o'clock. The walls opposite the Russian troops were manned by soldiers and armed citizens.

While this expulsion was being effected, some of the patriots were employed in the city in choosing a military chief. They agreed to offer the command to Chlopicki.[13]

Towards eleven, General Chlopicki was led by the people, with acclamations, to the hotel of the Minister of Finance, where many senators and other persons were assembled to take measures respecting a Provisional Government, the security of public order, &c. Chlopicki was received with acclamations by the chiefs of the nation; and after all had declared their consent, he was proclaimed Commander-in-Chief. He was addressed on this occasion by Professor Lelewel, one of the patriots, who, after drawing the picture of our past sufferings, and comparing it with our hopes of the future, concluded with the following words, addressed directly to Chlopicki. "Brother—take the sword of your ancestors and predecessors, Czarnecki, Dąbrowski, and Kosciuzko. Guide the nation that has placed its trust in you, in the way of honor. Save this unhappy country." This ceremony concluded, Chlopicki was shown to the assembled people from the balcony. They received him with shouts of "Our country and our liberator Chlopicki forever!" Many cried, "Chlopicki, rely on us, and lead us to Lithuania!" The general thanked them for their confidence in him, promised never to abuse it, and swore that he would defend the liberty of Poland to the last moment.

The patriots now proceeded to choose members of the Provisional Government. Prince Adam Czartoryski,[14] Radziwiłł,[15] Niemcewicz, and Lelewel were elected, and one of the old ministers, Lubecki, was retained to assist them. This arrangement was made public about noon, in order to tranquilize the people.

The first step taken by the new government was to send deputies to the Grand Duke. They were instructed to demand whether he meant to depart peaceably, or to attack the city. Among the deputies were Lubecki and Lelewel. They found the Grand Duke encamped, with his army, in the fields of Mokotow.

The deputies represented to Constantine the consequences that would result from an attack on the city, as well in regard to himself as to the nation. They informed him that the army had already joined the people, and proposed to him that he should depart unmolested, on a prescribed route. They promised that he should find every possible accommodation provided on that route, for himself and his troops. The Grand Duke demanded some time for reflection, and finally gave the deputies the following answer in writing.

ART. I. The Grand Duke declares that it was never his intention to attack Warsaw. In case he should find himself under the necessity of so doing, he will give the authorities notice of his intention forty-eight hours before the attack.

ART. II. The Grand Duke will entreat the Emperor to grant an amnesty for the past.

ART. III. The Grand Duke declares that he has sent no orders to the Russian forces in Lithuania to pass the frontier of the kingdom.

ART. IV. Prisoners will be exchanged.

The deputies returned to Warsaw with this answer, at three o'clock. It was immediately published, but did not satisfy the people. They demanded to know the day and hour of the Grand Duke's departure.[16] If he should refuse to obey, they declared that they would attack him. It was finally concluded to allow him two days for his necessary arrangements, and then to send a second deputation to insist on his instant departure.[17] The Provisional Government immediately set about restoring order to every department of the administration. The Bureau of Police was abolished, and a council of citizens was substituted in its place, under the direction of the aged and worthy Wengrzecki. This man bad been president of Warsaw in the times of the Grand Duchy. He was compelled to leave this office, by certain persecutions, which he brought upon himself by not being sufficiently in the spirit of the Russian Government. At the same time the National Guard was established, and placed under the command of Count Lubinski. The guard began their service on the very same day. They mounted guard at the bank and the public treasury, and their patrols maintained order in all parts of the city. Their duties were performed with the utmost punctuality. All the shops were opened, and the city wore as peaceful an aspect as if there had been no army before it.

At the same time the Provisional Government sent proclamations into all the provinces, to inform the nation of these events. They began with the following beautifully figurative expression: "Poles! The eagle of Poland has broken his chains, and will soon have burst through the clouds into those purer regions in which nothing shall shut from him the light of the sun." The military government issued proclamations to the troops at all the distant stations, ordering them to repair forthwith to Warsaw. The divisions of chasseurs received orders in case of an attack from the Grand Duke, to fall on his rear and cut off his retreat. The city itself was put in a better state of defense; the barriers were fortified, and guarded by strong detachments; all was prepared for an attack. The government made proper provision for the care of the Russian prisoners, of whatever rank, as well as of the ladies of the Russian civil and military officers who had left Warsaw. The royal palace was assigned for the residence of the officers and ladies; the privates were lodged in barracks. At a later period, they were permitted to go about the streets and earn money by their labor, in addition to their usual allowance. The Russians were so touched by this generous treatment, that they swore, with tears, never to forget it.

These details of the first day of our revolution, for the correctness of which I pledge myself, may serve to answer the accusations of some journalists, who have stated that the commencement of the national struggle was marked with the greatest atrocities, and that more than forty field officers, many subalterns, and large parties of privates were butchered for declining to engage in the cause.

These impeachments of the Polish nation are unjust and false. As has been said before, the foreigners in Warsaw could not sufficiently praise the admirable order with which our first movements were conducted. Our enemies accuse the people of having robbed the public treasuries. I affirm that not a gilder was lost—neither public nor private property was pillaged.

As the enemy was still encamped before the city on the first and second of December, and had as yet given no decisive answer respecting the time of his departure, the people, as well as the army, were still under arms and upon the walls. At this time, the twelve companies of students, called the Academic Legions, were organized. It was heart-stirring to see these noble youths assembled in arms to defend their country. Many of them had just been rescued from prison, and could not walk without difficulty. This did not dampen their ardor; the hope of fighting successfully for the liberty of Poland renewed their strength. The Academic Legions requested to be sent to the posts nearest the enemy. These two days passed in entire quietness.

In the afternoon of the second of December, General Schenbeck arrived from Plock with the 1st Chasseur Regiment. At the same time came Colonel Sierwski from Scherok, with his regiment. Both were received with great enthusiasm. New detachments from the provinces marched into Warsaw every day. A truly affecting sight it was to see more than a thousand peasants, and about fifty peasant girls from the country about Warsaw, marching into the city with clubs, scythes, and weapons of every description. They were escorted by the shouting populace to the Bank, and there welcomed by the National Government. At the request of the people, another deputation was this day sent to the Grand Duke, to urge his departure, and to inform him that an attack would be the necessary consequence of his refusal. The Grand Duke saw the necessity of compliance, and decided to commence his march on the following day, by the prescribed route of Pulawa. He issued a proclamation[18] to the Polish nation, wherein he promised never to fight against those, "whom," to use his own expression, "he had always loved." He adducted his marriage with a young Polish lady as proof of his affection for the nation. At the same time, he promised to entreat the Emperor to obtain amnesty, and to take, in general, the mildest measures. He begged the Poles to deal gently with the Russian prisoners, their families, the ladies, and in short with all Russian subjects remaining in Warsaw.

NOTES

13. General Chłopicki, a man of rare merit, began his career the struggle for liberty under Kosciuzko. In 1807, he was colonel commandant of the 1st Vistula Legion Regiment, under Napoleon. He had the command of a brigade, and after¬wards of a division, of the same legion in Spain. This general distinguished himself at the storming of Saragossa, where the Poles performed prodigies of valor, as well as at the battle of Saginta. Under the Russian Government of Constantine, Cholpicki left the army, not being able to endure his commander's brutal deportment. The Grand Duke censured the general on parade, in an unbecoming manner, saying that his division was not in order. Chłopicki replied, "I did not gain my rank on the parade ground, nor did I receive my decorations there." He asked his discharge the next day. In later times the Emperor Alexander and the Grand Duke himself endeavored to induce him to return to the service, but Chłopicki never consented, he pre¬ferred a retired life to the splendor of Russian slavery. This gained him the esteem of the whole nation.

14. Prince Adam Czartoryski was born on the 14th of June 1770. He is the oldest son of Prince Casimir Czartoryski, Palatine of Russia, and Princess Elizabeth Fleming, daughter of Count George Fleming, First Treasurer of Lithuania and Palatine of Pomerania. The Czartoryski family are descended from the Gedimines, who reigned over Lithuania in the thirteenth century, a descendant of whom, Jagiellon, reigned long and gloriously in Poland. At the last partition of Poland, Adam Czartoryski and his brother Constantine were sent to St. Petersburg as hostages. While residing in the Russian capital, Prince Adam was on terms of friendly inti¬macy with the Grand Duke Alexander. This friendship influenced, perhaps, his political career. He was sent as an ambassador to the Sardinian Court, and when Alexander ascended the throne, he was recalled, and entrusted with the portfolio of foreign affairs. He declined this charge for a long time, and at last accepted it at the earnest entreaty of Alexander, on condition that he should be allowed to retire as soon as the discharge of his official duties should militate against the interests of his country. At the same time, he was appointed Curator of the University of Wilna, and yet another important duty devolved on him, which was the establishment of schools in all the Russian provinces of Poland. Though the Russians cannot see a Pole in so honorable a station without jealousy, the conduct of Prince Adam was so noble as to win the hearts of all. He did not surround himself with parasites; his course was plain and upright, and he scorned the idea of receiving rewards from government. He would not even accept a salary.

In 1808, Czartoryski resigned his ministerial office, but retained his place over the university, hoping to do more good in it. He increased the number of elementary schools and those of all classes of instruction. He reformed the antiquated institutions of the university, and gave the whole course of instruction a more simple and convenient form, which was also better adapted to the wants of the middle classes of the people. By these means he hoped to develop and elevate the national character, in these classes.

The events of 1812 showed but too plainly that the misfortunes which then befell France was owing to the same cause to which the previous distress of Russia was attributable; viz. the non-ex¬istence of Poland. If Poland had remained independent in her original extent, the two gigantic powers could not have come in contact, and the equilibrium of Europe, now entirely lost, would have been preserved. It was, then, a true and necessary policy to bring forward the question of the independence of Poland again. This was the object Prince Adam Czartoryski kept in view during the war between France and Russia, and it was in the hope of effecting it that he accompanied Alexander to Paris in 1314. He was not anxious without reason. The Emperor Alexander satis¬fied him, in part, and proposed to the Congress of Vienna to erect the Grand Duchy of Poland into a kingdom. This kingdom received a constitution and several other national institutions. An entire freedom of trade with the remaining Polish provinces under Russia, Austria, and Prussia, was assured to it. All these promises were published and confirmed by Alexander at Warsaw in 1816. Yet, in the very act of confirmation, several privileges which the Emperor had promised to Czartoryski were retracted; and this was owing to the influence of the other powers, and the principles of the Holy Alliance. Russian policy made these restrictions more and more sensibly felt, and unfortunate Poland beheld, one after another, the instructions so solemnly guaranteed to her, vanishing away.

Indignant at these breaches of promise on the part of Russia, Prince Czartoryski resigned the Curatorship of the university of Wilna, in 1824, in which he had been the means of effecting much good, particularly in the cause of patriotism and liberty; and in order to free himself from all connection with the intriguing cabinet of Russia, he went, with his whole family, on a journey to foreign countries.

This prince was proprietor of the beautiful town of Pulawa, which Nature and Art have united to make one of the finest in Europe. The reader will, perhaps, be pleased with a short de¬scription of this place, which no traveler in the north of Europe will fail to visit. The little town of Pulawa is situated about eighteen leagues south of Warsaw, on the main road to Lemberg in Gallicia, on the right bank of the Vistula. The windings of this noble stream are so happily turned as to present a prospect of both its sides, till it reaches the horizon. The breadth of the river near this town is nearly three English miles. Its shores are broken into little hills covered with wood, in the intervals of which fine villages meet the eye, and in the distance, are seen the picturesque ruins of Gasimir. The town of Pulawa itself is situated on the declivity of a high bank, which declines toward the river in the form of an amphitheatre. This declivity is laid out as a garden in the purest taste, terminating, toward the river, in extensive meadows, planted with groves of oaks and poplars, and enlivened by herds of Tyrolian cattle, cottages, shepherds' cabins, &.c, in various styles of building. This garden surrounds Pulawa, and is itself surrounded by great parks, which extend several leagues beyond it in every direction. These are intersected by beautiful avenues of linden trees. Among the many works in marble, statues, obelisks, &c. the temple of Sibylla, with its magnificent statue of alabaster, is distinguished, as is also the statue of a nymph in one of the grot¬tos, a masterpiece of sculpture. The palace, consisting of a main building with two wings, is a noble piece of architecture. Its apartments are rich and splendid. Prince Czartoryski has the largest library in Poland, and the greatest private library in Eu¬rope, which is open to the public.

Czartoryski happened to be in Pulawa when the revolution broke out. Summoned to the helm of state by the nation, he hastened to devote his exertions to his country. Laudable as his previous career had been, it was excelled by his conduct during the strug¬gle, in which he represented the beau ideal of virtue and patriotism. Through all the stormy changes of popular opinion he continued firm and unwavering, having but one view, one aim, the good of his country. He carried to the chief magistrate's seat the same calmness, the same mildness which had characterized his private life. He was never actuated by passion. He considered all Poles as brethren. Though in the sixtieth year of his age, he did not shrink from the fatigues of war, but constantly accompanied Skrzynecki, to whom he was much attached, in his marches, and was at his side in many battles. His whole character was essen¬tially noble.

15. Prince Michael Radziwiłł was born in Lithuania, on his family estate called Nicswiez. He is nephew of Prince Anthony Radzi¬wiłł, Governor-General of the Grand Duchy of Posen, and brother-in-law of the King of Prussia. This prince was commander of a brigade in the time of Napoleon, and distinguished himself at the siege of Danzig. He retired from service under the Russian Government, and lived privately in Warsaw. He was a man of quiet character, and a sincere patriot, but not of eminent military talents.

16. The Grand Duke's army at Mokatow consisted of the following regiments:

		Bns	Sqns	Infantry	Cavalry	Artillery
1	Grenadiers		2		2,000	
2	Light Infantry	2		2,000		
3	Instruction Battalion	1		1,000		
4	Podolia Cuirassiers		4		800	
5	Cesarowicz Uhlans		4		800	
6	Grodno Hussars		4		800	
7	Horse Battery					12
8	Foot Battery					12
	Total	5	12	5,000	2,400	24

17. Of Polish soldiers, he had six companies of grenadiers of the Foot Guard, and one regiment of Chasseurs of the Guard. These regi¬ments, however, returned to Warsaw and joined the nation on the second of December. The true cause of the Grand Duke's demand for time was that he hoped to exert a secret influence on those of the Polish troops who had not yet joined the people. This fact was confirmed by two captured spies, one of whom he had dispatched to the light-horse in Lowicz, and the other to the division of hussars of Siedlec. The letters they carried to the commanders of these forces urged them, with promises of great rewards, to join the Grand Duke.

18. These proclamations, which were immediately published in the Warsaw papers, contain clear proof that the Grand Duke had no injuries on the part of the Polish nation to complain of, and that he himself felt that the Poles were constrained.

CHAPTER III

The Patriotic Club commences its session. - Character of that association. - The Grand Duke departs for the frontier. - Particulars of his march. - The Polish regiments which had remained with him return to Moscow. - Their reception. - Krazynski and Rornatowski. - Deputation to St. Petersburg. - Demands to be laid before the Emperor. - Sierawski made Governor of Warsaw, and Wasowiez chief of the staff. - Order respecting the army - Arrival of volunteers from the interior. - Opening of the theatre. - Religious solemnities at Praga. - Chlopicki nominated and proclaimed Dictator.

ON the third of December, the Patriotic Club began its session, under the guidance of very worthy persons. The object of this society was, to watch over all the departments of the administration, to see that the measures adopted were congenial with the wishes of the people, and in the spirit of the revolution; and to promote fraternity and union throughout the nation. They desired to repress all manifestations of selfishness or ambition, to discover and bring before the people the persons best qualified for public offices, and, in short, to promote the best interests of the nation with unwearied zeal. If this club was, at times, led by the fervor of patriotic feeling to adopt measures considered rigorous by many, their acts were never inconsistent with the love of country, or their own views of the national honor. At this time, a committee was also appointed for the trial of the spies.

On the morning of the third of December, the Grand Duke commenced his march towards Pulawa, according to agreement,[19] and the Polish regiments which had remained with Constantine up to this time, now returned to Warsaw. These troops were at first regarded by the people with feelings of indignation. Such feelings were, however, soon dissipated by the explanations which were given. They had been misled by their generals, Krasynski and Kornatowski. As to General Zimyrski, who commanded the grenadiers, he was entirely blameless. He had intended to join the patriots at first, but was detained as a prisoner by the Russians. The other two generals persuaded their men that the revolutionary movements were only disturbances of the mob, excited by the students, and would quickly come to an end. They ought not, they told them, to forsake their legitimate government and the Grand Duke. It was impossible afterwards for these regiments to learn the truth, as they were closely surrounded by the Russians, and cut off from all communication with others.

Early on the third of December, when the Grand Duke had resolved to depart, he visited these troops in person, and declared before them that he left Warsaw only to avoid useless bloodshed, and that order would soon be restored. He requested them to go with him, as they were regiments of guards, in whom the Emperor had peculiar confidence. "Soldiers," he said, "will you go with us; or stay and unite with those who have proved faithless to their sovereign?" With one voice the whole corps exclaimed, "We will remain - we will join our brethren and fight for the liberty of our country. We are sorry that we could not do so from the beginning, but we were deceived."

The people who had assembled to gaze at these unfortunate men, with unfavorable and unjust feelings toward them, were disarmed of their resentment at the very sight of them, and rushed into their embraces. They were surrounded by the multitude, and taken, with joyful acclamations, to the Place of the Bank. But though the people forgave the soldiers, their indignation remained unabated against their generals, and the greatest efforts of the leading patriots were required to save Krasynski and Kornatowski from their rage. It was dreadful to behold these generals riding with downcast looks, not daring to look on those whom they had intended to betray. Death would certainly have been preferable to thus meeting the curses of a justly incensed people. Mothers held up their children, and, pointing at the two generals, exclaimed, "See the traitors!" Arriving at the Bank, the people demanded that Krasynski and Kornatowski should give their reasons for having acted as they had done; and as the wretched men could say nothing in their own defense, a general cry arose of "Death to the traitors!" Nothing but the love of the people for Chlopicki and Schembeck, who interceded, could have hindered them from carrying their wishes into immediate execution. Several excited individuals made their way toward the culprits with pistols in their hands, and, after aiming at them, fired their weapons into the air, crying, "You are unworthy of a shot from a Polish hand. Live - to be everlastingly tortured by your consciences!" The unfortunate men entreated that they might be permitted to serve in the ranks, as privates. They were immediately deprived of their commissions, and from that time they lived in retirement during the war.[20]

The people were this day informed that Prince Adam Czartoriski had been nominated President of the National Government; that the eighteenth of December was appointed for the opening of the Diet; that till that day the rights of the Emperor Nicholas would be acknowledged; and that Lubecki, Osvowski, and Jezierski would be sent to St. Petersburg!), as a deputation, to inform the Emperor of all that had happened. They were also to lay before him the following demands:

1st. That all Russian troops should be withdrawn from the kingdom forever, that a perpetual conflict between the two nations might be avoided.

2nd. That the privileges of the constitution should be again confirmed in their fullest extent.

3rd. That all the ancient Polish provinces incorporated with Russia should partake in the privileges of the constitution, as Alexander had promised.

The deputies were also instructed to entreat the Emperor to come to Warsaw and open the Diet, in order to satisfy himself respecting the actual state of affairs. The deputies left Warsaw that very evening.

The Commander-in-Chief appointed General Sierawski governor of the city of Warsaw, and Colonel Count Wonsowicz Chief of Staff. These officers were both beloved by the people, and proved themselves able and zealous defenders of their country through the whole campaign. The Commander-in-Chief also published an order that the army should consist of 200,000 men. Each Voivodeship (principality[21]) was to furnish 9,000 infantry and 11,000 horse. There are eight wayewodeships in Poland. The army already existing, the volunteer forces, and the regiments raised and equipped by some of the noblemen, were not reckoned in this estimate, nor did it include the volunteers which were to be expected from the Polish provinces under other foreign governments.

The fourth, fifth, and sixth of December were remarkable days in the history of our revolution. Soldiers and peasants flocked in from all sides - from all quarters of the country. In a short time, more than five\ thousand peasants, armed with scythes, axes, and other weapons, were counted. Among them were more than two hundred peasant girls, with sickles. These were days of real joy, when all united in the defense of Poland, without distinction of rank, age, or even sex - when rich and poor, nobles and peasants, met, as friends escaped from common sufferings, and embraced. Tables were spread with refreshments for those who arrived, in the streets. The fourth was remarkable for the opening of the theatre.[22] Religious solemnities took place in Praga on the fifth, and on the sixth a Dictator was nominated.[23]

When, on the sixth of December, the National Government notified Chlopicki of his nomination as Generalissimo, he replied, that they had no power to place him in that station that in such critical times the civil and military power ought to be vested in one person, and that he felt himself entitled, by his long services, to nominate himself Dictator. His powers, he said, he would lie down on the assemblage of the Diet. In the afternoon of the next day he was proclaimed Dictator in the Champ de Mars, amidst the acclamations of an immense multitude. After this, he took a public oath to act in accordance with the spirit of the people, and to defend the rights and privileges of Poland.

NOTES

19. The details of the Grand Duke's march may not be uninteresting to the reader, and at the same time they will serve to refute the false report that he was pursued by the Poles.

Early on the morning of the third of December the Grand Duke left his camp at Mokotow, and marched on the route of Kosienire and Fulawa. Agents had been sent in advance in this direction, to procure for him every convenience, which he found uniformly prepared. In a village between Koseinice and Graniza, where he halted with his troops, he met Intendant General Wolicki, who was on his way from Lublin to Warsaw. Wolicki waited on the Grand Duke, in the hope that he might render him some service. Constantine had quartered himself in the house of the curate of the village, and received the Intendant General in the parlor, where the Grand Duchess Lowicz was present. Wolicki requested his orders with regard to the accommodation of the troops. Constantine coldly thanked him, and immediately began to complain of the Poles; in which he was joined by his lady. He reproached the nation with the benefits he had conferred on them, and seizing Wolicki violently by the hand, added, "And for all this they wanted to assassinate me!" When Wolicki, in the most delicate manner, represented that his residence had been entered with the best intentions toward his person, the Grand Duke, with yet greater exasperation and fury, exclaimed, "They have chased me out of the country—but I shall soon return." In his rage he again seized Wolicki's hand, saying, "You shall stay with me, as a hostage for my generals retained in Warsaw." Notwithstanding the expostulations of Wolicki, he was arrested and detained. He however was not long a prisoner, for he soon found means to regain his liberty. The Grand Duke passed that night at the village of Graniza, some of the inhabitants of which Wolicki knew. He found opportunity to speak with one of them in the night, told him what had befallen, and desired him to raise a false alarm, as if the Poles were at hand. It was done. The citizens began to shout in the streets, and Wolicki, profiting by the fright and disorder of the Russians, escaped.

He arrived at Warsaw on the following day, and related his adventure, which was published as an illustration of the Grand Duke's perfidy and inconsistency. This conduct, together with his threats, would have justified the Poles in pursuing and taking him, with his whole army, prisoners. But the nation generously suffered this opportunity for revenge to pass by, and adhered to the promise of a free passage.

On his arrival in Pulawa, Constantine was received by the Princess Czartoriska in the friendliest manner, as he also was in Lubartow by the Princess Lubomirska. In the latter place, General Roszniecki, who accompanied the Grand Duke, demanded an apartment in a pavilion adjoining the palace, which was designed for the suite of Constantine. The Princess answered, in the presence of the Grand Duke, "There is no room for traitors to their country in my house."

On the way to Lenczna, the Russian army met a division of Polish lancers, marching to Siedlec. They halted in order to go through the ceremony of saluting. The Grand Duke, with his suite, approached them with an air of perfect friendship, shook hands with several, and endeavored to persuade them to return with him. "Uhlans," said he, "do not forget your duty to your monarch, but set your comrades a good example." He then offered them money and other rewards. Indignant at his proposals, the lancers replied, "Prince, we thank you for the money and promises you offer us, but there is no command more sacred in our eyes than the call of our country; no greater reward than the privilege of fighting in her cause!" With this, they wheeled, and continued their march past the Russian troops, singing patriotic songs.

The Grand Duke passed the frontier with his forces on the thirteenth of December, and crossing the Wadowa, entered Volhynia, an ancient Polish province, now incorporated with Russia.

I cannot forbear to record the noble conduct of colonel Turno, a Pole, and aid-de-camp to the

Grand Duke. This officer had been fourteen years with Constantine, and was one of the few honest men in his suite. His long endurance of his chief's follies and rudeness could have had no other motive than the hope of doing good to others, and preventing mischief. Constantine loved him, valued him highly, and was firmly convinced that Turno -would remain with him. What was his surprise, when, at the frontier, Turno rode up to take his leave! At first, he was unable to answer. After some time, he said, with an expression of heartfelt grief, "Turno, and will you leave me - you, upon whom I had placed my greatest hopes - whom I loved so much - who have been with me so long?" Turno answered, with dignity, "Your Highness may be assured that I am sorry to part with you. I have certainly always been your friend, and I am so still. I should never leave you in another cause - no, not in the greatest distress: on the contrary I should be happy to share every misfortune with you. But, your Highness, other circumstances and duties call me now - the highest and weightiest duty - the duty a man owes to his country. Your Highness, I have done all that honor and duty commanded as your aid-de-camp - I have accompanied you to the frontier, that I might be your guide as long as you should remain on Polish ground, and preserve you from every possible danger. Now you need me no longer. You are in your own country, and my duty as your aid-de-camp being at an end, it is now my sacred duty as a Pole to return at the summons of my country."

The Grand Duke marched with his corps toward Bialystok, where he remained till the beginning of the campaign. In the war, he was not ashamed to accept the command of a corps of the army, and to fight against those who had treated him so generously, his promises to the contrary notwithstanding.

20. These Polish regiments and generals are, doubtless, the same as who were reported by the Berlin State Gazette to have been butchered. So far from that, the nation received them kindly, and forgave them. Prussians! you know little of the Poles, or of their feelings. The time may come when we shall know one another better.

21. In fact a *Voivode* was akin to a province

22. This was the first time the theater was opened during the revolution. A patriotic piece was performed, viz. "The Krakovians and Guralians," or "The Union of the Two Tribes." This play had been prohibited before. As early as six, P. M. the theatre was crowded. No distinction was observed in regard to places. Before the play began, one of the patriots addressed the audience with a speech, in which he called to memory all the outrages by which the revolution had been rendered necessary, and informed them what measures the National Assembly had taken to insure the success of the good cause. "Poles I Brethren!" he said, "we have sent deputies to the Emperor, to represent our sufferings for fifteen years—our oppressions—which drew neither attention nor relief from Russia, while our rights were trampled upon, and our innocent brethren tortured. Perhaps the Emperor, surrounded by bad men, has been kept in ignorance of our wrongs, and will be astonished to hear of all this injustice from the mouths of our deputies. Perhaps he will take measures to redress all these villainies without delay. If the grace of God has granted him to reign over Poland, he may follow the steps of our good kings of old; of whom no one ever tarnished the throne with tyranny. As for us, brethren, let us forget past dissensions, and unitedly and patiently strive with one accord for the redemption of our country." After this speech, which was joyfully received, the orchestra played Kosciusko's march, which had not been heard for fifteen years. At first, the music was drowned in the shouts of the audience - "Hail, our country - our father Kosciusko! France, and Lafayette the friend of Kosciusko, forever!" After this, the Marseilles hymn was played, and then the Mazur of Dombrowski. The play was full of patriotic songs, and the audience joined their voices to those of the actors. But when, at the end of the play, three standards, with the armorial bearings of the ancient provinces of Poland, were brought in, and were folded into one in the

embraces of the actors who represented the three chief tribes, the exultation of the audience surpassed all bounds. One of the favorite actors addressed the spectators in these words - " The monster tyranny, terrified by the sudden light of liberty, which he could not endure, has left the den from which he has hitherto spread death and affright. Oh that, scared by this light, he may be driven farther and farther, nor be suffered to rest on any of the fields of Poland. May he retire to the dark, icy regions of the north, whence he came, and God grant that he may never return to us."

After this, those of the patriots who had been most actively distinguished on the first night of the revolution and after, and those who had suffered in dungeons for their love of country, were presented to the assemblage. They were received with infinite joy, and carried about on the shoulders of the people with shouts. Many ladies were then brought forward, who had followed the patriots in arms on the first night, or had sacrificed their wealth on the altar of patriotism. At first sight, these beautiful and noble beings might have been taken for angels sent down for the redemption of unhappy Poland.

These scenes surpass description - they can only be felt by hearts truly free. These were moments to unite the whole nation. Persons who had shunned each other for years, each fearing a spy in the other, explained themselves and embraced. These scenes will live eternally in the memory of every Pole. Beholding his countrymen in this ecstasy of joy, there was none who did not weep - none who did not feel ready to die on the morrow, having seen them thus happy. The prisoner condemned to death, when unexpectedly rescued, and permitted to breathe the free air, laughs, weeps, and endeavors to express his gratitude, and cannot. Such was the feeling of Poland in these blessed moments.

23. On Sunday, the fifth of December, prayers were offered up in all the churches of Warsaw by the people from the provinces as well as the inhabitants. The blessings of the Most High were implored on our arms. Of all the religious solemnities, those of Praga were the most edifying and affecting. A mass was said in the open air, at an altar erected on the spot where the victims of Suvarov had been buried. This altar was surrounded by more than 50,000 men, who sent up one voice to God. The twelve academic legions formed the innermost circle, among whom those who had been imprisoned for assisting on a similar occasion were conspicuous. In the intervals of divine service, and after its termination, several speeches were delivered, one of which was by one of the liberated prisoners. Recalling the cruelties perpetrated by Suvarov, as well as those which we had lately suffered, he observed, "Brethren, we were lately forbidden - nay, it was accounted a crime, to pray for our unfortunate" murdered ancestors. Today, under the free vault of heaven, on the grave of our fathers, on the soil moistened with their sacred blood, which cries to us for retribution, in the presence of their spirits hovering over us, we swear never to lay down our arms till we shall have avenged, or fallen like them." The assembled multitude then sung a patriotic hymn.

The sixth of December was remarkable for the nomination of Chlopicki to the Dictatorship; - the union of the supreme civil and military powers in his person. The authority of the Provisional Government was thus at an end; everything was referred to the Dictator. In the afternoon, more than 100,000 persons assembled in the Champ de Mars and the space around it. The greater part of the army, too, was present. Chlopicki came with the senators, and was received by those who had entrusted him with their defense with shouts of joy. His aspect was, indeed, venerable. His silver head, grown white in the service of Poland, bespoke the confidence of all.

CHAPTER IV

The Dictator enters upon his duties. - Plans for the enrollment of new forces - System of officering them. - Want of energy in the execution of his plans. - Fortifications neglected. - The people supply the deficiencies of the administration - Discovery of the correspondence between the ministers Grabowski and Lubecki. - The march of the army delayed. - Answer of the Emperor Nicholas to the Deputies, - His proclamation. - Its effect on the nation. - The Diet demand of the Dictator an account of his trust. - The result of their investigations. - Chlopicki deprived of the Dictatorial power. - The civil administration entrusted to Prince Adam Czartoryski, and the command of the army to Prince Michael Radzivil, each subordinate to the Diet

ON the seventh of December, the new Dictator took possession of the residence which had been prepared for him. A guard of honor was assigned him, consisting of a company of the Academic Legion. The twelve companies of which this legion was composed mounted guard in succession. The nation had conceived the highest hopes of Chlopicki; they expected, above all, the most energetic measures in regard to the armament and organization of the forces. These hopes were not fulfilled. At the very commencement of his administration, it began to be seen that this man, either from his advanced age or the original inadequacy of his talents to the demands of such a situation, would fail to satisfy the wants of the nation. Indeed, the union of so many different duties in the hands of one individual demanded abilities of no ordinary strength and compass. As might have been expected, the evident incapacity of Chlopicki early became the occasion of dissension in the patriotic association already referred to, accusations being preferred, as a matter of course, against those who had been active in procuring his investment with such high powers. The succeeding events will enable the reader to decide for himself of the justice of such accusations.

On assuming his post, the Dictator adopted the following arrangements in. regard to the enrollments of the new forces, and other objects of military administration. He estimated the army already in existence at 25,000 men, and sixty-two pieces of cannon. This army was constituted as follows: - The infantry was composed of nine regiments, of two battalions each, and a battalion of sappers, making a total of 19,000 men. The cavalry was also composed of nine regiments, each regiment consisting of four squadrons, 7,200 men in all. The artillery was divided into nine battalions, of eight pieces each, in all seventy-two pieces, exclusive of the artillery in the fortresses of Modlin and Zamosc.

This force the Dictator proposed to augment in the following manner: - Each existing regiment was to receive a third battalion; and he intended to form fifteen new regiments, of three battalions each. This would have increased the total of infantry to 54,000 men, without taking into the account the National Guard of Warsaw and the other cities, amounting to 10,000 men. The cavalry was to be augmented by 8000, making a total of 15,200. To the artillery were to be added twenty-four pieces of cannon, making a total of ninety-six pieces.

In this estimate the Dictator did not include the aid that might be calculated upon from the provinces of Prussian, Austrian, and Russian Poland, the volunteers of every kind, and the regiments raised and equipped by the large landed proprietors.

For each of the eight palatinates into which the kingdom was divided, an officer was appointed, whose duty it was to superintend the organization of the military forces, of which from seven to eight thousand infantry, and one thousand cavalry, were to be furnished by each palatinate. These officers were subordinate to two others, who had the supervision of four palatinates each, and bore the title of *Regimentarz*. These last had the power of appointing all the officers of the new forces.[24]

The augmentation of the army was to have been completed by the twentieth of January, 1831. But all these arrangements were only made on paper - the government did not press their execution. In fact, such a degree of negligence existed, that in some places where the people assembled to be enrolled, they found no officers to receive them, and, after waiting some time, they returned to their homes. It was, in truth, only by the energy of the nation, which supplied the deficiencies of the administration that our forces were ever in any degree augmented. The volunteer force was in an especial manner liberally furnished by the people. A similar state of things existed with regard to the fortifications; and here again the energy of the people atoned for the negligence of the administration. This was especially the case at Warsaw and Praga, where all the citizens labored on the works of defense, without distinction of age or sex.

The construction of barricades in the different streets of Warsaw, and of mines in several parts of the city, was commenced by the citizens. The Dictator, however, instead of occupying his attention with these warlike preparations, devoted it to diplomatic negotiations, and dispatched emissaries to the neighboring courts, charged with propositions made without the knowledge or the wish of the nation, and even, in some cases, incompatible with its honor, and inconsistent with the design of the revolution. All the measures, indeed, of the Dictator, however well intended they might have been, indicated much weakness and indecision.

Such was the state of affairs when an event occurred that seemed to augur well for our prospects. This was the discovery of the correspondence between the ministers Grabowski and Lubecki, the former being Secretary of State for Poland and a member of the Cabinet at St. Petersburg, the latter Minister of Finance of Warsaw. This correspondence afforded the clearest evidence that Russia had intended to declare war against France, and that she was prepared to commence that war the following December.[25]

These letters were sent to Paris in the early part of December, by an express, and ought to have convinced the French Government of the hostile intentions of Russia. They should have satisfied France that our revolution, and the war that was to follow, were a part of the great struggle in which her own existence was concerned.

The existing army was, through the activity of the general officers, brought into such a state, by the middle of December, that it could then have taken the field against the enemy. The soldiers were eager for the struggle, but the delay of their march gave color to the supposition that an answer from the Emperor was waited for. It was even rumored that the Emperor was coming to Warsaw in person. All this tended to damp the excitement of the moment. What, then, was the astonishment of the nation, when it was found that the monarch, far from admitting the severity of the oppression under which we had suffered fifteen years, - far from giving a paternal audience to the deputies which the nation had sent to him, and who, in its name, had presented the most moderate demands, (limited, in fact, to the ratification and observance of the constitution granted to us, and the union of the Polish provinces under one government, as had been promised by Alexander), - far from consenting to repair to Warsaw, as the deputies had entreated him to do, as a father among his children, to hear their complaints and satisfy himself as to their justice, - far from all this, - in a word, discarding all paternal feelings, he applied the term "infamous" to the sacred effort we had been forced to make by the oppression under which we had so long suffered.[26]

The Russian Generals Benkendorf and Diebitsch, in a conversation, of which our revolution was the subject, and which took place in an interview with Colonel Wielczynski who was one of the deputies sent to the Emperor, spoke of a general war as impending after Poland should be crushed.[27] Colonel Wielczynski returned from St. Petersburg in the latter ,part of December, bringing with him the proclamation which has already been given to the reader, and which, being published, was received by the people with the utmost indignation. It was an insult to the honor and character of the nation, which demanded vengeance. The day of the promulgation of this document was a day of terrible agitation. The cry of "To battle! To battle!" was heard in every quarter. The nation demanded to be led against the enemy at once. The word had gone forth "there is no hope of peace."[28] It was with difficulty that the people could be restrained from rushing at once to the field and be persuaded to wait for convocation of the Diet fixed on the 17th of January. This delay was another error, for the time which intervened was uselessly employed. This Diet in the opinion of the nation could decide upon nothing short of war. Upon a just interpretation of the spirit of the Emperor's proclamation, no other course could be taken consistently with the national honor. It was in consequence of this proclamation, of so criminal, so unjust, so insulting a character, that Nicholas Romanoff and his successors were declared to have forfeited all claims to the throne of Poland, and that that throne was declared vacant. The Poles could no longer submit to a King, who, far from being willing to hear their complaints, far from guaranteeing the rights secured by the constitution, went the length of insulting that national honor to which all history has borne testimony. To what a future must Poland, under such a king, have looked forward?

Better were it to risk the bloodiest conflict, nay, to be buried under the ruins of our country, then to remain the vile slaves of a man, who, relying on the force which he could control was willing to take advantage of his strength to be unjust.

The Diet demanded of General Chlopicki an account of his trust, in regard to the military and civil administration generally, and in a particular manner in regard to the preparation of the forces. The result of this inquiry was to satisfy them that there had been a general negligence of his duties, especially in regard to the increase and organization of the army. On examining the military reports, it was found that only the fifth part of the amount of force ordered to be levied was as yet enrolled. Two months had been wasted. The Dictator, as has been already stated, occupied himself principally with diplomatic affairs, and seemed to forget that the country was to be defended. The Diet saw that General Chlopicki was hoping to finish the war by conferences, and that his eagerness for peace was betraying him into a forgetfulness of what was due to the national honor. In fine, a correspondence with the Emperor Nicholas was found to have been carried on by him.[29] The Dictator, it was seen, had been equally neglectful of the different fortifications. Except at the principal points, Praga, Zamosc, and Modlin, no works of defense had been constructed. The important places of Serock, and Zegrz, the former on the Narew, and the latter below the confluence of the Narew and the Bug, were forgotten, as were all the positions on the great road, which leads from Warsaw to Brzese, upon which, or in its vicinity, our principal operations were to be executed. No point on the frontier was strengthened. The country was left entirely open. The Diet, considering all these circumstances, resolved to send a deputation to the Dictator, to demand of him, for the last time, what his intentions were, and to require of him to take the field forthwith. As the Dictator would not submit himself to this expression of the will of the Diet, and even opened to Prince Adam Czartoriski, who was one of that deputation, propositions deemed inconsistent with the national honor, the Diet deprived him of his trust.

The affairs of the civil administration were confided, as before the Dictatorship, to the senate, under the presidency of Prince Czartoriski, and the post of Commander-in-Chief of the army was given to the Prince Michael Radzivil. All these powers were subordinate to the Diet. In this manner ended the Dictatorship of Chlopicki, who afterwards took a place in the suite of Prince Radzivil, and was admitted into the counsels of the administration of military affairs.

58

NOTES

24. A very important circumstance, which either escaped the notice of the Dictator, or was willfully neglected by him, respected the nomination and rank of officers. As the army was to be considerably augmented, a proportionally greater number of officers was requisite. All arrangements upon this subject were confided to the Regimenitarz, with whom the important power of making these appointments was entirely left. This course soon led to trouble. The Regimentarz, not having the power to transfer the older officers of the existing army, excepting in cases where the offer was made by those officers, were compelled to appoint new officers to newly formed regiments. These newly levied soldiers were thus placed under officers who were but learners themselves. The evil effects of this injudicious system were indeed sensibly felt in the first actions of the campaign. Besides the evil here alluded to, a degree of jealousy between the old and new officers resulted from the operation of these arrangements. It was natural for those who were old in service too see with dissatisfaction recently commissioned officers placed above them in rank. Instead, then, of studying to preserve the utmost harmony between those who were going forth together to shed their blood in the cause of their common country, that course was in fact taken, which if it had been designed to disturb this harmony, would have been deemed the most efficacious.

Arrangements for officering the army might have bees made in such a manner as the following, to the satisfaction of all parties. After dividing the officers into three classes, the first, consisting of those actually in service, the second of those who had been in service, but had given up their commissions and were in retirement, and the third of the newly commissioned officers; a military commission might have been formed, who should have before them lists of officers, showing their periods of service. This commission could have designated the rank of each upon an examination of these lists, placing the retired officers in the grades in which they stood at the time of their retirement. The new regiments should have been officered from the two first classes, advancement being made in the grade of each officer. The third class, or the new officers, should have been appointed to the vacancies thus left in the old regiments. Besides the justice which such an arrangement would have done to the officers of older standing, it would have had this good effect: the experienced officers would have been more widely distributed through the army, and the new regiments would have advanced more rapidly in organization and discipline. General Skrzynecki clearly saw the defects of the actual arrangement; but once made, it was difficult to reform it. He took, however, every opportunity that offered to transfer the older officers to advanced grades in the new regiments.

25. *Letter to Prince Lubecki, Minister of Finance at Warsaw, dated St. Petersburg, the 18th of August* 1830. "My Prince, - His Majesty the Emperor and King directs me to inform you that the Polish troops being now in marching condition, you are requested to provide the necessary funds, without delay, upon which the public treasury may count as occasion may require, to support the expenses of the movement of the army, and of the approaching campaign."

(Signed) "TURKUL, *Secretary of State.*"

In an answer to this letter, dated the third of September, Prince Lubecki renders an account of the means at his command. "Poland," he says," has 9,000,000 gilders in its treasury, and 1,000,000 in the bank of Berlin. She is then ready to undertake the necessary preparations."

Extract of a letter addressed to Prince Lubecki by Count Qrabowski, Secretary of State for Poland, at St. Petersburg. "The official correspondence which, by the order of His Majesty, I have the honor to communicate, to you, my Prince, and which directs the placing of the Polish Army on the war establishment, was, undoubtedly, even more unwelcome to you than to myself. I suffer, truly, in seeing the progress of our financial arrangements thus arrested. Our treasury would have been in the most perfect condition, but for the expenses of this war, which will absolutely exhaust its coffers; for on this occasion our geographical position places us in the front line."

"*Dated St. Petersburg, 15th October* 1830.

(Signed) "GRABOWSKI."

FROM THE SAME TO THE SAME. *Dated October 18th,* 1830. "Having been this day informed by His Excellency, the aid-decamp of His Majesty, Gzerniszew, that orders have been given this royal highness the Caesarowicz, to place on the war establishment all the troops under his command, without excepting those of the Polish Kingdom, and that these orders are to be carried into effect by the 22nd of December, I have the honor, my Prince, to communicate this information to you, by His Majesty's order, so that the necessary funds may be furnished without delay to the Minister of War. And I further request you, my Prince, by the order of His Majesty, to have the goodness to assign to His Imperial Highness the Caesarowicz all the funds for which he may have occasion in the execution of his orders.

(Signed) " GRABOWSKJ."

FROM THE SAME TO THE SAME. *Dated 20th November* 1830. "The return of Marshal Diebitsch will determine what measures it will be necessary to take. He has received orders to pass through Warsaw, on his return from Berlin, with the view to consult with the Grand Duke Constantine, in an especial manner upon subjects connected with the movement and subsistence of the army. The Emperor wishes that you would see the Marshal, as soon as possible after his arrival in Warsaw, in order to consult with him on all these subjects; and he authorizes you to execute all the arrangements which may be determined upon by Marshal Diebitsch and the Grand Duke, without waiting for further orders from His Majesty. You will conform strictly to the wishes of His Imperial Highness. His Majesty, in conclusion, orders me to invite you to repair to St. Petersburg as soon as the army shall have com-menced its movement and the war shall have been declared, so that you may receive in person the orders of His Majesty. We are now in the month of November, the distances are great, our armies cannot be ready before the spring, and events follow each other so rapidly that God only knows what may happen before that time. The rapidity of their succession has made it impossible to receive intelligence of events in season to influence their course. It is this which has caused the unfortunate state of affairs in regard to Belgium. And here, again, is opened a train of events, in reference to which it is useless to act, for the next courier may bring us intelligence of an entirely new state of things."

26. The proclamations of the Emperor on the 17th and 24th of December were in effect the same. There was a perfect correspondence between them in severity of language and spirit. We will give the last.

"By the grace of God, We, Nicholas the First, Emperor and Autocrat of all the Russias, make known to all our faithful subjects that an infamous treason has convulsed the Kingdom of Poland, which is united to Russia. Evil-minded men, who had not been disarmed of their bad passions by the beneficence of the im-mortal Emperor Alexander, the generous restorer of their country, under the protection of the laws he had given them, have secretly concerted plots for the subversion of the established order of things, and began to execute their projects on the 39th of November last, by rebellion, effusion of blood, and attempts against the life of our well beloved brother the Caesarowicz Grand Duke Constantine Paulowicz. Profiting by the obscurity of the night, a furious populace, excited by these men, precipitated themselves upon the palace of the Caesarowicz; while, spreading throughout the city of Warsaw the false report that the Russian troops were massacring the peaceable inhabitants, they collected the people about them and filled the city with all the horrors of anarchy. The Caesarowicz, with the Russians who were about his person, and the Polish troops who remained faithful to their duty, determined to take a position in the vicinity of Warsaw, and not to act with hostility, in order that, avoiding all occasion, of shedding blood, they might prove in the clearest manner the falsehood of the report which had been circulated, and give the authorities of the city time and means of bringing back to their duty, in concert with the well-intentioned citizens, those who had been misled, and to restrain the discontented. This hope was not fulfilled. The council of the city was unable to re-establish order. Incessantly menaced by rebels, who had formed some illegal union among themselves, and had gained an influence in the council by separating from it some members named by us, and filling their places with others named by the chiefs of the conspirators, there was no course left to it but to beseech the Caesarowicz to send back the Polish troops who had left Warsaw with him, to protect the public and private property from new pillage. Soon after this council was entirely dissolved, and all its powers were united in the hand of one general. In the interval, the news of the revolt was spread through all the provinces of Poland, Everywhere the same means were employed. Imposture, menaces, falsehood were used to inveigle the pacific inhabitants into the power of the rebels. In this unfortunate and serious state of things, the Caesarowicz considered it indispensable to yield to the request of the government. He permitted the small body of Polish troops which remained faithful to him to return to Warsaw, in order to insure as far as possible, the security of persons and property. He himself quitted the kingdom with the Russian troops, and entered on the 13th December the town of Wlodawa, in the government of Volhynia.

"Thus, was executed a crime which had been resolved upon, probably, for a long time before. After so many misfortunes, and when at least in the enjoyment of peace and prosperity under the protection of our power, the people of the Kingdom of Poland have plunged themselves again into the abyss of revolt and misery, and multitudes of credulous men, though already trembling in fear of the chastisement which awaits them, dare to think, for a moment, of victory; and propose to Us the condition of being placed on an equality with ourselves! Russians, you know that we reject them with indignation! Your hearts burn with zeal for the throne. Already you appreciate the sentiments we feel. At the first intelligence of the treason, your response was a new oath of unshaken fidelity, and at this moment We see but one movement in the whole extent of our vast empire. But one sentiment animates all hearts; the desire to spare nothing, to sacrifice all, even life itself, for the honor of the Emperor and the integrity of the Empire. We witness with deep emotion the strong manifestation of the love of the people for ourselves and for their country. We might, indeed, answer you with tranquility, that new sacrifices and new efforts will not be necessary. God, the protector of right, is with Us, and all-powerful Russia will be able, with a decisive blow, to bring to order those who have dared to disturb her tranquility. Our faithful troops, who have so recently distinguished themselves by new victories, are already concentrating upon the western frontier of the Empire. We are in readiness to punish the perjured; but we wish to distinguish the innocent from the guilty, and to pardon the weak, who, from inconsiderateness or fear have followed the current. All the subjects of our Kingdom of Poland, all the inhabitants of Warsaw, have not taken part in the conspiracy and its melancholy consequences. Many have proved, by a glorious death, that they knew their duty. Others, as we learn by the report of the Grand Duke, have been forced, with tears of despair, to return to the places occupied by the rebels. These last, together with the misguided, compose, no doubt, a great part of the army and of the inhabitants of the Kingdom of Poland. We have addressed ourselves to them by a proclamation on the 17th of this month, in which, manifesting Our just indignation against the perjured men who have commenced this rebellion, we gave orders to put an end to all illegal armaments, and to restore everything to its former footing. They have yet time, then, to repair the fault of their compatriots, and to save the

Polish kingdom from the pernicious consequences of a blind criminality. In pointing out "the only means of safety, we make known this manifestation of our benevolence toward our faithful subjects. They will see in it our wish to protect the inviolability of the throne and of the country, as well as the firm resolution to spare misguided and penitent men. Russians! the example of your Emperor will guide you, the example of justice without vengeance, of perseverance in the combat for the honor and prosperity of the Empire, without hatred of adversaries, of love and regard for the subjects of Our Kingdom of Poland who have remained faithful to the oath they have made to Us, and of an earnest desire for reconciliation with all those who shall return to their duty. You will fulfill Our hopes, as you have hitherto done. Remain in peace and quietness; full of confidence in God, the constant benefactor of Russia, and in a monarch who appreciates the magnitude and the sacredness of his duties, and who knows how to keep inviolable the dignity of His Empire, and the honor of the Russian people.

" Given at St. Petersburg the twenty-fourth of the month of December, 1930.

(Signed) "NICHOLAS."

27. The following is part of a conversation, in the presence of the Emperor, between Generals Field Marshal Diebitsch and Benkendorf, and Colonel Wielezynski, (one of the deputies sent by the Polish Dictator), at the close of a short interview, which took place at a council on the affairs of state to which those generals had been called by the Emperor.

"Well, gentlemen of Poland," said Marshal Diebitsch, "your revolution has not even the merit of being well timed. You have ' risen at the moment when the whole force of the Empire was on the march toward your frontiers, to bring the revolutionary spirits of France and Belgium to order."

When the Colonel observed that Poland thought herself capable of arresting the torrent long enough to give Europe the alarm, and to prepare her for the struggle, Marshal Diebitsch answered,

"Well, what will you gain by the result? We had calculated to make our campaign on the Rhine; we shall now make it on the Elbe or the Oder, having crushed you first. Consider this well."

28. According to the testimony of Colonel Wielczynski, the proclamation of the Emperor was in contradiction to the sentiments he expressed in the conversation above mentioned. The tone of that conversation was anything but severe. He even conceded that the Poles had just reason to be discontented, and admitted many of the barbarities of his brother, the Grand Duke Constantine. He promised Colonel Wielezynski that he would act with the strictest justice, and would consider it a duty to inquire scrupulously into, and carefully distinguish all the circumstances of the case, in regard to which a manifesto should shortly be published. As he took leave of the Colonel, in presence of Diebitsch and Benkendorf, he declared that he loved and esteemed the Poles, and that these his feelings should be the basis of his course with regard to them. How inconsistent such language was with that of the proclamation!

29. Some letters of the Emperor Nicholas were found among papers of Chlopicki, in which the Emperor expressed his thanks to him for having taken the Dictatorship, and for the service which he had done to him, by the preservation of public tranquility. The Emperor exhorted him to follow "the conditions which had been prescribed to him." The conditions here referred to could not be found.

The reader will permit me to dwell, for a moment, upon mode of conduct, on the part of the Emperor Nicholas, which is here indicated

What conditions could Nicholas propose to the Dictator, which the nation should not know of? If those conditions were compatible with justice and with the honor of the nation, why was all this secrecy necessary? If they were incompatible with justice and our honor, the Dictator certainly could not have it in his power to make the nation accept of them. On the contrary, the nation who had given him its confidence, the moment that it should have been convinced that the Dictator had intended to compromise its honor, would have despised him as a traitor, and he would have fallen a sacrifice to its indignation. To wish to induce him, on his own responsibility, to commit acts contrary to the honor of the nation, is to be willing, for selfish ends, to induce him to do that which would render him infamous in history.

Is this a course becoming a King? A conduct so insincere, Machiavellian, and even malignant, is based on the system of intrigue, and is in correspondence with the accustomed policy of the Russian cabinet, - a policy which has always brought divisions and misery upon the nations who have been under her power. Such a system, however, is far from being ultimately favorable to the interests of Russia herself, for it can never lead to a sure result. Sooner or later duplicity will be discovered, and the more a nation has been deceived, the deeper will be its determination of vengeance.

The letters referred to, which, I believe, are now in the hands of some of our countrymen, will be, in the eyes of the world, a new justification of our revolution.

CHAPTER V

Remarks on the policy of the late Dictator - System of operations adopted. - The army leaves Warsaw. - Statement of the existing forces. - Of the forces proposed to be raised. - Unfortunate consequences of the delay in the preparation of the forces. - Statement of the voices with which the war was actually commenced.

THE DICTATORship had exercised a most unpropitious influence upon our affairs.[30] Every movement had been retarded, and the most invaluable time was lost. Instead of offensive operations, the defensive was now necessarily taken. We awaited the enemy on our native soil, and exposed that soil to his insults and outrages. Even, however, at this point, the patriots called on the government to take the offensive, but it was too late. An immense Russian army was concentrated upon our frontiers, and was ready to pass them. Our forces were not strong enough to defend every point against the enemy's entrance. It was decided to keep our troops concentrated, and presenting to him always a narrow and recurvated front, to lead the enemy to the environs of Warsaw, and to give him a decisive battle there. On about the 20th of January, Prince Radzivil renewed the orders for the most rapid organization of all the different corps, and directed those corps which were already organized to hold themselves in readiness for marching. A division of lancers which was in the environs of Siedlce, augmented by some regiments of newly raised light cavalry, occupied, as a corps of observation, all the country between Wlodawa and Ciechanowiec, and were ordered to watch every movement of the enemy in that region. On about the 25th of January, the troops began to leave Warsaw and the other towns of the department, and to concentrate themselves upon a line embracing the towns of Siedlce, Ostrolenka, and Lukow.[31]

STATEMENT OF THE EXISTING ARMY, AND OF THE NEW FORCES PROPOSED TO BE LEVIED.

The whole Polish force under the Russian Government, consisted, of *Infantry*, nine regiments of two battalions each, 19,000 men, and a battalion of sappers of 1,000 men, in all, 20,000; *Cavalry*, nine regiments of four squadrons each; in all, 7,200; *Artillery*, six batteries of eight pieces each, and two batteries of light artillery, also, of eight pieces each; in all, sixty-four pieces. According to the plans of the Dictator, the infantry was to be aug-mented in the following manner: To each of the existing regiments was to be added a battalion of 1,000, making a total of 9,000 men. He then proposed to form fifteen new regiments, thus increasing the number of regiments of infantry to twenty-four. Each one of the new regiments was to be composed of three battalions of 1,000 men each. The total of these new regiments would then have been 45,000 men, and the grand total of the new levy would be 54,000 men. This body of recruits was to be made up from those of the exempts (their term of service[32] having expired) who were yet under the age of forty, and from all others under that age, and above that of sixteen.

Of this force, six thousand men were to be furnished by Warsaw and an equal number by each of the eight palatinates. Besides this force, the enrollment of a national guard at Warsaw of 10,000 men was ordered; and in forming this body, no exemption was admitted except from age or bodily infirmity. Each of the eight palatinates was also to enroll a national guard of a thousand men. Thus, the whole National Guard was to consist of 18,000 men.

The cavalry was to be augmented as follows: From the whole gendarmerie, it was proposed to form a regiment of carabiniers, consisting of two squadrons of two hundred men each. To the nine existing regiments of cavalry it was proposed to add, as a reserve, four squadrons of two hundred each, making, in all, eight hundred. Ten new regiments were to be formed, of four squadrons each; so that the whole number of old and new cavalry would be twenty regiments. The whole augmentation of this army would amount to 9,200. The raising of this force, as in the case of the infantry, was to be equally divided between Warsaw and each of the eight palatinates.

The artillery was to be augmented by four batteries, of eight pieces each, making a total of thirty-two pieces.

RECAPITULATION

	Infantry	Cavalry	Artillery
New Forces	54,000	9,200	32 pieces
Existing Forces	19,000	7,200	64
Total	73,000	16,400	96
If we should add to this number the regiments formed by the land proprietors at their own expense, detachments of volunteers, foreigners, anddetachments of partisans, amounting perhaps to	6,000	2,000	
The total might be increased to	79,000	18,400	96

This force, although it would seem to be disproportionate to the resources of the kingdom, it was certainly possible to have raised; for the energy and spirit of the people were at the highest point, and everyone felt the importance of improving the favorable moment, which the general state of Europe, and the weakness of Russia, pre-sented. If the reader will anticipate the course of events, and remember what a struggle, against the Russian force of more than 200,000 men was sustained by the 40,000 only which we actually brought into the field, he may conjecture what advantages might have been expected from twice that number, which we should certainly have brought to the field, had the energy of the government followed out its plans. But from the incapacity of the Dictator for the energetic execution of his trust, these forces were never raised, and it was soon seen that Chlopicki, by assuming a duty to which he was unequal, gave the first blow to the rising fortunes of his country. The Dictator, as we have seen, had not even taken a step towards the organization of these forces, and one would have thought that he had thrown out these plans merely to blind the eyes of the nation, without having entertained the thought of taking the field. Two months passed away, the inevitable moment of the conflict arrived, and the nation was obliged to march to the fight with half the force which, under an energetic administration, it would have wielded. If we add to this unfortunate state of things, that, besides the threatening forces of our gigantic eneiesy, Prussia and Austria, at this late moment, and especially the former, had began to take an attitude of hostility towards us, and thus all hope of sympathy from her neighbors was lost to Poland, the perilous nature of the crisis to which the delay of the Dictatorial government had brought us, thus unprepared, may be imagined. But Poland did not suffer herself to be discouraged by all these unpropitious circumstances. Trusting to the righteousness of her cause, she went forth to the contest, determined to fall or to be free.

STATEMENT OF THE FORCES WITH WHICH THE WAR WAS ACTUALLY COMMENCED.

A great exactitude in the computation of these forces would be obviously impracticable, as the precise number of the detachments of volunteers, occasionally joining the army, serving in a particular locality only, and often perhaps for a limited period, cannot be ascertained; but it will not be difficult to make a pretty near approximation to the truth.

At the beginning of the campaign, the forces were divided into four divisions of infantry, four of cavalry, and twelve batteries of artillery, of eight pieces each.

The whole infantry consisted of: The nine existing regiments,
enlarged by one battalion to each regiment, making in all.................. 27,000
One battalion of sappers 1,000
A tenth regiment of two battalions, called the "Children of Warsaw" ... 2,000
A battalion of volunteers, added to the 4th Regiment 1,000
Different detachments of volunteers, as the detachments of
Michael Kuszel and the Kurpie or Foresters, etc. 1,600

Total of Infantry... 32,600

The four divisions of infantry were nearly equal, consisting of from 7 to 8,000 men each. To each of these divisions a corps of 250 sappers was attached. The divisions were commanded as follows; 1st Division by General Krukowiecki; 2nd Division, General Zymirski; 3rd Division, General Skrzynecki; 4th Division, General Szembek.

The cavalry consisting of the nine existing regiments	7,200
Four squadrons added to these as a reserve	800
Two Squadrons of Carabiners	400
Two regiments of Krakus or light cavalry of Podlasia and Lubin	1,600
Two regiments of Mazurs	1,600
Six squadrons of Kaliszian cavalry	1,200
Two squadrons of Zamoyski Lancers	400
Total of cavalry	13,200

This cavalry, which was composed of 66 squadrons, was divided into four nearly equal bodies. They were commanded as follows: 1st Division, by General Uminski, consisting of 15 squadrons; 2nd Division, General Stryinski, 15 squadrons; 3rd Division, General Lubinski, 15 squadrons; 4th Division, making the reserve, under General Pac, 17 squadrons. Besides these divisions, four squadrons were designated for the corps of General Dwernicki.

The artillery was divided into 12 batteries of eight pieces each, making in all 96 pieces.

The general statement of the forces with which the campaign was commenced is then as follows:

Infantry, 32,600. *Cavalry*, 13,200. *Artillery*, 96 pieces.

This incredibly small number marched to the combat against a Russian force of at least 200,000 men and 300 cannon. In fact, by the reports of Field Marshal Diebitsch, found after his retreat, and the detailed statements confidently made in the *Berlin Gazette*, the Russian forces amounted to 300,000; but we reject one third on the supposition that the regiments had not been entirely completed. If the very thought of commencing a war with such disproportionate means, against so overwhelming a force, should seem to the reader to be little better than madness, he will appreciate the energy and courage with which it was supported, when he learns that in *twenty days*, from the 10th of February to the 2nd of March, thirteen sanguinary battles were fought with the enemy, besides twice that number of small skirmishes, in which, as we shall see, that enemy was uniformly defeated, and a full third part of his forces annihilated.

NOTES

30. The Dictatorship may be said to have been the first of our misfortunes. The Dictator, acting in contradiction to the spirit of the revolution, did not take advantage of that enthusiasm with which the revolution commenced and by which prodigies might have been achieved. But not only did he neglect to make use of that enthusiasm, or to foster it, he even took measures which had a tendency to repress it. The first fault with which he was reproached by the Patriotic Club, was his having given permission to the Grand Duke to leave the kingdom with his corps, taking with them their arms and accoutrements, which were really Polish property. The retaining of the Grand Duke would have been of the greatest importance to us. No historian could have blamed such an act; for if the justice of our revolution be once acknowledged, every energetic and decisive act which would favor this happy result must also be justified in the view of history. The Russians indeed have regarded our conduct on this point as an indication of weakness and timidity rather than as an act of delicacy and magnanimity, in which light Chlopicki intended that it should be considered. That same corps, attached to the Grand Duke, consisting, as we have said, of 7,000 men and 24 cannon, with the Grand Duke himself, did not regard it in this light, for they fought against us in the very first battle. Another fault of General Chlopicki was, not to have taken immediately the offen-sive, passed the Bug, and entered the brother provinces which had been incorporated with Russia. The Russian troops, especially those in Lithuania, were not in a state to resist the first impetuosity of our national forces. The Russian soldiers, as the reader probably knows, are not, except in the large cities, concentrated in barracks, as in other states of Europe, but are dispersed in quarters throughout the country, in small bodies; so that sometimes a single regiment may be spread to a circumference which may embrace eighty to a hundred villages, with perhaps from ten to thirty soldiers only, in each. In fact, the soldiers of a company may have often from six to twelve miles march to reach the quarters of their captain. All this made the concentration of these forces an affair of time and difficulty; and one regiment after another could have been fallen upon, and their whole forces annihilated in detail and that without much effusion of blood. Besides this, the Russian corps of Lithuania was composed, in part, of our brethren enrolled in that province, and even commanded, in part, by officers who were natives of that province. They would of course have united themselves with us, and the revolution would have spread, with the rapidity of lightning, to the very borders of the Dwina and the Dnieper; and after this, not four million alone, but sixteen millions of Poles, would have been united in one cause. At a later period, all this was no longer possible. Russia began to become alive to the danger of the occurrence of such a state of things, and all the regiments with Polish soldiers in their ranks were withdrawn into the interior, and three hundred Polish officers in the Russian service were sent to take commands in regiments posted in the regions about the Caucasus, in Asia. The Dictator, who gave as a reason for not having taken the above course, that the neighboring cabinets would have taken umbrage at it as a violation of a foreign territory, can with diffi-culty be conceived to have really felt that this would have been the case. Even if such apprehensions were well founded, are diplomatic formalities to be regarded, on an occasion like this? Should we, in such a cause, forbear, from apprehensions of this kind, to press onto the delivery of our brethren from the despo-tism under which they were suffering? But, in fact, the true interests of those cabinets were to be found in, what every sagacious observer of European history has pointed out as the great safeguard of Europe, the establishment of the Polish Kingdom as a barrier against the threatening preponderance of our barbarous enemy. It was indeed ridiculous to require of the Poles that they should regard, as their only limits, the little kingdom into which the violence and fraud of the combined sover-eigns had contracted them. The Poles, in entering those provinces, would have been still on the soil of their ancient country; and, in fact, the revolution was equally justifiable at Wilna, Kiev, and Smolensk, as at Warsaw. The patriots, indeed, who began the latter, did not think of their own sufferings alone, they bore in mind also the even greater sufferings of their brethren who

were more absolutely in the power of despotism. It was indeed the great end of the patriots and of the nation, the union of all the provinces of ancient Poland, which was abandoned by the Dictator. Nothing else, in fact, but the forcing of the frontiers, would have subdued the arrogance of the Emperor, and forced him to listen to our claims. The unanimous voice of sixteen million of Poles could not have safely been despised. This compulsory amelioration of our condition would have also spared Nicholas the remorse with which he must reflect on the sacrifice of nearly 900,000 lives, and the death or suffering to which he has condemned, and is still condemning, the best spirits of Poland.

31. I cannot forebear to dwell for a moment upon the occasion of the departure of our troops from Warsaw and the other towns. It was one of the fine and touching moments of our revolution. Every friend of liberty would have desired to have brought together all the autocrats of the world to witness the animation with which our national troops went forth to engage in the combat for liberty. Perhaps they would have been involuntarily struck with the conviction that this liberty must be a blessing when men will sacrifice themselves so cheerfully to achieve it. When the march was commenced, all the inhabitants of the neighboring country left their homes to witness the departure, and all the plains about Warsaw and the roadsides between Warsaw and Siedlce were covered with people. The soldiers, in marching through the streets of the city, passed between lines of people composed of senators, officers of the government, the clergy, children from the schools, the members of the National Guard, and in short, an immense assembly of both sexes, reaching even to two miles beyond Praga. All the regiments passed in review before the General-in-Chief, and each regiment took the oath to defend their country to the last drop of their blood. Exclamations such as these were constantly uttered: "Dear General, if you see us turn from before the enemy, point the artillery against us, and annihilate our ranks." The 4th Regiment, the bravest of the brave, knowing that our magazines were ill provided with powder, refused at first to receive any cartridges; but on the remonstrance of the chief, they agreed to take thirty each man, (half of the compliment for one battle), saying that they would furnish themselves afterwards from the Russians. They then entreated the Commander-in-Chief never to send them against a smaller body of the enemy than a division, and to use them wherever a decisive blow was required. "Forget, dear general," said they," that we have no powder; but trust ' to our bayonets!"

It was truly affecting to witness the parting of the soldiers from their friends and relatives, fathers taking leave of children, children of fathers, husbands of wives and to hear the cries of sorrow mingled with animating shouts and patriotic hymns. These are moments of which I am unequal to the description; but which every freeman will form a conception of moments of the struggle between domestic happiness and public duty; moments which show that the love of country is the most powerful of all sentiments and that men will sacrifice everything under its impulses.

32. A service of ten years in the army, in person, or by substitute, was required by law of every citizen.

CHAPTER VI

Entrance of the Russian forces into the Kingdom. - Proclamation of Marshal Diebitscn. - Their effect. - Disposition of the Russian and Polish forces - Plan of operations of the Poles.

THE Russian forces, simultaneously with the Polish, began to concentrate themselves on the frontiers of the kingdom, (See Plan No. I), particularly at Bialystok and Grodno. Four general points were designated for the entrance of this enormous force, viz. Zlotoria, Ciechanowiec, Brzesc, and Wlodawa.

Marshal Diebitsch, on entering the kingdom, published a proclamation to the Poles, a copy of which is given in the notes.[33]

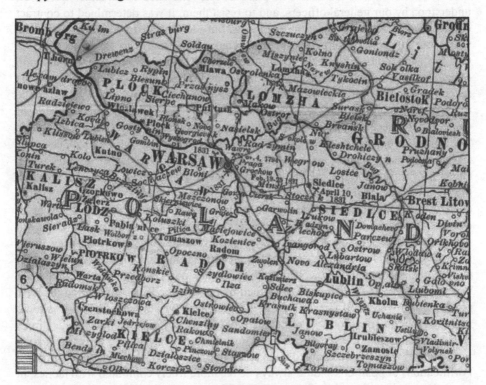

PLAN I

Those proclamations were published in the latter part of January. The people were disgusted with their promises and their menaces, and rejecting all idea of reconciliation on such terms as these proclamations set forth, they entreated to be led to the struggle in which they had once decided to engage, preferring every sacrifice to so degrading a submission.　　They demanded that an answer should be sent to Diebitsch, informing him that they were ready to meet him, and called upon the government to commence hostilities without a moment's delay.[34]

The Russian forces, [See plan No. 1.[35]] consisting, as we have already mentioned, of about 200,000 men and 300 pieces of cannon, had, on about the 5th of February, passed the Polish frontier at the four general points above named above Their different commanders, besides the Marshal Diebitsch, were, the Grand Duke Constantine, Generals Rosen, Pahlen, Geismer, Kreutz, Prince Württemberg, and Witt. The chief d'etat major was General Toll, the most skilful of the Russian generals. The space designated for the entrance of the different detachments of the Russian corps embraced an extent of ninety-six English miles. This space was almost wholly occupied by either small or large detachments. General Diebitsch, meaning to attack our centre at Siedlce with a part of his army, intended to outflank us with the rest, and to march directly upon Warsaw, and thus, following the plan of Napoleon in the campaign of Prussia, in 1806, at Jena and Auerstadt, to cripple our front, and to put an end to the war in a moment. The plans of this renowned commander were well understood by our general officers, and to resist them, it was determined to contract our forces into a line of operations, narrow, but concentrated and strong; a course which our inferiority of force seemed to require. This line was posted as follows: Our left wing, consisting of the fourth division of General Szembek and a division of cavalry under General Uminski, was in the environs of Pultusk. This wing sent its reconnaissances towards Ostrolenka. In the environs of the town of Jadow was the division of General Krukowiecki; and in the environs of Wengrow, the division of General Skrzynecki, with the division of cavalry commanded by General Lubinski. The centre of our position was about half way between the two latter places. Our right wing was at Siedlce, and was composed of the 2nd Division of infantry under General Zymirski, and the 2nd Division of cavalry under General Stryinski. To cover the right wing, a small corps under the command of General Dwernicki was posted at Seroczyn. That corps consisted of 3,000 infantry, 800 horse, and three pieces of cannon. Different patrols of cavalry were employed in observing the enemy along the whole space between Sokolow, Miendzyrzec, and Parczewo. The rivers Narew, Bug, and Liewiec, covered the whole line of our operations, and made it sufficiently strong. Our centre, especially, was well posted between Jadow, Wengrow, and Siedlce. It was protected by the great marshes formed by the Lieviec River. Excepting in a few points, which were well fortified, these marshes were wholly impassable. It is to be regretted that this position was not made still stronger by more ample fortifications. Besides making the passage of this point cost a more severe loss to the enemy, such fortifications would have enabled us to spare one whole division for other purposes. Fortifications of positions should always be the more freely combined with tactics, in proportion to the inferiority of a force.

In the above-mentioned position, we were to await the first shock of the enemy, after which the army was to retire slowly towards the environs of Praga, and in such a manner that each corps should always be on the parallel with the rest. In this retreat, each corps was required to profit by every opportunity, to cause the utmost loss to the enemy, and to harass him as much as possible. By a retreat of this nature, it was intended to draw the enemy onto the walls of Warsaw, and, having weakened him during such a retreat, to give him a decisive battle there.

NOTES

33. Proclamation of the Field Marshal Count Diebitsch Zabalkansky to the Poles.

POLES! His Majesty the Emperor and King, our august sovereign, has confided to me the command of the troops destined to put an end to the deplorable disorders which afflict the Kingdom of Poland. The proclamation of His Majesty the Emperor and King has already apprised you that the Emperor has wished, in his generosity, to distinguish His faithful subjects who have respected their oaths, from the guilty instigators of disorder who have sacrificed to their odious ambition the interests of a happy and peaceful community. Nay, more, He wishes to extend his benevolence and His clemency to the unfortunate persons who through weakness or fear have lent themselves as the accomplices of a deplorable enterprise. Poles! Hear the voice of your sovereign and your father, the successor of the august restorer of your country, who like Him has always desired your happiness. Even the guilty will experience the effects of his magnanimity, if they will trust to it with confidence. Those only who have dipped their hands in blood, and those who still more guilty perhaps, have excited others to do this; will meet the just punishment to which the law condemns them.

1. Ac the moment of entering with the troops which I command, into the Kingdom of Poland, I wish to convince you of the principles which will guide all my steps. A faithful soldier, and a conscientious executor of the orders of my sovereign, I will never depart from them. The peaceful inhabitants, who shall receive us as friends and brothers, will find their friendly dispositions reciprocated by the troops placed under my orders. The soldiers will pay a fair price for everything which shall be furnished to them, and if circumstances require that the troops shall be provisioned by the inhabitants, or if we shall be forced to make requisitions (which we shall endeavor to avoid as far as possible), in such cases the inhabitants will receive payment in printed certificates, which will be taken as money at the offices for the payment of imposts. Prices will be established for the provisions furnished according to the current value of the articles in the different districts.

2. On the approach of the Russian troops, the inhabitants of the towns and villages, who have taken arms in obedience to the orders of the government which has been illegally instituted, will be required to surrender their arms to the local authorities, if those latter shall have returned to their duties. In other cases, they will be required to give up their arms upon the entrance of the troops of His Majesty the Emperor and King.

3. Every inhabitant, who, forgetting the duties which he owes to his sovereign, shall persevere in the revolt, and shall be taken with arms in his hands, will have to meet the utmost rigor of the law. Those who shall attempt to defend themselves against the troops shall be delivered over to a council of war. The towns and villages who shall dare to resist His Majesty the Emperor and King, will be punished according to the degree their resistance shall have been carried, by an extraordinary contribution, more or less heavy. This contribution will be principally levied upon, those who shall have taken part in a criminal defense, either by carrying arms themselves, or by exercising others to that crime. In case of relapse from a return to duty, and of rebellion in the rear of the Russian Army, the insurgent places shall be treated with the utmost military rigor. The principal instigators shall be punished with death, and the others exiled; but the greatest care will be taken to distinguish and protect those who shall have had no part in the crime.

4. To prevent such evils, I invite all the authorities, civil as well as military, who may be in the towns and cities, to send deputies to the commanders of the Russian forces, when these forces shall arrive. Such deputations will bring with them as a sign of submission to their legitimate sovereign, a white flag. They will be expected to announce that the inhabitants submit themselves to the benevolence of His Majesty the Emperor and King, and that their arms have been deposited in some place which shall be designated. The Russian commanders will then take the necessary measures of security. They will maintain the civil authorities, which existed before the revolt, as well as those which shall have been instituted afterwards, if they have taken no active part in the rebellion. The Sedentary Guard of Veterans will be continued, if they have not engaged in the resistance, or given manifest proofs of treason towards their legitimate sovereign. All those authorities, civil as well as military, will be required to renew their oaths of fidelity. Conformably to the orders of His Majesty the Emperor and King, an amnesty and pardon for the past will be given to all of those who shall submit without delay, and shall comply with the conditions which have been above mentioned.

5. The Russian commanders shall organize, as circumstances may require, in the places, where no Russian garrisons may remain, a civil and municipal guard, who shall be chosen from among the most faithful of the veterans, and the inhabitants shall be entrusted with the interior police, as far as may be necessary to secure order and tranquility.

6. The organization of the administration of the Palatinates, arondissements, and communes, will remain upon the footing on which it was before the insurrection. It will be the same with all the direct and individual taxes. The authorities will remain in their places after they shall have complied with the above conditions. In other cases, new authorities will be established by the choice of the commanders of the Russian forces. That choice will fall principally upon the individuals who may unite, with the necessary capacity, an established moral character, who shall have given proofs of their fidelity to their legitimate sovereign. All those will be excluded who shall have taken any part whatever in the rebellion, as well as those who after the entrance of the Russian troops into the kingdom shall persist in an organized opposition against legal order. The proprietors of land and houses who may remain tranquil in their habitations, and shall submit to the conditions above announced, will be protected in their rights, as well by the local authorities as by the Russian troops. In other cases, the property of all those who shall remain in the revolutionary ranks will be sequestered, as well as that of those who shall have continued to exercise the functions entrusted to them by the illegal government, or in some who shall have openly taken part in the revolt. Such are, Poles, the principles which will direct the army which His Majesty has deigned to confide to my command. You have to choose between the benefits which an unqualified submission to the will of our magnanimous sovereign assures to you, and the evils which will be brought upon you by a state of things without object as well as without hope. I hold it an honor to have been called upon to make known to you these resolutions, emanating from the generous intentions of the Emperor and King. I shall execute them scrupulously, but I shall not fail to punish criminal obstinacy with inflexible severity.

(Signed)   THE MARSHAL COUNT DIEBITSCH ZABALKANSKY.

They shall have complied with the above conditions. In other cases, new authorities will be established by the choice of the commanders of the Russian forces.

Proclamation of the Count Diebitsch Zabalkansky to the Polish troops.

GENEROUS POLES! Twenty-five years since, your country was implicated in the wars which the gigantic plans of a celebrated conqueror had kindled. The hope, often awakened, and always disappointed, of an illusory regeneration, had connected you with his fortunes. Faithful, although unfortunate, you answered those deceptive promises by the sacrifice of your blood. There is scarce a country, however distant it may have been, that has not been wet with that blood which you have prodigally shed for interests altogether foreign to the destiny of your country. Great events brought at last, at a remarkable epoch, an end to your misfortunes.

After a contest, forever memorable, in which Russia saw you among the number of her enemies, the Emperor Alexander, of immortal memory, obeying only the impulse of his magnanimous heart, wished to add to all his other titles to glory, that of being the restorer of your country. Poland recovered her name, and the Polish Army a new life. All the elements of national welfare, of tranquility, and of prosperity, were miraculously united, and fifteen years of uninterrupted progress prove, to this day, the greatness of the benefits for which your country is indebted to the paternal solicitude of the sovereign who was its restorer, and to the no less earnest concern of him who has so nobly continued the work of his predecessor.

Polish Warriors! His Majesty the Emperor and King has trusted to your gratitude and your fidelity. A short time since he gladly did justice to your devotedness and your good will. The exemplary conduct of all the Polish officers, without exception, who partook with our armies the fatigues and the glory of the Turkish war, had given a high satisfaction to His Majesty. We accepted with pleasure this fraternity of arms which became a new bond between the Russian and Polish troops. The best hope of reciprocal advantages should connect with that union, which was founded upon all that is sacred in military honor. Those hopes have been cruelly deceived. A handful of young men, who have never known the dangers of battle, of young officers who had never passed through a campaign or even a march, have shaken the fidelity of the brave. The latter have seen committed in their ranks the greatest of crimes, the murder of their commanders; they have not arrested the revolt against their legitimate sovereign. What unhappy blindness, what criminal condescension has been able to induce these veterans to permit the consummation of the greatest of offences, and to join themselves with those whose hands were stained with blood! Can it be possible that the design of rendering a service to their country has been made for a moment a pretext for such conduct? That country can answer that for a long period she had never enjoyed so much happiness. She had attained much, and she could still hope much from her fidelity, and the support of public order. She exposes herself to the loss of all these advantages by engaging in an unequal struggle, in revolting against a sovereign whose firm and energetic character is well-known, and in braving a power which has never been defied with impunity.

Polish Warriors! Rebellion would stamp upon your front the stain of dishonor. Put away from you such an ignominy. History will one day relate that, in the hope of serving your country, you have been faithful and devoted to the man who promised you everything, and kept his promise in nothing. Shall it also say that, paying with ingratitude and perjury, the sovereign who has generously granted you everything which you had any right to hope for, you have drawn down upon your country new misfortunes, and upon yourselves an indelible disgrace? If some grievances existed, you should have had confidence enough in the character of our august sovereign to have laid before him your complaints, in a legal manner, and with that frankness which characterizes the true soldier. And I too, Poles, I speak the sincere language of a soldier; I have never known any other. Obedient to the orders of my sovereign, I reiterate, by His wishes, all the propositions which, in His clemency, He has already made to you by his proclamation of the 17th of December. Our august sovereign has witnessed, with marked satisfaction, the fidelity of the brave Light Cavalry of the Guard, of the greater part of the Grenadiers of the Guard, and of the sub-officers of the cavalry. He does not doubt that the greater part of the troops cherished the desire to remain faithful to their oaths, and that many others were hurried away only by the impulse of the, moment. Let each one hasten to execute the orders which are contained in the proclamation of His Majesty. But if unforeseen circumstances do not permit you to follow the course which has been pointed out to you at least, on the approach of the faithful armies of our common sovereign, remember your duties and your oaths. It is not as enemies that the troops placed under my command enter the Kingdom of Poland. It is on the contrary with the noble object of re-establishing public order and the laws. They will receive as brothers all persons, either in civil or military life, who shall return to their duties; but they will know how to subdue, with the constancy and courage which they have ever manifested, the resistance which evil-minded men may attempt to oppose to them, men who, trampling underfoot the sacredness of their oaths and the laws of honor, sacrifice to their ambitious and even criminal projects the dearest interests of their country. It is to you especially, generals and colonels of the Polish Army, that I address myself with confidence; to you, whom I have been accustomed to regard as my worthy brothers-in-arms. Return from the momentary error to which you have been capable of surrendering yourselves, that you may, in joining the rebellious, bring them back to their duties, and serve your country without violating your oaths. Experience will have disabused you of your error: return to the path of fidelity, and you will by that restore the happiness of your country. You know the clemency of our august sovereign: return to him. Weigh well the immense responsibility which you will take upon your heads by a criminal obstinacy. Join yourselves to your brothers-in-arms. Show that you are still worthy to be the commanders of the troops which your sovereign has entrusted to you. You will be received as brothers. An amnesty of the past is assured to you. The troops which I command will fulfill with loyalty the intentions of our sovereign, and the gratitude of your country, restored to tranquility, will be a delightful reward for your return to your duty. But if there are found among you men hardened in crime, who cannot be persuaded to trust in magnanimity, because they know not the elevated sentiments in which it has its origin, let all the bonds of military fraternity between you and them be broken; the all-powerful hand of God, the protector of the good cause, will bring down upon their heads the punishment due to their crimes.

(Signed)   THE MARSHAL DIEBITSCH ZABALKANSKY.

34. To the proclamations of General Diebitsch, one of our countrymen made a reply, in the form of a letter, which was published in the gazettes, and which, as far as my memory serves me, was in nearly the following terms: "General, your proclamations, which breathe the spirit of injustice, arrogance, and cruelty—the menacing tone of which is backed by the colossal force you have led to the invasion of our territory, and which you are to wield as an instrument for establishing a new tyranny and inflicting new sufferings upon a country of freemen, these proclamations, general, prove that the favorable opinion which Europe entertained of you was ill-grounded, and that you too, like the rest, are willing to lend yourself an easy and vile instrument in the hands of the oppressor. Diebitsch! Can it be you who so recently passed the Balkans, to deliver a nation from the yoke of barbarism, an action which gained for you so great a name in history?

"Do you remember the proclamations which you published on that occasion, how different from these, filled with noble thoughts, and in which you felicitated yourself on being placed in command of an army destined to deliver the unfortunate Greek nation from the barbarism which was oppressing it? What a contrast! There you went to deliver the unfortunate; here you come to increase the sufferings of a nation which has for fifteen years been oppressed in a manner, which was well known to you, and which it is horrible to think of. General, have you forgotten how you were received at Warsaw, after your return from the campaign of Turkey? Have you lost the recollection of those looks of welcome and of joy at the sight of the man who had effected the deliverance of an unfortunate and oppressed nation? You were then touched, for the sentiments of the Polish nation were in harmony with those which you yourself then entertained. All those recollections you have turned away from. Dazzled by false ideas of greatness, arrogance has driven from your heart those noble sentiments which would have made you truly great. Diebitsch! Poland once had confidence in you. Many Poles had hoped that you would act as a mediator between your monarch and us. No one could be in a more favorable situation than yourself to set before that monarch the nature of our sufferings, and the claims which we had upon his justice. You would have been in a situation to persuade him that the time had come to aid the cause of civilization, and to promote his own happiness, by conceding to a nation those rights which are essential to its happiness and prosperity. Poland had such expectations of you. You alone, who are so near the person of the monarch, and to whom his character is so intimately known, you could have done this. Such conduct would have added indeed to the glory you had already acquired. Who then would have equaled you? But, for your misfortune, you have chosen another course, and by acting as a servile instrument of tyranny you have tarnished all your former glory. Know then, Diebitsch, that the Poles despise you. Spare both your promises and your menaces; for with neither will you effect anything. They long for the approach of your colossal masses, that they may give you an example of what freemen can do."

35. Editor: This is not the original map provided with the text. That map was of extremely poor quality. Though the quality of this map is superior, there will be discrepancies in the spellings of various Polish city names. They are not, however, so different that the text cannot be followed on it.

CHAPTER VII

The opening fire- - Affairs of the 10th and 11th February. - Combat of Stoczek. - Disposition in consequence of that battle. - Battle of Bourne. - Retrograde movement to Dobre. - Combat of Makowiec - Passage of the Orsyca. - Combat of Dobre. - Attack on the right wing at Minsk.

THE tenth of February 1831, was the first day, after an interval of fifteen years, of the encounter between the Russian and Polish arms. Mendzyrzec (18) was the place in which the first fire was given; and the little skirmish which took place there was of good presage. On the morning of that day, two regiments of Cossacks showed themselves upon the plain before the town, on which were posted two regiments of Krakus, or light cavalry, and the 4th Lancer Regiment, as an advanced guard. Our cavalry were impatient to engage with the enemy, and begged of their commander to be allowed to attack him. When it was seen that this body of the enemy was detached from his larger force, permission was given to one of the two new regiments of light cavalry, supported-by a squadron of the old cavalry as a reserve, to throw themselves upon the enemy. In a moment, our cavalry were among the ranks of the Cossacks. Both of the enemy's regiments were dispersed, and one squadron, with six officers, was taken prisoners. The enemy was not pursued, our troops being satisfied with this successful attack, and with having excited the first consternation in the enemy's ranks. After this skir-mish, our cavalry, in obedience to previous instructions, retired to the environs of Siedlce. In this town was a little garrison consisting of a regiment of light infantry and a detachment of riflemen, formed and commanded by Michael Kuszel. On the 11th, at about mid-day, the whole of the advanced guard of the Russian centre, which was commanded by Diebitsch in person, reached the environs of Siedlce, and took position there. Before the night set in, other Russian columns began to place themselves upon the same plain. Their advanced guard then recommenced the march, throwing their tirailleurs forward, who began a warm fire, which was answered by our own light troops, who were placed in the suburbs and the sides of the town. The brave detachment of Kuszel's riflemen, who were finely trained and equipped, caused a great loss to the enemy. The Russian artillery, to protect their tirailleurs and the columns of infantry which followed them, commenced a heavy fire upon the suburbs occupied by our infantry. This fire of the Russian artillery was ineffectual; but our own fire, as the Russians were exposed in an open plain, was very destructive. The action continued until dark, when our infantry began to evacuate the town and marched to rejoin the divisionary camp, which was about a mile in the rear.

At 8 o'clock, General Zymirski, supposing that the enemy had taken possession of the town, determined to make an attack, with two regiments, upon the town and the Russian camp, at the point of the bayonet. The 7th Line Infantry Regiment and the 4th Light Infantry Regiment, which were designated for this object, fell with impetuosity upon the enemy, whom they found in a wholly unprepared state. A few hundred prisoners were the fruits of this attack, after which our forces evacuated the town. These little advantages gained in those two days, retarded the advance of the enemy. He remained inactive on the 12th and 13th. On the 14th, the Russian corps under the command of General Kreutz, composed of 15,000 men and 24 pieces of cannon, attacked the small corps of observation on our right, under the command of General Dwernicki.

COMBAT OF STOCZEK.   [See Plan II.]

General Dwernicki, although aware of the vast superiority of the enemy's- force, yet, trusting in the strength of his own position, determined to meet his attack, and give him battle. The position of Stoczek (a) was strong in several respects; first, from its commanding elevation; secondly, from the circumstance that the town is protected by the Swider River (6), which forms marshes that are not passable but by a dyke (m) at a short distance from the city, in the direction in which the Russian army was approaching. That dyke was defended by the whole artillery of our corps, consisting of three pieces (e); and the declivity descending toward the dyke was occupied by two companies of light troops dispersed in favorable positions as sharpshooters, and in such a manner as to act on the dyke. General Dwernicki divided his forces into the smallest possible bodies, to give an appearance of extent to his line, and thus mask his inferiority of force. Leaving a battalion of infantry (rf) to protect the artillery and prevent the passage of the dyke,—which passage, he was sure that the enemy could not possibly execute rapidly, and that this small force was sufficient, if not to prevent at least to retard it,— he t6ok the two battalions (rf) which made the remainder of his force, and throwing them upon the right bank (A) of this river, in the forest, where an easier and safer passage was open to the enemy, he there awaited the enemy's movements. The first step of the Russians (g, h) was to place all their artillery (f) at the nearest possible point to our position, and to commence a warm fire upon the town. Under this fire they thought to affect the passage of the dyke. General Dwernicki ordered his artillery not to fire, until the Russian columns should make their appearance on the dyke, and then to open a fire of grape upon them. In this manner some hours passed, during which the Russian artillery kept up an ineffectual fire, and the Russian corps executed various maneuvers in attempting to force the passage of the dyke, and in pushing their attack in the direction of the forest. General Kreutz, seeing that his attempts to force the dyke were attended with severe loss, and thinking that in the other direction the passage would be much easier, decided on a general attack in that quarter. He divided his corps, leaving one part before the dyke, and with the remainder advanced to the attack of our right (A). Strong columns of Russian infantry and cavalry marched against it. As soon as this maneuver was observed by Dwernicki, the idea was conceived by him of prevent-ing the attack, by throwing himself with the utmost impetuosity upon the enemy before he had taken a position and while on the march. He renewed his orders to defend with the utmost firmness the passage of the dyke; and, taking all the cavalry with him, he passed over towards the forest; and, with the united force of this cavalry and the infantry who were concealed in the forest, he threw himself upon the Russian artillery, and the cavalry which was protecting it. In a moment both artillery and cavalry were completely overthrown and dispersed, and seven pieces of cannon remained in our hands. The disorder communicated itself to the columns which were on the march, who thought no longer of following up their attack, but retreated as fast as possible, and in fact a general and disorderly retreat commenced. The ruin of their left wing caused consternation in the forces composing their right, who, not knowing what had happened, ceased their fire, quitted their position, and joined in the general retreat. Besides the killed and wounded, more than 1,000 prisoners, with twenty officers, were taken, together with a great quantity of ammunition, baggage, &c. among which were several voitures containing the chapels of the camp.[36]

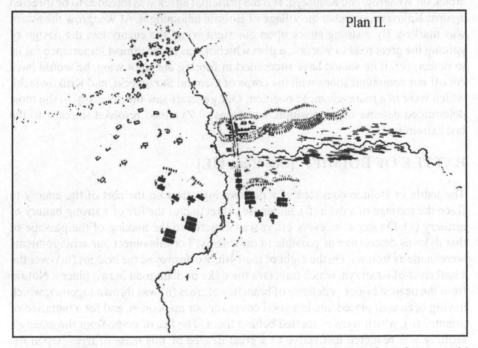

Plan II.

The enemy was followed a short distance only, as the inferiority of our force would not of course admit of an extended pursuit, and it was an important object also with General Dwernicki not to permit the enemy to discover that inferiority. He contented himself therefore with having destroyed nearly a third part of the enemy's corps, and with having thrown his whole force into the greatest consternation. This brilliant affair was the com-mencement of the remarkable career of General Dwernicki; and it was a propitious opening for our campaign.

General Dwernicki resumed his former position at Stoczek, where he awaited the orders which the Commander-in-Chief might issue on receiving the report of what had taken place. To make this position stronger, he ordered a barricade of trees to be made at the termination of the dyke and at the other points where the approach was easy, and, in order to keep a close observation upon the enemy, he sent patrols in the direction of Kock and Zelechow. While thus occupied, he received orders to leave his position immediately by a rapid march in the direction of Zelechow and Macieiowice, then to pass the Vistula and meet the Russian corps under the command of Prince Württemberg, who, after having crossed that river at Pulawa, had made a demonstration on its left bank, and was approaching Warsaw.

On receiving these orders, General Dwernicki left Stoczek on the same night.

In consequence of the enemy's attack upon Dwernicki's corps, which covered our right wing, that wing was inclined and withdrawn towards Kaluszyn, in order not to, be exposed to the enemy's demonstrations upon its flank or rear. The town of Minsk was also occupied by a detachment. On the 15th the Russians made a simultaneous attack on Wengrow and Kaluszyn. But the principal attack was intended to be directed against Kaluszyn, or rather the village of Boimie adjoining it. At Wengrow the attack was masked. By a strong attack upon our right wing, the enemy had the design of gaining the great road to Warsaw, a plan which it was of the utmost importance for us to defeat; for, if he should have succeeded in forcing our right wing, he would have cut off our communications with the corps of General Skrzynecki, and Krukowiecki, which were in a more advanced position. Our generals saw the necessity of the most determined defense of the position, and General Zymirski resolved to resist to the last extremity.

BATTLE OF BOIMIE.   [See Plan III.]

The battle of Boimie consisted of a persevering effort on the part of the enemy to force the passage of a dyke (ft), under the protection of the fire of a strong battery of artillery (e). On our side, every effort was directed to the making of the passage of that dyke as destructive as possible to the enemy. For this object our arrange-ments were made as follows: On the night of the 14th, we destroyed the bridges (m) over the small river of Kostrzyn, which traverses the dyke or main road in two places. Not far from the nearest bridge, a defense of branches of trees (n) was thrown together, which having been well placed, made a good cover for our marksmen, and for a battalion of infantry (o), which were concealed behind them. The fire of grape from the enemy's artillery was rendered ineffective to a great degree by this mass of trees. Upon the nearest elevations of ground (B), General Zymirski placed eighteen pieces of cannon (a), the fire of which was concentrated upon the dyke. By this means every attempt of the enemy to re-construct bridge was made to cost him a severe loss, and was rendered ineffectual. The main body of our forces was placed without the reach of the enemy's artillery. On the left of our position, at the distance of about half a mile, a small road (p) led to Dobre, and that road was intersected by the small river above mentioned. The bridge which continued the road over this river was destroyed by us, and a small detachment placed there to prevent its reconstruction and its passage by the enemy.

Such was the distribution of the small force which, profiting by the strength of its position, was able to meet the attacks of the numerous body of the enemy commanded by Marshal Diebitsch in person, and which were renewed during the whole day.

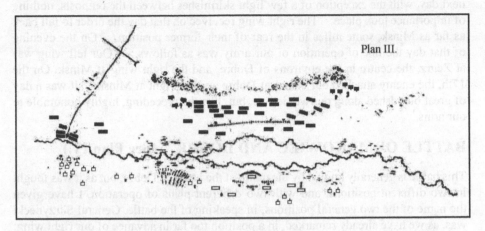

Plan III.

The details of the action are as follows: - At about 9 o'clock on the morning of the 15th, the Russian force commenced debouching from the forests which border the main road, between Mingosy and Boimie, and deploying to the right and left, took position. In a short time, the field was covered with the enemy's masses. His force consisted of twelve regiments of infantry (f), six of cavalry (g), and sixty pieces of cannon. It was at about noon that the enemy placed his artillery upon the heights (A) above the bridge and commenced his fire. After continuing for some time this fire, which was but occasionally answered by our artillery, the enemy sent several battalions in column, upon the bridge, a part of which force engaged in the repair of the bridge, and the rest attempted to make the passage. Every approach of the enemy was met with a warm fire from behind the defense of trees above mentioned, and our artillery at the same time opened a destructive fire of grape upon the bridge. The attempts of the enemy were renewed for some hours, in vain.

Finding the impossibility of forcing this passage, he directed his efforts to that on his right (D), and sent a cloud of light infantry and cavalry to attempt to pass the marshes, and ford the stream. But this passage was equally impossible, and several Russian regiments, who were engaged in the attempt, exposed themselves to a severe fire of platoons from our troops, and several staff officers of the enemy were killed at the head of those regiments. In these renewed and bloody attempts, the day passed away, and as the night approached, our troops quietly evacuated their position, and took another a few miles in the rear.

As to the affair at Wengrow, it was only an engagement with the rearguard of the corps of General Skrzynecki. That general, knowing his position to be too far advanced, decided to retire as far as the environs of Dobre. This retreat was so orderly that it seemed rather an evolution than a retreat. All the movements were executed with perfect coolness, and the alternate retreat and fire of the different battalions, the displaying and closing of the columns, the change of front, &c. were executed with such precision that it impressed the enemy with a certain degree of respect, and though three times superior in force he did not attempt to push his attack. In this manner, the corps arrived at the village of Makowiec, where it took position. On the next day, with the exception of a few light skirmishes between the outposts, nothing of importance took place. The right wing received on that day the order to fall back as far as Minsk, some miles in the rear of their former position. On the evening of that day the line of operation of our army was as follows: — Our left wing was at Zegrz, the centre in the environs of Dobre, and the right wing at Minsk. On the 17th, the enemy attacked our centre at Dobre and our right at Minsk. It was a day of great bloodshed along our whole line, but, like the preceding, highly honorable to our arms.

BATTLE OF MAKOWIEC AND DOBRE. (See Plan IV.)

This battle is generally known by the name of the battle of Dobre; but as it was fought in two different positions, and with two different plans of operation, I have given the name of the two general positions, in speaking of the battle. General Skrzynecki was, as we have already remarked, in a position too far in advance of our right wing; and as the enemy on that day had attacked, as we have also stated, the right wing and the centre simultaneously, and could have made, as will be seen by the plan, a demonstration on Stanislawow, and thus have acted on the rear of Skrzynecki, which was nearest to him, that general had two objects to effect. First to make the attack of the enemy as costly to him as possible, and next to arrange his retrograde movement in such a manner as to be able to reach Stanislawow by night. Both of these designs were exceedingly well executed. Upon each of his positions he was master of his own movements, and quitted them at his own time. This affair of the 17th of February was the occasion of the first development of the remarkable talents of this commander. It was then that he first awakened the high expectations and gained the confidence of the nation, which soon after committed to him the trust so honorably and faithfully executed by him. In regard to the first position at Makowiec, the reader will observe, on examining the plan, that the Polish forces were principally engaged in defending a triangular space embraced between the two roads (f) which lead from Wengrow and Kaluszyn and meet behind Makowiec (h). This space over which small elevations covered with brush-wood were scattered, afforded good positions for artillery as well as infantry: but the principal advantage of this peculiarity of the ground was, that it concealed the inferiority of our forces. In this position, the village of Makowiec was made a point d'appui upon our left wing, and it was defended by five companies (rf), under the command of Colonel Dombrowski. Six pieces of artillery (e) placed in the rear of this village, reached with their fire the village and the plain in front of it. The Russian position was an open plain.

The enemy commenced by an attack upon the two roads from Wengrow and Kaluszyn; and as the attack was met with a strong resistance, he began to deploy upon the plain between the two roads, and to take order of battle. Nearly 30,000 Russians, with fifty or sixty pieces of cannon (c), in a short time were seen upon that plain, and commenced a terrible fire of artillery and musketry along their whole line, directed principally against the village and the wooded ground. Several battalions (a), in column, attempted an attack upon these points. Those attacks were witnessed by Colonels Dombrowski and Boguslawski with perfect indifference. They even ordered our artillery not to fire. Our tirailleurs, and all the infantry in that position, formed themselves into detached columns (k) of half battalions, and the Russian columns approached. Our artillery then commenced a fire of grape, and this fire was a signal for our columns, with the brave Colonels Boguslawski and Dombrowski at their head, to leave their cover and to throw themselves upon the enemy. The 4th Regiment immortalized itself in that attack. One of its columns threw itself upon three of the-enemy, the fire ceased, and a terrible carnage at the point of the bayonet commenced. The enemy repeatedly renewed his attacking force, but he found it impossible to move our position.   At about midday, having suffered so much from loss and exhaustion, he discontinued the attack. General Skrzynecki, profiting by the cessation of the enemy's fire, took the opportunity to pass the Liwiec, and ordered a light fire of tirailleurs to be kept up, under cover of which his columns commenced executing the passage. When the greater part of the corps had passed, the tirailleurs began to make a retrograde movement, and were undisturbed by the enemy. Six squadrons of cavalry (c), left as a rearguard, protected the passage of the river by the light troops. In this manner, the position was slowly evacuated, the bridge destroyed, and by about two o'clock the whole corps were on the march for Dobre. The six squadrons above named, to which were added nine pieces of light artillery (H), prevented for a long while the reconstruction of the bridge by the enemy, and did not quit their position until the corps was at a safe distance, after which they followed rapidly and overtook the corps at about four o'clock, and with it took position in order of battle near Dobre.

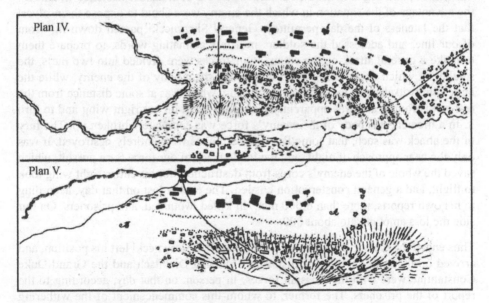

BATTLE OF DOBRE.   [See Plan V.]

The position of Dobre was more advantageous for us than the former. It was protected in front by two ponds of considerable size, which lost themselves at their extremities in marshy ground. The only passage which led between those two ponds was easy of defense and General Skrzynecki posted upon it twelve pieces of artillery of large caliber (a). The remaining part of this position was, like the former, covered with scattered clumps of brush-wood. The principal circumstance, however, which made this position eligible, was the declivity of the ground, inclining towards the marshy ponds above mentioned.

General Skrzynecki collected all, his cavalry upon his right wing, to hinder the enemy from gaining the road that leads to Minsk (A). The left of his position (B) he laid open to the enemy. The position in that direction was surrounded by marshes, upon which, if the enemy should advance, it would be impossible for him to extricate himself without being exposed to fight on the 'most disadvantageous terms.

On this oblique front, General Skrzynecki awaited the approach of the Russian force. In about half an hour after our position was taken, the enemy arrived, and began to debouch between the two ponds, which he was allowed to do, under a very light fire of our artillery. Every maneuver, however, upon our right was met with desperate charges of the bayonet, and the fire of our whole artillery. All his attempts in that quarter were ineffectual. In the repulses of these attacks, two of our bravest Colonels, Boguslawski, commander of the 4th Infantry Regiment, and Ziemiecki, commander of the 2nd Regiment of Uhlans, (the former fighting on foot with his carbine in his hand at the head of his regiment), were severely wounded. At last, after these ineffectual attempts on our right, the enemy fell into the plans of General Skrzynecki, and began to act on our left, when our commander hastened to take all the advantage of the situation in which the enemy were about to expose themselves, that the lateness of the day permitted. General Skrzynecki passed down the front of our line, and addressed the soldiers in a few animating words, to prepare them to make a general attack on the enemy. Our forces were divided into two parts, the smaller of which occupied, by their attack, the main body of the enemy, while the larger threw itself upon the enemy's right wing, which was at some distance from the rest of his forces, and was apparently intending to act on our right wing and to turn it. In a moment this body of the enemy's force was completely broken up. The fury of the attack was such, that some Russian battalions were entirely destroyed. It was only the near approach of night, and the inadequacy of our force for a pursuit, which saved the whole of the enemy's corps from destruction; for his entire right wing took to flight, and a general consternation ensued. The enemy lost on that day, according to his own reports, more than 6,000 men, in killed, wounded, and prisoners. On our side the loss amounted to about 800.

Thus ended the memorable battle of Dobre. General Skrzynecki left his position, and arrived on the same night at Stanislawow. Marshal Diebitsch and the Grand Duke Constantine were with the Russian forces, in person, on that day, according to the report of the prisoners. The former, to whom this commencement of the withering of his laurels had led to a state of the greatest exasperation, often led the columns in person to the fire - but all in vain.

On the same day, as we have already remarked our right wing was attacked at Minsk. The enemy supposed that our main force was there, and it was for that reason that he chose to attack Dobre, being more confident of piercing our line at that point. The Russian corps under General Rosen, which attacked our right wing, satisfied themselves with keeping up a fire of artillery on Minsk, and the day passed without any attempt to force the position having been made. Our troops were in the same position at night as in the morning, and nothing of importance occurred, although occasionally severe losses were sustained on both sides.

NOTES

36. It was in this battle that the celebrated Matuszka (in Russian Mamyuika), or the image of the Holy Mother, fell into our hands. This image was held in great veneration by that superstitious people. In the campaign of Turkey, many of their successes were attributed to the Mamyuika. Its loss occasioned a general sensation in the Russian army, and was-regarded by them as a most unfavorable presage. We often heard the prisoners whom we afterwards took, attribute all their misfortunes to the Holy Mother having abandoned them.

CHAPTER VIII

Retrograde movement of the 18th of February. - Details of this movement, and of the actions which took place. - The army reaches the field of Praga - Its reception at Warsaw. - Position of the army. - Battle of Wawr and Bialolenka. - Operations of General Dwernicki against the corps of Prince Württemberg. - Defeat of that corps by General Dwernicki at Swiena. - Renewal of the enemy's attack on the main army on the 20th. - Its successful resistance. - Review of the events of the preceding days. - Examination of the plan of operations of the Polish Army.

ON the 18th, our whole line was ordered to make a retrograde movement, [See Plan VI.] The utmost order and tranquility was to be observed in this movement. The several corps were required to preserve a constant communication with each other and to keep themselves uniformly on the same parallel. General Zimirski, commanding the right wing (A), and who remained on the main road, received orders to take advantage of every good position which he should meet with between Dembe-Wielkie (13) and Milosna (12). Two points in particular were recommended to his attention, Dembe-Wielkie (14), and Milosna. Nature presents at those points commanding positions surrounded by forests. In each of those positions, the enemy would be exposed to the fire of our artillery, on debouching from the intervening forests; and it was designed to make the attack of those positions as costly as possible to the enemy.

The centre (B), which was commanded by Generals Skrzynecki and Krukowiecki, was to retire upon the road which leads from Stanislawow (9) to Okuniew (11). Upon this winding road, which traverses thick forests, the means of defense was easy.

The left wing (C), commanded by Szembek and Uminski, which was in the environs of Zegrz (4), received orders to gain Jablonna (16), and Zombke (15), on the same night. The great bridge over the Narew at Zegrz was to be destroyed, and a small detachment to be left at Zagroby, for the purpose of observing the enemy.

Conformably to the above orders, our entire line commenced the evacuation of its position, and an incessant fire was kept up throughout the line, during the whole day. In the morning, two squadrons of light cavalry, which were sent from Minsk to Stanislawow, met a Cossack regiment, who were making a reconnaissance, after having traversed the forest of Jakubow. The cavalry threw themselves upon them, dispersed them, and took two hundred prisoners with their horses. Upon the position of Dembe, our cavalry threw themselves upon some Russian artillery which appeared upon our right, and were marching in a direction from Ruda. Six chests of ammunition were taken, and four pieces of cannon were spiked. At Stanislaus, the 2nd Regiment of Uhlans and the 4th of the Line performed prodigies of valor, throwing themselves continually upon superior masses of the enemy. The division of General Zimirski repelled two successive attacks from a superior force of the enemy at Konik, upon the road between Dembe-Wielkie and Janowek. Twelve pieces of artillery, placed upon the elevated points of the road, poured an incessant fire of grape upon the masses which were advancing to the attack, and which were enclosed by forests on both sides, as well as impeded in their progress by the trees which had been placed across the road to obstruct them; and, although the enemy constantly renewed his attacking columns, he was not able to force our position, which indeed was not evacuated until the movement of the general line required a corresponding withdrawal of this division.

Our left wing fought with equal advantages at Nasielsk. From this town, which was entirely in flames, the attacks of the enemy were repeatedly repulsed. Our artillery distinguished themselves by acts of daring valor. They drew their pieces into the midst of blazing streets, in order to pour a more effective fire upon the masses of the enemy, who had entered at the opposite extremities.

The 1st Light Infantry Regiment, having at their head the brave Szembek, threw themselves upon a part of the town occupied by a whole division of the enemy, and drove them out. Even in the midst of the burning town, our chasseurs fell upon and destroyed the different parties of the enemy. The enemy, on quitting the place, was exposed to continual attacks from our cavalry, under the command of General Uminski, who took on that day some hundred prisoners, and among them several officers.

Our right wing, in its last position at Milosna (12), held the enemy in check before that town. General Zimirski placed his artillery upon the heights behind the town, from which the town and the adjoining plain were commanded. Every attempt of the enemy, every debouchment from the forest, cost him a severe loss. The enemy in vain took positions with his artillery to act upon us. He was not permitted to occupy Milosna until night approached.

At Okuniew, the road passes a marshy forest for more than half a mile. The enemy was imprudent enough to push his columns upon this road. General Skrzynecki awaited them at a point not far distant on the opposite side. The advanced guard of the enemy, imprudently composed of several regiments of Cossack cavalry, had already passed the dyke, when the 4th Regiment threw themselves in columns upon them.

The enemy was thrown into the utmost consternation. Their only escape was into the marshes on either side, where some hundreds of them were taken prisoners without resistance. The arrival of the night terminated the scene, and saved this advanced guard of the enemy from total destruction. Thus, ended a sanguinary day, on which, in every part of our line, our troops were victorious, and the enemy was subjected to immense losses. Our generals had made the best choice of their positions, and had profited by them to the utmost.

96

The enemy's loss on that day, in killed, wounded, and prisoners, amounted to at least 10,000 men. On our side the loss did not exceed 1,000.[37]

On the night of the 18th our army took the following position. [See Plan VII.] Our left wing was between Jablonna (16) and Zombki (15), and sent out its reconnaissances as far as Zagroby (i), upon the Narew (N), the bridge over which at that place they destroyed. Our centre was between Okuniew (11) and Zombki (15). Our right wing was at Wawr (17).

After two such bloody days, as the preceding had been for the Russians, we cannot sufficiently express our astonishment that Marshal Diebitsch should have allowed his army no repose, but should have again pushed his attack, without any new plan, on the 19th and 20th. These operations of Diebitsch, without an assignable end, indicated a blind confidence in numbers, or the headlong fury of a man inflamed by the renown which he had acquired, and who was determined to make the event bear out as nearly as "possible, whatever sacrifice it might cost, the rash boast which he is said to have made, that he would finish the war in twenty-four hours. But he sacrificed his thousands in vain.

On the 19th an action took place, not only with the Grand Army under the walls of Warsaw, or on the fields of Praga, but also on the left bank of the Vistula at Swierza [(7) PL VI.], forty miles from Warsaw, where General Pwernicki beat Prince Württemberg, who, as we have already mentioned, had passed the Vistula at Pulawa [(6) PL VI.], and was approaching Warsaw [(1) PL VI].

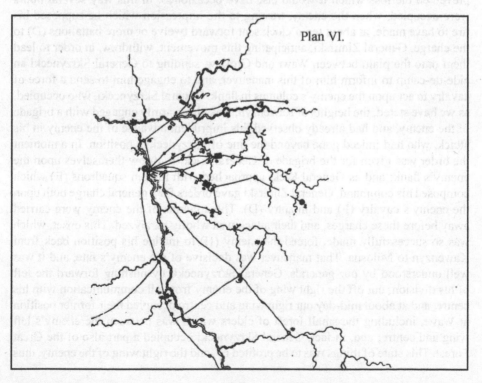

Plan VI.

BATTLE OF WAWR AND BIALOLENKA. [PL VIII and IX.]

At the break of day, upon every point, the right wing, the centre, and the left wing, our line was attacked. We mlight remark in regard to the positions of the two armies on that day, that our right wing (A), which was at Wawr, was unprotected, while on the other hand the left wing (C) of the enemy, opposite to it, was very advantageously placed on heights covered with woody between Milosna and Wawr. Our centre (B) was better posted at Kawenzyn. It occupied this village, (which was in a commanding position), and the declivity descending from it to the village of Zombki. Our left wing at Bialolenka was advantageously covered by little wooded hills, having two dykes in front leading toward them.

The Russians on that day directed their strongest attack upon our right wing, which occupied the weakest position. With the view of carrying this position, they sent against it some forty battalions of infantry and some thirty squadrons of cavalry, supported by seventy pieces of artillery. Our position was defended by a division of about ten battalions of infantry and fifteen squadrons of artillery, supported by twenty-four pieces of artillery. This enormous disproportion did not discourage our soldiers. Their energy supplied the place of numbers. The enemy commenced his attack by a warm fire of light troops and a fire from his artillery, which commanded the plain. The skillful maneuvers of General Zimirski, in displaying his front, contracting it, dividing it into small parties, and withdrawing or advancing, as the direction of the enemy's artillery required, and thus avoiding the effect of his fire, prevented the loss which it would else have occasioned. In this way several hours were occupied, when the enemy, trusting to the impression which he supposed his fire to have made, at about ten o'clock sent forward twelve or more battalions (D) to the charge. General Zimirski, anticipating this movement, withdrew, in order to lead them onto the plain between Wawr and Grokow, sending to General Skrzynecki an aide-de-camp to inform him of this maneuver, and to engage him to send a force of cavalry to act upon the enemy's columns in flank. General Skrzynecki, who occupied, as we have stated, the heights of Kawenzyn, was also warmly engaged with a brigade of the enemy, and had already observed this imprudent advance of the enemy in his attack, who had indeed gone beyond the line of Skrzynecki's position. In a moment the order was given for the brigade of General Kicki to throw themselves upon the enemy's flank; and as General Kicki approached with the ten squadrons (E) which composed his command, General Zimirski gave orders for a general charge both upon the enemy's cavalry (F) and infantry (D). The columns of the enemy were carried away before these charges, and their attack was wholly paralyzed. This onset, which was so successfully made, forced the enemy (H) to incline his position back from Kawenzyn to Milosna. That maneuver was decisive of the enemy's fate, and it was well understood by our generals. General Skrzynecki, by pushing forward the left of his division, cut off the right wing of the enemy from all communication with his centre, and at about mid-day our right wing and centre occupied their former position at Wawr, including the small forest of elders which was between the enemy's left wing and centre; and, in fact, General Skrzynecki occupied a part also of the Great Forest. This state of things was to be profited by, and the right wing of the enemy, thus separated, was to be attacked before the enemy should be able to renew his attack upon Kawenzyn, and the forest of elders, and our right wing. To execute this plan, the two divisions of Krukowiecki and Szembek, composing our left wing, which was fighting at Bialolenka [See Plan IX.], received orders to push a strong attack against the enemy's front, at the same moment that a brigade (B) of Skrzynecki's division, supported by some pieces of cannon, operated upon the road (a) leading from Kawenzyn (6) to Zombki (k). By this maneuver the enemy was menaced with being taken in the rear.

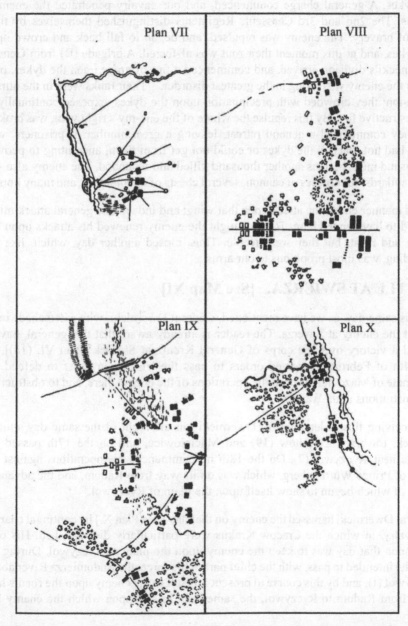

The left wing, as we have said, wad warmly engaged with the superior force of the Russians; who, by placing some fifty pieces of cannon (f) behind the two dykes (e) above named, kept up a sweeping fire of grape upon our artillery (d) and infantry (C), which were defending the passage of the dykes. A considerable body of the enemy had already reached the hither side of the dykes, when General Uminski, with a brigade of cavalry (D), advanced to the charge, and at the same time communicated the orders to the two divisions to commence the general attack. Under a warm fire of grape, our cavalry threw themselves upon the enemy's infantry, which had debouched #over the dykes. A general charge commenced, and our cavalry penetrated the enemy's masses. The 2nd and 3rd Chasseurs Regiments distinguished themselves by their feats of bravery. The enemy was repulsed, and began to fall back and crowd upon the dykes, and at this moment their rout was af-fected. A brigade (B) from General Skrzynecki's division arrived, and commenced a fire of grape upon the dykes, over which the enemy was flying in the greatest disorder. Their ranks were in the utmost confusion; they crowded with precipitation upon the dykes, exposed continually to our destructive fire. By this repulse the whole of the ene-my's right wing was broken, and they commenced a general retreat, leaving a great number of prisoners, who either had not reached the dykes or could not get from them, amounting to perhaps a thousand men, besides another thousand killed and wounded. The enemy also lost two standards, four pieces of cannon, several chests of ammunition, and many horses.

In this manner ended the attack upon that wing; and indeed, the general attack might be said to have ended here. Towards night the enemy renewed his attacks upon our centre and right, but they were feeble. Thus, closed another day, which, like the preceding, was most propitious to our arms.

BATTLE AT SWIERZA.   [See Map XI]

On this same day, as we have mentioned, General Dwernicki, with a detached corps, fought the enemy at Swierza. The reader is already aware that this general, having gained a victory over the corps of General Kreutz at Stoczek [Plan VI. (18)], on the 14th of February, received orders to pass the Vistula, in order to defend the palatinate of Mazovie, to check the operations of the enemy there, and to obstruct his demonstrations upon Warsaw.

On receiving this order, General Dwernicki, on the night of the same day, quitted Stoczek, traversed Zelechow (19) and Macieiowice, and on the 17th passed the Vistula near Ryczywol (7). On the 18th he commenced his operations against the corps of Prince Württemberg, which was on its way from Radom, and the advanced guard of which begun to show itself upon the plain of Ryczywol.[38]

General Dwernicki harassed the enemy on that day [See Plan X.] by continual charges of cavalry, in which the Cracow Krakus were particularly distinguished. His only plan upon that day was to keep the enemy upon the plain of Ryczywol. During the night he intended to pass, with the chief part of his force, the Radomierza River above Ryczywol (f), and by this course to present himself to the enemy upon the road which leads from Radom to Ryczywol, the same road in fact upon which the enemy had advanced, and attack him both on his flank and rear, the Vistula being on his front. In executing this movement, General Dwernicki left two squadrons of cavalry (A), one battalion of infantry (A), and two pieces of cannon, at the side of the river, under the command of Colonel Russyian.   He then quietly left his position, and crossed the river in its fordable places (f) about half a league above.   Colonel Russyian, who as we have said remained on the position at Ryczywol, was ordered to commence a light fire of skirmishers at break of day, but to retrograde constantly, and to allow the enemy an easy passage over the bridge.   On the 19th, the enemy (D), who had no suspicions of the maneuver, commenced in the morning his debouchment upon the bridge, having the expectation of engaging with our whole force in a decisive battle upon the field of Ryczywol.   His astonishment may be imagined, when, as the day commenced, he found both upon his flank and his rear a force marching against him to the attack (B). The enemy stopped passing the bridge, and attempted to turn and meet the attack, but this was not permitted him. Our cavalry threw themselves with impetuosity upon that part of his forces which were attempting to place themselves in position; and our artillery, which was boldly brought near the enemy's columns, poured a terrible destructive fire of grape upon them. The utmost consternation ensued, and a general and disorderly flight was commenced in the direction of Nowawies (N), to which place our corps continued the pursuit of the enemy (R).

This day, which may he called one of the most brilliant in our war, cost the enemy, besides his killed and wounded, two thousand prisoners, with more than twenty officers, four standards, ten pieces of cannon, some hundred horses, and about thirty chests with ammunition, with officers' baggage, &c. The Prince Württemberg with the remains of his corps retreated by forced marches to the small town of Granica, where he repassed the Vistula and reached Pulawa. Thus, by a single battle, the whole country on this side of the Vistula was cleared of the presence of the enemy.

General Dwernicki permitted to his corps, who were really much exhausted by fighting and marching, to repose by a slow march as far as Kozie-nice, where he remained stationary, sending out, however, his reconnaissances as far as Pulawa.

NOTES

37. I cannot pass over this occasion of describing the manner in which the nation received that army, which had but a month before left the walls of Warsaw, and had, after so many glorious actions, returned to give there a decisive battle to the enemy, and to fall or conquer there before the eyes of the nation. Those were moments rare in history, and should be handed down to posterity, to demonstrate to what a height the feelings of the nation were exalted, and what unanimity was felt in the great cause that warmed all hearts. The thunder of the cannon which, during the 15th, rolled over the fields of Milosna and Okuniew, was heard at Warsaw, and announced the approach of the army. At nightfall, when our first detachments began to show themselves from the forests of Milosna and Jablonna, and to deploy upon the plains of Wawr and Bialolenka, the whole population of Warsaw began to leave the city, and go forth to meet and hail their defenders. The Senate, whose estimable president, Czartoriski, was with the army, left the city also. In a short-time the fields were covered with an exulting multitude. When the army took its position, and all was quiet under the protection of night, the people drew near and entered the camp. What a touching scene was there presented! Here a father and a mother, seek their son, who, meeting them presses them to his bosom. There a wife, leading her children, finds her husband and their father, and throws herself into his arms, while the children cling around the knees of their delighted parents. A melancholy contrast was presented by those who sought in vain for son—husband—parent. But no complaint was heard. The tears falling for those who were no more, were checked by the thought that they had died for their country.

The Senate, in the name of the nation, and in the most touching language, thanked the Commander-in-Chief and his officers for the services which they had rendered to their country, and requested them to communicate these sentiments to the whole army. They finished their address in nearly the following terms: "Preserve brave compatriots, this noble energy, and in a short time the throne of despotism will fall, and upon its ruins civilization and public happiness will rise." The people continued with the army, furnishing them with every comfort, and regardless of the fire which was commenced the next day from the enemy's artillery. Under this fire, vehicles with provisions and ammunition were continually arriving from the city, and some of them were destroyed by the enemy's shot. During the actions before Warsaw, the inhabitants made it a duty to be at hand, to bear off and succor the wounded; and among those who engaged in these offices were some of the most distinguished ladies of Warsaw. The strangers who were then there, and who witnessed the enthusiasm which animated the people, and seemed to unite them into one family, exclaimed that such a nation could never, and ought never be conquered.

The following days, the 21st, 22nd, and 23rd of February, in which no action took place, were devoted to thanksgiving to God, for his favor in protecting the Polish cause thus far. In all the churches the people assembled to offer prayers for the welfare of the country; and the army employed this period of repose in the same manner. On that field, over which the three hundred cannon of the enemy were pointed in battle array; while the first line was in position, the rest of the army were engaged in these devotional exercises. At each assemblage of troops, the ministers of religion administered patriotic oaths, and animated the soldiers to perseverance in the holy struggle. Those sacred ceremonies were followed by hymns, which were sung along the whole line, and which, mingling with the solemn sounds of the bells of Warsaw tolling for the assembly of the people in the churches, produced an indescribably impressive effect. These exercises ended in the general shout of "Poland forever!"

To convince the Russians that the Poles were not blindly fighting against them as Russians, but for that cause of civilization and happiness which was of equal moment to themselves, several hundred white flags were prepared with inscriptions in the Russian language, in terms such as follows: "Russians, brother Sarmatians! We march to combat not as your enemies, but to fight for your welfare as well as our own." Each regiment received from ten to twenty of those flags, which during the combat, were to be distributed among the tirailleurs and flankers. They were directed to throw them, as occasion might offer, among the Russian ranks. Many of those volunteers, in rushing forward to plant those flags among the Russian skirmishers, met their death at the hands of those whom they wished to save from tyranny. The Poles had done all that their duty required of them in this holy contest, to convince the world that the general cause of civilization and happiness was the great end of their struggle. They sought not their own aggrandizement by conquests from the territory of another nation, for their ancient boundaries are wide enough for them. They fought for that liberty which they had for ages possessed; and that ancient liberty and those ancient limits they will sooner or later regain.

38. The Prince Württemberg, who commanded the corps against which general Dwernicki was sent, had served in the Polish Army as brigadier-general. He was cousin to the present King of Württemberg, and nephew of the late Emperor Alexander, who married his aunt. This prince commanded the 3rd and 4th Regiment of Uhlans, of the first of which regiments general Dwernicki was Lionel. In this way the prince was perfectly well known to general Dwernicki, and was held by him in very low esteem, as a man of vanity and pretension, and a tyrant over his subalterns. The vices of his character developed themselves sufficiently during our revolution. At the breaking out of the revolution at Warsaw, this man was at Krasny-staw, a small town in the Lublin Palatinate, in which his brigade was posted. On the arrival of the news of the revolution his first care was to secrete himself. Afterwards, finding that it was impossible to keep concealed, he began to tamper with the brigade, and tried to persuade his soldiers to adhere to the service of the Grand Duke, and to refuse to join the cause of their country. These false persuasions, coming from him, a general in the Polish service, in open defiance of the will of the nation, and in opposition to its holiest efforts, afforded a sufficient ground of accusation against him, to have brought him to judgment as a traitor. Besides all this, by his tyrannical conduct as a general, he had deserved severe treatment. But all these offences were forgotten, and the nation spared him, merely ordering him to quit the country. He exhibited his gratitude for this delicate treatment, by departing for Russia and the Polish provinces, and pointing out for arrest some of the most respectable citizens, who were known for their patriotic sentiments. He passed several days at Wlodawa, a small frontier town between the Polish kingdom and the Grodno Government. There he was guilty of the mean act of intercepting the correspondence between the different patriotic individuals.

This was not enough. In the campaign, he took the command of a Russian corps destined to act in the very Lubin Palatinate where he had held his Polish command for fourteen years, and where all the proprietors had treated him with the greatest kindness and delicacy. Arriving there with his corps, he left at every step the traces of his tyranny. On reaching Pulawa, the estate of the beloved Czartoriski, the President of the National Government, the residence of that family from which he had himself received so many kindnesses, and in which every virtue reigned, he did not scruple to give orders to burn the town; he did not scruple to take the name in history of "the devastator of Pulawa"—of that beautiful spot on which the labor of ages had been expended, and which was so celebrated for the charms with which nature as well as art had enriched it. His cruelties were carried to such a height, that he actually caused to be beaten with the knout, a young lady, a friend of the Princess Czartoriski, who had manifested her patriotic sentiments by the sacrifice of her jewels to aid the cause of her country. Even the Princess Czartoriski, who was already at an advanced age, was not spared the insults of this gross man, who, to put the finishing stroke to his barbarity, on his second visit to Pulawa, directed a fire of artillery upon the palace, which he knew was occupied only by the Princess and her ladies. Even the Russians themselves regarded these actions with abhorrence. In regard to his military talents, they were of the lowest order. General Dwernicki promised that in a few weeks he would dispatch him; and he in fact kept this promise to the letter.

CHAPTER IX.

Renewal of the enemy's attack on the 20th. - Its result. - Review of the events of the preceding day. – The enemy's loss. – Examination of the plan of operations of the Polish Army. – Neglect of fortifications. – Want of concert in the different operations. – Advantageous offensive operations neglected. – Acts of the National Government. – Provision in lands for the soldiers. – Abolition of the Corvee, &c. – Marshal Diebitsch remains in a state of inactivity. – Negotiations are opened by him. – His propositions are declined. – Position of the 24th, and battle of Bailolenka.

On the 20th of February, our main army was engaged with the enemy the whole day upon the same position as on the preceding. This repetition of his attack, without a change of plan or position, was a great weakness in the enemy. On that day, feeling sensibly the loss of a part of the great forest opposite Kawenzyn, as well as that of the small forest of elders, the enemy commenced his attack upon those points. Some twenty battalions were incessantly pushed forward to the attack, against which eight battalions on our part kept an effectual stand for several hours. This day, although uninteresting and indecisive in maneuvers, was bloody. No important blow was attempted by us, but every attack of the enemy was met with a vigorous and sanguinary repulse. It was a day of glory for the 4th Regiment - the day on which that celebrated regiment, though already distinguished, began to take its high place in our reports; and on which it fought with a degree of valor that could never have been surpassed. Without even waiting for orders, this brave regiment was seen constantly pushing itself towards the points of the greatest danger; and its companies were often fighting singly in the very midst of the thickest masses of the enemy.

By the unsuccessful and costly attacks of the enemy the whole day was occupied, and at its close, after the loss of thousands of men, he had not gained a foot of ground.

Thus, ten days had passed in continual and bloody actions upon the same position, during which the Polish Army had been uniformly successful, and at the end of which the enemy discontinued his attacks, thus giving the most convincing proof of the extent of the losses he had suffered on all points, during that period, amounting, in fact, in killed, wounded and prisoners, to a full 30,000 men. In this space of ten days, the whole Russian army had been engaged, and that army amounted, as we have already said, and as will be confirmed by all the official reports, to more than 150,000 infantry, 50,000 cavalry, and 300 pieces of cannon. To this force was opposed a handful, comparatively, of Poles, consisting of 30,000 infantry, 12,000 cavalry, and 96 pieces of cannon; a sixth part, in fact, of the Russian force.

This memorable commencement of our war will show to the world what can be affected by a nation fighting in defense of its liberty and to throw off an oppressive yoke. Those bloody combats, and that enthusiasm, to which my feeble pen cannot render justice, but which some better historian will present to the world in their true colors, should convince men that the immense mercenary forces which a despot may lead on, and by which he trusts to enforce his will, may avail him little. His enormous masses are like a heap of sand, which a little stone can pierce. Without animating motives, and therefore without energy - a machine scarcely to be trusted - that army itself, upon the slightest change of circumstances, may become terrible to the despot, of whom and of whose creatures it was to have been made the unhappy sacrifice.

The reader will pardon me, if I fatigue him with further reflections upon this stage of our affairs. I shall not exaggerate in saying that this enormous mass of the enemy's forces would in an equal period have been absolutely annihilated, if we had then had a Commander-in-Chief of greater talent, and a general plan of operation differently arranged, for the different operations in detail were, generally speaking, perfectly executed. The Commander-in-Chief, Prince Radzivil, was an individual of the most estimable character, but as he afterwards himself avowed, not possessed of military talent. General Chlopicki, who was always near him, and who in fact virtually commanded, if he had in the early part of his life exhibited military talent, in his present advanced age had certainly lost much of his energy, and was unfit to undertake things which demanded the most active intellect, and the most absolute devotedness of mind and body to the cause. We cannot too strongly express our astonishment that General Chlopicki, who had formed the plan and a very judicious one it was, of drawing the enemy onto the walls of Warsaw, to give him there a decisive battle, should have neglected to fortify the natural positions upon his route, by which the enemy's loss would have been doubled or even trebled. Serock and Zagroby (4) [See Plan VI.], situated upon points of the greatest importance, especially the first, were evacuated by our forces, for the want of proper defenses. Not the slightest fortification was constructed at the different passages of the Narew (N), the Bug (B), the Liewiec (L), and the Swider (S), nor upon the region between those rivers, which was full of forests and impenetrable marshes, and in which proper fortifications would have presented the most important obstructions to the enemy's passage. No concealed passages or by-roads through those forests were constructed, as they should have been, by which a body of troops could be led in ambuscade and brought to act suddenly on the enemy's flanks or otherwise, in critical moments, and with decisive effect. Such works would have required but little expense, and could have been made by the Jewish inhabitants, of whom there are some millions in Poland (twenty thousand in Warsaw alone) and who could have no claims for exemption, for they render no service to the country, but on the contrary, lead a life of profitable fraud and deception, practiced upon the inhabitants. The Jews, indeed, with some very few exceptions, did not in the least aid in the war, but often frustrated our exertions by their espionage; and there are in fact instances of their having fought against us —against those who had given them an asylum upon their soil. In the towns of Nasielsk and Makow this occurred. This part of our population, who had an equal interest with us in the protection of the country, as far as property was concerned, could have been thus employed with perfect justice and propriety. If, by such arrangements, a system of fortification had been properly united with tactics, and all the plans directed by a man of talents and energy, of which examples were certainly to be found in our ranks, with such troops to command, the reader will admit that the Russian forces could have been soon driven back to the frontiers.

The succession of victories which we have described were not the results of any general system: They were victories of detail, executed with energy and rapidity, and for which we were indebted to the generals of divisions and brigades, the colonels of regiments, &c. These successes were isolated, but, had they been made to bear upon each other, their advantages would have been much greater. For example, the battle of Dobre, which was so brilliantly gained by Skrzynecki, would have caused the total ruin of the corps opposed to him, if the 11th Division of Krukowiecki, which was in the environs of Jadow, had come to the aid of Skrzynecki during that action. And indeed, this was the expectation of Skrzynecki when he remained so long upon the position of Makowiec. But this division, instead of acting upon the rear of the enemy, as it might have done, having no orders to this effect, continued its retrograde march, although within the sound of the cannon of that action.

On the 18th there was not enough of harmony in the operations of the several divisions. On that day, if those operations had been directed from one point as from a centre, the enemy, who had been guilty of extreme imprudence in the advance which he had made into the marshy and wooded region between Stanidawow (9), Okuniew(ll), and the great road, could have been completely hedged in. [See Plan VI.] The maneuvers of General Zimirski, when the enemy made his rapid attack on the morning of the 19th, were executed at hazard, no general order having been given in anticipation of such an attack. These maneuvers were well executed by General Zimirski: but if the case had been thus anticipated by the Commander-in-Chief, and, at the commencement-of the action, our right wing had been withdrawn to Grochow, [See (A) Plan VIII.] an obstinate defense of the commanding position of Kawenzyn (B) being kept up, and the enemy had been thus allowed to follow our right wing with his left; by the same method of operation which was in fact executed by Skrzynecki and Zimirski, in concert, but with much larger forces; the enemy could have been attacked on his flank, and instead of the annihilation of his sixteen battalions, the same fate would have attended twice or thrice that number; - for, when a force is taken by surprise in flank and rear, numbers avail comparatively little in resistance; indeed, the greater the number, the greater is the difficulty of changing position, and the greater the disorder and consternation which follows.

The Russian army was thus early inspired with terror at the resistance which it had experienced, and the immense losses to which it had been subjected. It was of the utmost importance to profit by this consternation; but the vast advantages which might have been gained under such circumstances, by some general plan of offensive operations of bold and decisive character, were let pass.

Whilst the array was thus gloriously fighting, the National Government was laboring for the happiness of the people. Among other valuable institutions, it adopted a paternal guardianship over the defenders of the country by designating an allotment of lands for each soldier. Many of the wealthiest families contributed of their landed property for that object. Another act was to free the peasantry from the corvée, by purchasing the rights of the landholders over them. Each peasant was made a proprietor, and for the landholders an arrangement of compensation in the form of annual installments for a period of years, was made by the government. Other institutions for the public welfare, as the establishment of schools, &c. received also the attention of the government.

When, after so many battles, the Russian commander discontinued his attacks, it may be supposed that besides the repose which his army required, he had another object, viz. to wait the arrival of a new corps, consisting of 20,000 men, and 36 pieces of cannon, under Prince Sczachowski. He evidently wished to concentrate all his small detachments and all his reserves, in order to strike, with his whole force, a decisive blow; and the attempt was, in fact, soon made.

Our army, which in the ten preceding days had lost about six thousand men, was reinforced by three regiments armed with pitchforks; amounting to about the number we had lost. Our whole army, infantry and cavalry, may have amounted to 40,000 men, and, with the pieces taken from the enemy, 100 cannon. The Russian army, with the new corps of Sczachowski, amounted to 188,000 men and 316 pieces of cannon, deducting the artillery which had been lost or dismounted.

Marshal Diebitsch, before commencing hostile operations, opened negotiations, and, for this purpose, sent a general of division, Witt, with a flag of truce to our headquarters. This general was stopped at our advanced post, whither General Krukowiecki was sent by the Commander-in-Chief, with full powers, to meet him. General Witt commenced with expressions of the greatest sensibility, and enlarged much upon the friendship which ought to exist between the Poles and the Russians as brother nations. He then spoke in very flattering terms of the heroism of the Poles, lamenting that it was not displayed in a better cause. After much complimentary language, he insensibly passed to the ideas of duty and obedience to the monarch. General Krukowiecki, who understood perfectly well all these professions, which he knew to be insidious, answered nearly in the following laconic terms: "General, after the sad circumstances which have taken place, after the bloody combats to which we have been forced by the tyranny of fifteen years, by the refusal of justice, and in fine by the violation of our frontier, and the laying waste of our territory —upon this territory we can make no arrangements. You know well what are the frontiers of Poland. Upon the banks of the Dnieper, four hundred miles hence, we may enter into negotiations."

Thus, all was ready for the sanguinary battle of two days, which followed, and one memorable in the annals of war. It commenced by a combat on the 24th at Bialolenka, and ended on the 25th on the plain of Grochow.

POSITION ON THE 24th, AND BATTLE OF BIALOLENKA.

The position of the two armies, on the 24th, was as follows: The Polish Army occupied the same ground as when they ceased firing on the 20th; but the force was disposed in a different manner.—The right wing was reinforced by the division of General Szembek; and although Bialolenka, Kawenzyn, and Wawr composed the line of combat, there was this difference, that, while before, the centre was at Kawenzyn, and the left wing at Bialolenka, at present the left wing was at Kawenzyn; the forces which were at Bialolenka were posted as a detached corps, and the centre of the army was at the forest of elders. The right wing occupied the space between the great road and the marshes of the Vistula, called the marshes of Goclaw. This arrangement made our line more concentrated. The 1st Division under Krukowiecki, which was at Bialolenka, with the division of cavalry under Uminski, was directed to observe the great road from Jablonna, and all the roads leading from Radzimin and Zombki to Warsaw. Between Kawenzyn and Bialolenka the debouchment of the enemy was prevented by extensive marshes.

The Russian army was upon the same points as on the 20th. Their greatest force was opposed to our right wing at Wawr.

On the afternoon of the 24th, the enemy attacked with impetuosity the 1st Division at Bialolenka. The corps of the enemy which made this attack was that of the Prince Sczachowski, which had recently joined the main army, and for which Marshal Diebitsch was supposed to have waited. This corps, as was afterwards ascertained, had missed their road, and became unintentionally engaged with our forces on that day. The orders of that corps were to traverse the forests between Radzimin and Zombki, and to join the army without being observed by our forces. It was the false direction which they took that brought on the engagement at Bialolenka.

This battle consisted, like the former actions at this place, of an attempt by the enemy to force the passage of the dykes, which were defended on our side by about eight battalions, protected by some twenty pieces of cannon. This small force repulsed the enemy in three successive attacks upon the dykes. At about 5 P. M. another Russian corps, under General Pahlen, came to the succor of Sczachowski, and as the first corps attempted to pass the road leading from Radzimin, the latter attempted to force the passage of the two dykes leading from Zombki, and at both points under the cover of a terrible fire of artillery. If the reader will consider that our small force, consisting of only eight battalions and fifteen squadrons, stood their ground against two Russian corps of nearly 40,000 men and 60 pieces of cannon, the efforts which were made on that day may be appreciated. Our plan of action consisted chiefly in allowing a part of the enemy's forces to pass the dykes, and then falling upon and cutting them up by successive charges of cavalry and infantry, supported by an effective fire of artillery. By such efforts this handful of brave men repulsed the attacks of the enemy until night, when his attacks ceased. At the approach of night, General Krukowiecki sent small reconnoitering parties upon the roads from Radzimin and Zombki. These patrols, pushing as far as, and even beyond Zombki, saw nothing of the enemy, and in fact learnt, to their astonishment, from the marauders whom they too the two

Russian corps had quitted their position, and were on their march, across the forest of Kawenzyn, to join the main army. This sudden withdrawal of the enemy's corps was an indication that they had received orders to join the Grand Army, and that a general attack was in contemplation for the next day. In expectation of this attack, a body of men was sent, during the night, to obstruct, by defenses, the three roads leading from Radzimin and Zombki. Small detachments were left on those roads, and the forces which were at Bialolenka quitted their position, to reinforce the larger corps upon the plain of Wawr.

CHAPTER X.

Position of the armies of the 25th. – Great battle of Grokow. – Details. – State of the Russian army after its defeat. – Examination of the plan of the battle of Grokow. – Remarks upon the course adopted by Prince Radzivil after that victory. – The Polish Army crosses the Vistula to Warsaw. – Its reception by the National Government and the citizens. – Resignation of Prince Radzivil.

The following was the position of the two armies on the 25th, the day of the memorable battle of Grochow. [See Plans XI. and XII.] The Russian army was distributed into eight divisions of combatants, and three divisions of reserves. Those eight divisions consisted of 126,000 infantry (a), 42,000 cavalry (6), and 280 pieces of cannon (c). The three divisions of reserve (E) were composed of 16,000 infantry, 4,000 cavalry, and 32 pieces of cannon. This enormous force, which occupied the space between Kawenzyn (A) and the Goclaw Marshes (B), a distance of about three English miles, was arranged in two lines of combatants (C, D) and a third of reserve. Their position was as follows: Their left wing was between Wawr (r) and the above marshes of the Vistula, and was composed of four divisions of infantry, of 47,000 men, four divisions of cavalry, 15,700, and 120 pieces of cannon. The centre, opposite the forest of elders, consisted also of four divisions, of infantry of 57,000 men, three of cavalry of 10,500 men, and 108 pieces of cannon. The right wing, opposite the village of Kawenzyn, consisted of three and a half divisions of infantry of 31,000 men, four divisions of cavalry of 15,750 men, and 52 pieces of cannon. Upon the borders of the great forest opposite the forest of elders, was placed the reserve, commanded by the Grand Duke Constantine. Against this force our inconsiderable army was posted in the following manner: The right wing (G), formed by the division of Szembek, consist-ing of about 7,000 infantry (d) and 24 pieces of cannon (f), occupied the space between the road and the marshes above mentioned. The centre (H) occupied the forest of elders, and touched upon the great road. It was composed of two divisions commanded by Skrzynecki and Zimirski, composed of about 15,000 infantry (d) and 60 pieces of cannon (f). The left wing (T) occupied Kawenzyn, consisting of the first division, commanded by Krakowiecki, composed of 6,500 men (d) and 12 pieces of cannon (f) . Four divisions of cavalry (g) consisting of 9,500 men, commanded by Uminski, Lubinski, Skarzynski, and Jankowski, were not posted on any fixed point, but stood in readiness to act wherever occasion might offer. Besides these, was a small reserve (K) of four battalions and eight squadrons, in all about 5,400 men, under the command of General Pac.

BATTLE OF GROCHOW.

On the 25th, at break of day, the fire commenced on our left wing, on the position of Kawenzyn. The enemy pushed forward all the forces which were collected on his right wing, and commenced a terrible fire of artillery and musketry, with the apparent determination to carry our wing by a single overpowering effort. Nearly fifty pieces of artillery opened their fire upon Kawenzyn, and numerous columns of infantry, under the protection of this fire, pressed forward to carry the position. But our forces prepared to meet the attack. Small as they were, consisting only of seven battalions with twelve pieces of cannon, they had formed the determination to die or conquer upon that ground. They could hope for no succor, for the whole line was in expectation of a general attack.

The brave Generals Krukowiecki and Malachowski made every effort to sustain the perseverance of their troops, and each of them, at the head of their columns, and on foot, threw themselves upon the enemy's ranks. Our artillery did not answer that of the Russians, but directed its fire of grape wholly upon the columns which were approaching. By the unparalleled bravery of our wing, of which every soldier seemed to have formed the resolution to fall rather than yield a foot of ground, this tremendous attack of the enemy was sustained for several hours, till at last he was obliged to slacken it.

During the whole of this attack upon our left wing, the centre and the right remained still in their positions, awaiting the expected attack. It was near ten o'clock when the fields of Wawr became, as it were, in one moment, covered with the forces of the enemy, which issued out of the cover of the forests overhanging the plain. Looking over that plain, between the forest of elders and the Vistula, one would have thought it was an undivided mass of troops which was in motion; for in that comparatively limited space, the eye could not distinguish the different divisions from each other.

Two hundred pieces of cannon, posted upon that plain, in a single line, commenced a fire which made the earth tremble, and which was more terrible than the oldest officers had ever witnessed. After having prolonged for some time this tremendous fire of artillery, the enemy made an attempt to carry our right wing; but in a moment all our cavalry were collected there, and fell upon and overthrew his columns, and his efforts were as fruitless here, as they had been against our left.

Having been unsuccessful in these two attacks on the wings, and hoping that he had weakened our line by the terrible fire of artillery, which he constantly kept up, the Russian commander collected the greater part of his forces opposite the forest of elders, and it was there that an attack was commenced which presented a scene unheard of in the annals of war. It could with more propriety be called a massacre of nearly four hours duration. The Russians brought together at this point one hundred and twenty pieces of cannon, posted in the rear and on the sides of that forest. Some fifty battalions were incessantly pushed to the attack, with the view to get possession of that forest. Had they been able to affect this, they would have divided our army into two parts, and thus could not but have ensured its destruction. It was the consideration of this important fact which prompted the horrible attack, and the desperate resistance which it met. The brave Skrzynecki, Zimirski Boguslawski, Cgyzewslu, and Rohland, defended this forest with fourteen battalions, whose admirably executed maneuvers, the change of front, the arrangement of the attack in columns and echelon, the concentration of force upon the points in which the enemy's line seemed to waver, a fire which was never lost, but was always reserved for the closest approach of the enemy - all were executed with an activity, order and coolness never surpassed. It was only by such conduct that the tremendous attack of the enemy could have been sustained for four hours, and that, after having nine times gained possession of the forest, he was as often repulsed with an immense loss.

Like the infantry, our artillery performed prodigies. All the batteries, protected by cavalry, which never abandoned them, pushed themselves in advance even of the line of the skirmishers, and approached sometimes within a hundred feet of the enemy's columns, in order to give their fire with the most infallible execution. The battery of the brave Colonel Pientka, which defended the border of the forest, was so far advanced that it was sometimes surrounded by the enemy, who, in his own disorder, did not become aware of the advantage. All the different operations indeed, of our artillery in this battle were truly admirable. Batteries, now concentrated upon one point, were in a moment hurried to another and distant one, where the enemy was wholly unprepared for them, and was thrown into disorder by their sudden attack. In the early part of the afternoon, when the enemy, after having been several times repulsed, renewed his attack with the greatest determination, and our 2nd Division began to give way, the four batteries of artillery of the brave Adamski, Maslowski, Hilderbrand, and Bielak, in concert with that of Colonel Pientka, advanced like cavalry to the charge, and, approaching close to the Russian columns, opened a fire of grape, which spread destruction and disorder in their ranks. Our infantry, thus animated to the contest, rallied, and threw themselves again upon the enemy, who then yielded before them.

Like the artillery and infantry, our cavalry, besides the different charges which they executed with so much bravery, was maneuvered with the utmost skill by our generals, and was made to fill the voids occasioned by the inferiority of our forces, so as always to present to the enemy an unbroken line.

By such maneuvers of the three arms, executed with the greatest determination, in which every commander performed his duty to the utmost, the enemy's plans were continually disorganized, and his enormous force, which at first sight would have been supposed capable to have absolutely crushed the small army opposed to it, was in effect only a great mass, making a continual oscillation, and which seemed to trust to do everything by a ter-rible fire of artillery, which was always kept up, whether necessary or not.

Thus, it was that fifty battalions of the enemy, amounting to over 40,000 men, supported by 120 pieces of artillery, in a concentrated attack upon one point, the forest of elders, the decisive point of the position, were nine times repulsed from that forest, which was left literally covered with their dead.

From eleven o'clock until three, these attacks continued through the whole line (the most powerful being in the centre), and the destruction of life was immense. At the last named hour, our generals, each of whom we may remark had had their horses shot under them, and several of whom were severely wounded, formed the plan of giving the enemy a decisive blow. Their plan was to withdraw from the fire the 2nd and 3rd Divisions, which had suffered most, and to make a general retrograde movement in such a form as to have the wings considerably in advance of the centre, which was to be drawn back as for as the Obelisk of Iron, at which there was a position more commanding. This plan had the following objects: The first was, to draw the enemy upon the open plain; the second was, to concentrate our force still more, and to place it in two lines, the inner one to be composed of the whole of the 2nd and a part of the 3rd Division, which were withdrawn for repose. A third object was, to lead the enemy to believe that a retrograde movement was forced upon us by our losses, and that we felt ourselves too weak to continue the defense of the forest.

To execute this maneuver, and to enable the 2nd Division to retire without being molested, the artillery was left with some twenty squadrons of cavalry to protect the retrograde movement. This artillery and cavalry were ordered afterwards to evacuate their positions gradually, and the former to take post in the centre under the protection of the whole of the cavalry, which were en echelon and prepared for a general attack. The maneuver was as admirably executed as it was conceived. The enemy had no suspicion of its object, but, presuming it to be a flight, undertook to profit by it. It was at this moment that Marshal Diebitsch, as if sure of victory, saw himself already at Warsaw, and, on the field of battle, he allowed these words to escape him: "Well, then, it appears that after this bloody day, I shall take tea in the Belvedere Palace."

It was at about 3 P. M. that our 2nd Division, in conformity with the plan adopted, began to retire by en echelon movement. To hasten the execution of this movement, it was ordered that the columns, retiring in succession, on reaching a considerable distance from the enemy, should quicken their pace as they proceeded, in order to form the second line as soon as possible, and to give space for the operations of the artillery and cavalry. It was at this moment that General Zimirski, who had lost several horses under him, and had just placed himself upon a fresh horse, to superintend this movement, was struck with a twelve-pound ball in the left shoulder, which carried away his arm, and caused his death in a few hours. The melancholy loss of this general was most deeply felt by the whole army, and particularly by his own division, but it did not interfere with the execution of these orders. The brave General Czyzewski immediately took command of the division, and continued the orderly movement of the division towards the rear, and he received great support from Generals Rohland and Zaluski. As soon as the last columns of this force quitted the forest, [See Plan XII.] the Russian troops began to debouch from it, and our artillery commenced a terrible fire. The brave Colonel Pientka, who was still far in advance, checked the debouchment from the forest near him. Seated with the most perfect sangfroid upon a disabled piece of artillery, this brave officer directed an unremitting fire from his battery. The artillery and cavalry, after having protected the retrograde movement of the centre, still continued to keep their ground, to enable the wings also to retire undisturbed. All our forces were then in movement, and the enemy pressed on. The

Russian columns had already, advanced beyond the position of Colonel Pientka, but that brave officer still kept up the defense.[39] By this time, however, the 2nd Division had already reached their destined position, and their battalions had commenced forming. Such was the state of things, when, between Kawenzyn and the forest, a cloud of Russian cav-alry were seen advancing to the attack, having at their head five regiments of heavy cuirassiers; a force in fact of some forty squadrons, or between eight and nine thousand in all. Colonel Pientka, with his artillery, supported only by a single regiment of Mazurs, still held his post, to give yet another effective fire upon this advancing cavalry, which was already between him and Skrzynecki's division; and then, to save himself from being cut off, he quitted at full gallop a post which he had occupied for five hours under the terrible fire of the artillery of the enemy. This rapid movement of Pieptka's battery and the regiment of cavalry which attended him, animated the Russian cuirassiers in their advance, and the infantry and artillery of the enemy followed their cavalry. At this moment Chlopicki was wounded by a grenade, and the army was without a head; but Generals Skrzynecki and Czyzewski had already formed their divisions into squares, and awaited the attack of the enemy.

The Russian cavalry (f) advanced upon the trot, and came in a direction perpendicular to the line of our battery of rockets (b), which was posted between the 2nd and 3rd Divisions (A). Suddenly a discharge from this battery was poured into their ranks, and enveloped them with flame and noise. Their horses, galled to madness by the flakes of fire which were showered over them, became wholly ungovernable, and, breaking away from all control, spread disorder in every direction. The enemy's ranks were soon in the most utter confusion, and in a short time this enormous body of cavalry became one disordered mass, sweeping along towards the fire of our squares. In a very few minutes that cavalry was almost annihilated. So nearly complete, in fact, was their destruction, that of a regiment of cuirassiers, which was at the head of the attacking force, called the Albert Regiment, and which also bore the designation of the "Invincible" inscribed upon their helmets, not a man escaped. The few who were not left dead upon the field were taken prisoners. In fact, some hundred horse of that regiment were whirled along through the intervals of our squares, and were left to be taken prisoners at leisure. The wrecks of this routed cavalry, closely pursued by our lancers, carried along in their flight the columns of infantry which were following them, and a general retreat of all the enemy's forces commenced. The battle was gained. The cry of "Poland forever!" arose along our line, and reached the walls of Warsaw, to cheer the hearts of its anxious inhabitants. Nothing was wanting but a skilful Commander-in-Chief to our forces, to have insured the entire destruction of the Russian army.

Two thousand prisoners, among them twenty officers of different grades, five pieces of cannon, and upwards of a thousand horses, were the trophies of that immortal day, the memory of which will be forever terrible to tyrants.

It was nearly 5 P. M, when the Russian army commenced a general flight, and even evacuated its first position, which it had occupied in the early morning. It is to be regretted that the order to follow up the pursuit was wanting. Szembek alone threw himself, at times, with his division, among the Russian ranks, and took a great number prisoners, baggage and chests of ammunition. According to the declaration of General Szembek, if, during the retreat of the enemy, a charge of cavalry and artillery had been ordered between the left wing and the centre of the enemy, a great part (P) of that wing, which was considerably detached from the centre, would have been cut off. This could have been easily done, for no part of our little reserve was brought into action during the day, and they were eager to be permitted to make the charge. The Prince Radziwill, after the withdrawal of General Chlopicki from the army in consequence of his wound, found himself without council; and not feeling himself sufficiently capable to risk any bold maneuver; seeing too that the army was much exhausted by the fighting of that day and the preceding; and fearing also that the Vistula might become impassable, and the bridges be endangered by the melting of the ice; in fine, being unwilling to take upon himself the great responsibility of attempting to pursue his advantages, decided to give the army an interval of repose, and to occupy the time in reorganizing it.

Some further details, and remarks upon this important battle may not be unacceptable to the reader. First, in regard to position: On examining critically the position of the Polish Army, we notice some great faults. The right wing was upon a plain entirely uncovered, and exposed to the commanding fire of the enemy's artillery. All the talents of the brave Szembek were required to prevent this wing from being unprofitably sacrificed. This same wing, if it had been withdrawn a thousand paces further to the rear, in such a manner as not to have leant on the marshes of the Vistula, but have occupied the small wooded hills on the right of the main road, and on a line with the village of Grochow, would have been then in a commanding position, and safe from the tremendous fire of the enemy. The enemy would probably have then occupied the plain, and thus, been disadvantageously exposed to our fire. His loss would have been doubled, and all the charges of our cavalry and infantry would have been much more effective. But what was above all unpardonable, was that, with a full knowledge of the enemy's intention to attack us, together with a consciousness of our own inferiority of force, and the nature of our position, which was wanting in strength, no fortifications whatever were erected, although four days and five nights were passed in that position, during which the National Guard of Warsaw, and all the unenrolled population, who would have cheerfully volunteered for the purpose, could have been employed in the construction of works to any desired extent.

In regard to the centre, we may remark, that it was indeed covered by the forest of elders, of which it occupied a part, but the attack of this forest by the enemy was thus made necessary, and their repulse cost us too great sacrifices. But besides the sacrifices which the support of such a position required, our troops were so incessantly occupied with repulse of the successive attacks of the enemy, that it was impossible to attempt any decisive maneuver. It was not there, in fact, as we have seen, that the battle was decided, but at the Obelisk of Iron, and by other means. The centre, like the right wing, should have been withdrawn so far as to have been on a line with the village of Grochow; and in such a manner as to profit by all the commanding positions between Targowek and Grochow, upon which our artillery (which, as the case was, were upon a low and exposed position opposite the forest), would have been very advantageously posted. In general, our whole position was too extended, reaching from Kawenzyn to the marshes of the Vistula at Goclaw. It ought to have been from the beginning more concentrated, and supported on the outermost circumvallations of Praga (B). It could thus have profited by the advantageous positions which adjoin those defenses. In consequence of this too great extent of position, our forces remained in a single line for five hours in succession, in most dangerous exposure.

In regard to the evolutions, although the details were admirably executed, it is to be remarked that the left wing did not yield a sufficient support to the other bodies. The communications with that wing were not well sustained—another effect of the too great extent of the position. The line of the enemy was encumbered with artillery, and there were favorable moments for a general attack on that artillery by our cavalry. Such opportunities were perceived by our generals of cavalry, and the attack suggested by them to the Commander-in-Chief, but nothing was done. The greatest fault of all, however, and that which perhaps saved the Russian army from entire destruction, was the neglect to follow up the enemy in his retreat, and by a judicious maneuver to cut off his right wing, as was perfectly practicable; - by such a maneuver, as it will be seen was, in fact, afterwards successfully practiced by Skrzynecki at Wawr, where a great part of that same force were taken prisoners.

The battle of Grochow cost the enemy in killed, wounded, and prisoners, according to the reports published by the Russians themselves, 20,000 men. On our side the loss amounted to 5,000. But to give the reader an idea of the terrible fire of that day, it may be remarked that there was not a single general or staff officer, who had not his horse killed or wounded under him. Full two thirds of the officers, and perhaps the same proportion of the soldiers, had their clothes pierced with balls, and more than a tenth part of the army were slightly wounded, though not unfitted for service. In this battle, the 2nd and 3rd Divisions of infantry suffered the most, and twenty of their officers were mortally wounded with grape-shot. I would not desire to present a revolting picture of the horrors of a battlefield, yet to impress upon the reader how great a scourge tyranny is to mankind, I could wish to point out to him, along the whole road from Kawenzyrt to the marshes of Goclaw, hillocks of dead at every step, especially in the forest of elders, where rank upon rank was seen prostrate upon the earth. Indeed, so strewed with bodies was this forest that it received from that day the name of *the forest of the dead*.[40]

With the twilight, our whole army began to evacuate their position, and to cross the Vistula to Warsaw. The passage of the river occupied the whole night. On the morning of the next day, all that remained of our forces upon the right bank, were two battalions of infantry, and thirty-six pieces of cannon, which were at the bridgehead of Praga. The Russians were well satisfied with our passage of the Vistula, for they felt the need of repose. It was at first presumed that in a few days the enemy would storm Praga. This, however, was soon found not to be their intention; and, for what cause we cannot conjecture, they continued in a state of complete inaction.

Such then was the end of the grand operation of Marshal Diebitsch, with his colossal forces, by which it was his purpose to put an end to the war in a few days! The boasted Crosser of the Balkan, with from 180,000 to 200,000 men, and 316 pieces of cannon, was not only unable to crush, as he proposed to do, an army of scarcely 40,000 men and 100 cannon, but was beaten by that small army, and only escaped a total ruin from the absence of a competent leader to the Polish forces. Such facts, so rare in history, cannot be too frequently impressed upon the mind of the reader, and they should be held up to the view of every despot, to teach him upon what a frail foundation his confidence in numbers may rest, and to convince him that his masses must melt away and be dispersed, before a people, who, on their own soil, are resolved to throw off the yoke of despotism, and who fight for liberty with the energy of despair.[41]

The nation and the army occupied this interval of repose in giving thanks to Providence for the successes of the preceding day. In all the churches Te Deums were sung, as well as in the chapels of the camp near Warsaw. The army was received by the people with solemnities. The Senate, accompanied by the inhabitants, repaired to the camp, where patriotic addresses were delivered, and a public fete given to the army. For three successive nights, Warsaw was illuminated, and the inscription "To the defenders of their Country," was everywhere seen. Unequal to the description of these moments of exultation of a people animated with the recovery of their freedom, I can only say that they were moments which will live forever in the heart of every Pole, and will satisfy him that a nation so united will be always capable of great efforts.

On the day after the religious ceremonies, the Provisional Government met in the National (formerly the Royal) Palace, where all the general officers of the army were also assembled to deliberate upon the measures to be adopted both in regard to military and civil affairs. It was on that occasion that the Prince Michael Radzivil, actuated by the noblest impulses, and having a single view to the good of his country, abdicated the chief command, surrendering his trust into the hands of the National Government, with the avowal that he did not feel himself sufficiently capable to continue to hold so responsible a post. This step, which showed a great elevation of character, impressed the nation with feelings of gratitude, and has given to Prince Radzivil a name in history.

120

NOTES

39. Admirable as was the conduct of all our artillery, every man in which deserved a decoration, yet among this artillery, the battery of Colonel Pientka must be distinguished. Without yielding a step of ground, that battery held its place for 5 hours, and it often happened during the battle, that this single battery was left exposed alone to the fire of thirty or forty of the enemy's pieces. It was computed that this battery alone caused a greater loss to the enemy than the entire loss that his whole artillery caused in our ranks; and I do not exaggerate in saying, that the fire, chiefly of grape, which Pientka kept up for five hours, and at the distance often of a few hundred paces only, must have cost the Russians from one .to two thousand men. What is most remarkable, this battery itself, during the whole of the fire, did not lose more than one officer and six men killed, six wounded, and ten or twelve horses, two of which were killed under colonel Pi-entka, whose clothes were pierced through and through with grape, and his casque (helmet) torn in pieces, while, as if providentially preserved, his person was not in the slightest degree injured.

40. Up to the 10th of March, when a reconnaissance was made, as far as the plain of Wawr, the dead were not yet interred, and all the confusion of a battlefield remained, proving that the enemy was too much occupied to give the ordinary attention to these duties. On that day several wagons filled with Russian cuirassiers were sent to Warsaw. Many ruined caissons of ammunition, many gun carriages, three deserted cannons, and several hundred carbines, sabers, and pistols, knapsacks, and helmets in considerable numbers were strewed over the field, and indicated the disorder in which the enemy had made his retreat. To prevent an epidemical malady, our government made a request to General Diebitsch to send a body of his men to aid in the interment of the dead, which was in fact done.

Contemplating these masses of Russian dead, the victims of a horrible despotism, what reflections were awakened! Those unfortunate men were dragged to the combat to be sacrificed. Not one of that mass of victims could see the justice of the cause for which they were thus sacrificed. What consolation could there be in the last agonies of suffering incurred in such a cause? There could be none. How different must have been the death of the Polish soldier, who felt the sacredness and importance of the struggle on which he had entered. His last moments were consoled with the thought that his life was sacrificed for the good of his country. If the death of the Russian and the Polish soldier were thus different, their lives are no less so. What reward awaits the Russian soldier? Is it a service of twenty-five years under the terror of the knout, in which service he most generally dies, or if he survives, is too much broken down to be able to gain a subsistence afterwards? The Russian soldier, besides the fatigues of the general service, is subject to a private service under any one of his superiors, the merest subaltern perhaps, who, far from rewarding him for such services, abuses him but the more freely. The full pay of a Russian soldier is a great day; and even out of this little pay his superiors exact a profit. The consequence is that the degree of his misery is excessive, and he would be in extremity if the proprietors of land where he is quartered did not succor him. What other recompense is given to these wretched men, who are thus led to the sacrifice of their lives for the self-will of a despot, who, while the soldier, covered with wounds, is groaning under his sufferings, spends his time in luxurious enjoyment, and perhaps mocks at the abjectness of men who are thus willing instruments of his pleasure? What other recompense for all this? Perhaps to this soldier is given a medal of brass, which, if his commander in a moment of good humor, as he passes down the line, may have addressed him with the title of "Staryk" or "old soldier," he receives as a token of his having been through a campaign.   Compare this with the recompense which awaited the Polish soldier on his return from the campaign.   He was received by his countrymen with the warmest demonstrations of joy.   Mothers lifted their children in their arms, and pointed him out to them as one of the defenders of their country. No anxiety for the future weighed upon him, for his country had made ample provision for him.

It was at his will to remain in the service, or to go to occupy the land designated for him by the National Government. He would find there all that his wants might require. Remaining in the military service, he enjoyed the respect of those about him. All were his brothers, and the greatest delicacy of intercourse was observed between him and his superiors. His service was an agreeable duty, in which, besides gaining an honorable subsistence, he received each day some new mark of friendship and esteem.

41. The courage of our forces that day was no doubt much animated by the vicinity of Warsaw for the battle was fought within view of the inhabitants, who covered the fields about Praga. Many of the equipages of the wealthy families attended to receive the wounded from the field of battle, and all the inhabitants, without distinction of rank, pressed forward to remove and succor them. Those of the wounded who could not be led to the carriages, were carried in the arms of the citizens, and among those' who performed this office were the highest members of the National Government, ministers of religion, and even ladies. How then could such an attachment of the nation to her defenders, fail to be answered by an enthusiasm in her defense which knew no bounds? The wounded soldiers, in order not to draw upon this sympathy, conquered their sufferings, and stifled their groans; and to check the tears of those who bore them, they even forced themselves to raise the patriotic shout, and sing the national hymn.

To the details illustrating the courage which was displayed upon that field, I may add the following: In one of the attacks upon the forest of elders, when the enemy had gained possession of it, there was an interruption to our advance from a ditch which had been cut across the road, and which it was necessary to pass. The Russian artillery, observing the effect of this obstruction, poured a heavy fire of grape upon the spot to add to the confusion. Lieutenant Czaykowski, who commanded a platoon of grenadiers of the 7th Regiment, in the attacking columns, had passed with his platoon this small ditch, when he received a grape shot in the leg, which threw him down. As he fell, he cried, "Grenadiers, advance!" and continued this cry, regardless of his suffering, as he lay prostrate on the ground. Those brave grenadiers, animated by this noble spirit, pushed their attack with such fury that they drove the enemy from his position.

Our artillery, which had so bravely fought, and which had to answer the terrible fire of the numerous artillery of the enemy, as well as to check the strong attacks of the Russian columns, were obliged often to change their place, to concentrate, and disperse, as occasion required. It was in one of those evolutions, that a battery, posted near that commanded by Captain Hilderbrand, was required to change its position. The Bombardier Kozieradzki was sent to give orders to this effect. He was on his way to execute this commission, when a ball carried away his arm. That brave man, however, continued his way, thus severely wounded, reached the battery, executed big commission, and then fell from the loss of blood.

The following incidents of this battlefield deserve to be mentioned, as indicating how little of national animosity mingled with the feelings of the combatants. It was often seen that the wounded soldiers of the hostile forces who happened to be thrown in each other's vicinity, would drag themselves towards each other for mutual relief, and engage in friendly conversation. "Why," would a Polish soldier say to the Russian, "why are we shedding each other's blood? The cause for which we have taken arms is that of your happiness, as well as our own." The Russian soldier could only answer, with tears of shame, "We have been driven to march against you." No stronger example could be given, of the kindest dispositions of the Poles towards the Russians, than the treatment of the latter in our hospitals. They were nursed and fed, like our own wounded, by the hands of those benevolent and patriotic females who had devoted themselves to these holy duties. On leaving those hospitals, the Russian soldiers swore never to forget the kindness they had experienced.

CHAPTER XI.

Passage of the Vistula to Warsaw. - Disposition of the Polish forces on its left bank. - Appointment of General John Skrzynecki to the chief commands-Proclamation. - Prompt attention is given to the reorganization of the army, the arsenals and manufactories of arms, the fortifications, etc - Deportment of the Commander-in-Chief towards the army. - General enthusiasm of the nation. - The patriotic offers of the Polish women. - New regulations established for conferring orders of merit - Disorderly state of the Russian army. - Attempt of Diebitsch to bribe the Polish soldiery. - General view of the en-couraging circumstances of this epoch. - The insurrection in Russia under Yermolov. - View of the state of the Polish forces when General Skrzynecki took the chief command. - He presses the organization of the new forces. - Their distribution and that of the General forces. - Positions of the Polish Army and the detached corps. - Russian position.

AFTER the memorable battle of Grochow, fought on the 25th of February, before the walls of Warsaw, a day on which we had defeated a force three times superior to our own, the Prince Radzivil made the passage of the Vistula to Warsaw and the left bank. The objects which he had in view in that movement we have already detailed. Two battalions of infantry, with thirty-six pieces of artillery, were left to defend the fortifications of Praga, on the right bank of the Vistula opposite to and separated by a bridge from Warsaw, and which were in the form of a hornwork, supported on each wing by the river.

The army was disposed in the following manner upon the left bank. The cavalry were posted in positions a few miles above and below Warsaw. The infantry and the artillery were either concentrated in Warsaw, or were encamped near the city. Upon receiving the resignation of Prince Radzivil, the National Government proceeded to the choice, of his successor, and on the 27th of February 1831, elected, by an unanimous voice, to the chief command of all the national forces, the hero of Dobre, General John Skrzynecki, a man of the most devoted patriotism, of great decision of character, and uncommon military talent. He was, above all, eminently possessed of that rapidity of *coup d'ceil*, that capacity of seizing conjunctures, which enabled him, in the midst of the most complicated movements, to perceive, and instantly to profit by, every advantage which offered itself. This general was, in the time of the Russian Government, and at the commencement of our revolution, colonel of the 8th Infantry Regiment of the line, a regiment by which he was regarded with an almost filial attachment. On the enrollment of new forces, after the revolution had taken place, he was made general of brigade. In the month of January, before the commencement of

125

the campaign, he was advanced to the rank of general of a division, and the command of the 3rd Division of infantry was confided to him, at the head of which division, as the reader already knows, he gained laurels in several brilliant actions.

On the 27th, at midday, proclamation was made of the abdication of the Prince Radzivil, and the appointment of General Skrzynecki, as Commander-in-Chief of the army. The nation to whom the great merit of this officer was already so well known, received this annunciation with the greatest satisfaction. No dissentient voice was heard. Even the oldest generals in the service warmly applauded the choice. General Skrzynecki, on receiving the chief command, addressed to the army, on the 28th of February, the following proclamation:

"Soldiers and brethren! God has willed that, through your choice, I should be made the instrument of his providence in the important trust to which I have been designated. The Senate, the Chamber of Deputies, and the National Government have honored me with a difficult task, which I cannot worthily execute, but as your valor and constancy shall second me. Soldiers! We have before us an enemy, proud of his former successes, of his strength in numbers, and of the influence which he exercises in Europe, but if, in one point of view, his power appears formidable, on the other hand, the outrages with which the Russian Government have oppressed us, render that enemy so guilty in the eyes of God and of man, that, full of confidence in Providence and the sacredness of our cause, we can boldly measure our strength with him. We have only to swear in our hearts that we will be faithful to that motto which we so often repeat. To conquer or die for our country,' and we shall surely serve as an example, in the annals of the world, of encouragement to the defenders of the sacred rights of the people. If we do not succeed in conquering our powerful enemy, we will not live to submit to him—to him who has violated in regard to us every obligation of good faith. There is enough of glory in the sacrifice which I call on you to make; and in this heroic career, and so full of danger, I offer you crowns of laurel. We shall be sure to gain them, if you will support me by your valor, your union, your subordination, and your promptitude in performing the orders which will be given you."

The first object, upon which the attention of the Commander-in-Chief was fixed, was the state of the army. Even from the first hour of his investiture with the chief command, prompt and energetic orders and instructions were issued, to form new forces, to complete those which were already in a state of formation, and to fill up the ranks of the regiments which had suffered in the late engagements. During the Dictatorship of Chlopicki, and under the command of the Prince Radzivil, all the arrangements of the military administration were sluggishly attended to, as the reader is well aware. At the time of the battle of Grochow there had been only ten thousand new infantry were levied, and even this infantry was neither well organized nor armed; the only armament of the greater part of them consisted of pikes or pitchforks. It was the same with the new cavalry, of which the number at the time of that battle did not amount to more than three thousand six hundred: and even these forces were not formed by the exertions of the government, but were volunteers. In the arsenals, the works were not conducted with promptitude. This department of the military administration had been made great account of on paper, but was in reality neglected. As we have before remarked, the time was occupied in useless diplomatic discussions, while the subject of the greatest importance, the armament of our forces, was lost sight of. General Skrzynecki was well aware of this neglect, and soon gave a new aspect to these matters. From the 1st of March, in which he commenced the inspection of the arsenals, he was daily occupied with this duty, entering into all the details (with which he was familiarly acquainted) and infusing a new vigor and promptitude into this essential department of the military administration. In fact, in the several manufactories of arms, six hundred muskets per day were soon made.

The soldiers, who before had but rarely seen their commander, and to the greater part, of whom indeed the former commander was personally unknown, were elated to meet their chief often among them, and their enthusiasm was augmented by the frequent words of encouragement with which he took every occasion to address, them. General Skrzynecki established a new regulation in respect to the conferring of orders of merit, which was, that none should be given either to the officers or the soldiers, but upon the expressed consent and approbation of the latter. By thus submitting the conferring of these honors to the judgment of the soldier, he encouraged his self-respect, destroyed the power of the personal influence of the generals, and added much to the value of those honors as a motive for exertion.[42]

The time at which Skrzynecki received the chief command, was indeed a happy period with us, and enthusiasm was then at the very greatest height. No stronger evidence of this could be given, than the fact that the women of Poland actually formed three companies of infantry, composed from their own sex.[43]

Our army was victorious and full of energy and being then at Warsaw, it enjoyed all the conveniences which could be required by an army in a state of war. Their arms of every kind were well constructed, and in good order. The Russian army, on the other hand, was in a most disadvantageous situation. Their number had been sensibly diminished, and was diminishing every day, from the difficulty of subsistence and shelter, situated as they were in the environs of Praga which had been sacked and burnt by themselves.

Marshal Diebitsch and his army began to be convinced, by the victories which had been gained over them, and the firm resistance which they had uniformly met, that they were fighting with a nation which had resolved to sacrifice everything for liberty and independence, and that this war, which Diebitsch expected, and even promised, to finish in a few weeks, would be long protracted, and presented to him as yet no hope of a fortunate issue. A certain degree of disorder also began to take place in the Russian army, caused by the physical wants and the severe treatment to which the soldiers were subjected. Their wounded and sick were left neglected, and were accumulated in great numbers in the ruined buildings of the half-burnt villages, exposed to the open air in the severe month of February. Desertions too began to take place. Every day, indeed, small parties of deserters, and among them even officers, arrived at Warsaw. Those men assured us that a smothered discontent pervaded the army. They stated that the soldiers had marched under the expectation that they were to act against the French and Belgians, and not against the Poles, whose revolution had been represented to them as merely the revolt of one or two regiments; and that, seeing the true state of things, great numbers of them desired even to unite with us, when a favorable moment should offer. These unfortunate men, who were in the most deplorable state, with tears in their eyes, addressed themselves to our soldiers in terms like these: "Dear Poles, do you think that we willingly fight against you? What could we do? We were compelled to march against you by the force of blows. Many of our brethren gave out, and, falling from exhaustion on the road, have died under the blows of the knout." These deserters stated also that such a severity was exercised in the regulations of the camp that some officers were shot, merely for having spoken on political subjects; and that it was strictly forbidden to any persons to assemble together to the number of three or four. Such information satisfied us, that, although the Russian army was strong in numbers, morally speaking, it was weak. Our own army began soon to conceive high hopes, and to dream of victory under its brave chief.[44]

At this period, with the exception of Prussia, who had publicly manifested her hostility to our cause, none of the great powers had directly injured us. Austria was occupied with Italy. From France and England, the Poles had even cherished hopes of a favorable interposition. From the former, especially, after the intelligence derived from the correspondence of the two ministers, Lubecki and Grabowski, found among the papers of Constantine, which has been presented to the reader (giving satisfactory evidence that Russia was in preparation for a campaign against her, and showing that our cause was the cause of France), we had certainly the right to cherish the strongest hopes. But more important still than all these circumstances, was the intelligence received of a revolution which had broken out in the Russian department of Orenburg, under the famous Yermolov, and the point of concentration of which was to have been the town of Samara, situated on the frontier of Europe and Asia. The highest expectations were entertained of the results of this movement, from our knowledge of the character of this celebrated general, and of his great influence, as one of that distinguished family of Yermolov, perhaps the most influential in the Empire (which, in fact, cherishes pretensions to the throne), and of the distinction which he had acquired as a bold and firm leader, in a service of many years.

His proclamations to the Russians, of which a few copies were found on the persons of their officers who were killed in the battle of Grochow, were full of energy, and breathed the sentiments of a true republican - of one who calmly and dispassionately aims at the good of his country.

These proclamations were published in all the gazettes of Warsaw on the first of March.[45]

This general was for a long while governor of the provinces beyond the Caucasus, Abassia, Migretia, Imiretia, and Georgia, provinces which were conquered from Persia and Turkey. Besides possessing a great degree of military knowledge, Yermolov was familiar with the duties of the civil administration. Those provinces were happy under his government. He ameliorated the state of the commerce by which they were enriched. The city of Tiflis, under him, rapidly increased to a great extent. That city became in fact a gen-eral depot of all the trade of Armenia, Persia, and Turkey in Asia. This general, who could have held a post of greater distinction, and nearer the throne, asked for this situation with the view to be removed as far as possible from that court which he despised, and the intrigues of which excited his abhorrence. Out of the reach of its influence, he could follow the impulses of his heart, and labor for the happiness of his fellow men. But this separation was not enough; those intrigues passed the barrier of the Caucasus to interrupt him in his benevolent labors. Several commissions were sent to make inquiries into his administration in various departments. Yermolov, to avoid these persecutions, sent in his resignation. General, now Marshal Paskevitch, filled his place. Yermolov, on quitting his post, retired to his own estates in the government of Orenburg, and lived there quietly in the bosom of his family. The breaking out of the revolutions of France, Belgium, and at last that of Poland filled his heart with joy. He hoped that the time was near at hand, when the people would have security for their rights, and would emerge from the darkness into which despotism had plunged them. He commenced the revolution in his part of the Empire, and (as we learnt at Warsaw) sustained himself for a long while against the superior forces which were sent against him. He was not, however, sufficiently supported by the people, and was too isolated to continue hostilities. It is to be regretted, that he did not commence this movement in the provinces which border upon Poland.

A VIEW OF THE STATE OF THE POLISH FORCES AT THE PERIOD OF SKRZYNECKI'S APPOINTMENT TO THE CHIEF COMMAND.

After the battle of Grochow, the Polish Grand Army was composed, as at the commencement of the war, of nine regiments of infantry, each consisting of three battalions. They amounted, after deducting the losses sustained during the campaign, to about 25,000. The newly formed infantry, which was in the battle of Grochow, amounted to about 6,000; from which are to be deducted about 500, lost in that battle. The whole force of infantry, then, amounted to 30,500 men. The cavalry was also composed of nine regiments, each comprising four squadrons; making, after the deduction of the losses by that battle, about 6,000 in all. The newly-formed cav-alry, consisting of eighteen squadrons, can also be estimated, after the losses at Grochow, at about 3,000; making, in all, 9,000 cavalry. The artillery was composed of ninety-six pieces of cannon.

Total of the Grand Army: - *Infantry*, 30,500. *Cavalry*, 9,000. *Artillery*, 96 pieces.

The detached corps of General Dwernicki consisted, at the beginning of the campaign, of one regiment of infantry, composed of three battalions, numbering, after the losses of the campaign, 2,800 men. The cavalry consisted of six squadrons, making, in all, about 1,000. The artillery, consisting at first of but three pieces, augmented by seven pieces taken from the Russians, amounted then to 10 pieces.

The small partisan corps under the command of Colonel Valentin, operating in the environs of Pultusk, consisted of 600 infantry and 100 cavalry.

The garrison of Zamosc consisted of 3,000 infantry and eighty-four pieces of cannon, that of Modlin, of 3,500 infantry and seventy-two pieces of cannon; and that of Praga, of 2,000 infantry and thirty-six pieces of cannon.

The total amount then, of disposable forces, (excluding, of course, the garrisons), on the 1st of March, the day on which Skrzynecki took the command, was: *Infantry*, 33,900. *Cavalry*, 10,100. *Artillery*, 106 pieces.

General Skrzynecki renewed the arrangements of the Dictator Chlopicki, in regard to the organization of new forces. These were, that each department should furnish from 6 to 8,000 infantry and 1,000 cavalry. When this arrangement was first made, four departments on the right bank of the Vistula were occupied by the enemy; viz: Augustov, Podlasia, Lublin, and Plock. Besides the forces which these departments should furnish, General Skrzynecki proposed to the nation, that in the other departments, on the left bank of the Vistula, viz. Mazovia, Ealisz, Sandomierz, and Cracow, a general levy should be made. These arrangements were executed with such promptitude, that six regiments of two battalions each, the formation of which had begun in December, and were but half formed on the 1st of March, were, by the 10th, in a complete state for service. Those regiments were distributed among the four divisions of the Grand Army. In addition to these, four regiments of cavalry, of four squadrons each, were also formed; and in this manner, the army received a reinforcement of 12,000 infantry, among which were 2,000 volunteer chasseurs, and of 3,200 cavalry. These newly levied forces, besides being well equipped and in fine condition, were full of spirit and energy. When Skrzynecki made the inspection of these new troops, they entreated of him to be led to the first fire.

In addition to the above forces, General Skrzynecki ordered the formation of eight regiments of infantry and four of cavalry, to be kept as a reserve to fill the ranks of the army as they should be wasted by the campaign. From this last body, was afterwards, (on the 1st of May), formed a fifth division. The infantry of the Grand Army was distributed into four divisions. They were formed and commanded as follows: -

The 1st Division, under General Rybinski, consisted of four regiments. The 2nd Division, under General Gielgud, three regiments. The 3rd Division, under General Malachowski, four regiments. The 4th Division, under General Muhlberg, four regiments. The total of the four divisions was about 45,000 men.

In this number are included the different small detachments of volunteers, who acted with the army.

Besides' this infantry, was the National Guard of Warsaw, amounting to 10,000 men.

The cavalry were also formed into four divisions, as follows: The 1st Division, under the command of General Uminski, 16 squadrons. The 2nd, under General Lubinski,

16 squadrons. The 3rd under General Stryinski, 16 squadrons. The 4th, which formed the reserve of 19 squadrons, was under General Pac. The whole force of cavalry amounted to about 14,000.

The construction and completion of the fortifications at Warsaw and Praga were not less actively pressed than the administration of the army; and, as the left bank of the Vistula, on which Warsaw is situated, commands the right, with Praga and its environs, General Skrzynecki placed on the left bank twelve pieces of cannon of 24-pound caliber, on the heights of Dynasow and Zoliborz. This battery covered with its fire the neighboring plain, to the extent of a circle of three miles in diameter, and could overpower any battery which the enemy might open against Praga. That town is divided into two parts, the first of which borders on the Vistula, and formed the bridgehead of the position; the other part, which is more distant, was not fortified. This latter part was taken possession of by the Russians, after the battle of Grochow, and was burnt by them. To the inhabitants this was a disaster; but for our defense it was a most favorable circumstance, as it left the enemy's approach unprotected, and opened a range for our fire. General Krukowiecki, who was appointed Governor of Warsaw, continued the works in the city and its suburbs with great activity. The rampart, which surrounds the city beyond the walls, had been constructed for a defense against musketry only; but at several points, it was now made defensible against artillery. The ditch was considerably widened and deepened. Beyond the ramparts, the city was surrounded by a chain of *lunettes*, placed in two lines, so as to alternate with each other, and afford a mutual support. The city itself was divided into six parts; each part being susceptible of an independent defense. The barricades in the streets were constructed with openings for the fire of the artillery, above which platforms were raised for the infantry. Mines were also prepared in different parts of the city.[46]

The positions of the army and of the different detached corps were as follows: - The infantry, the artillery, and the 4th Cavalry Division of the Grand Army, were at Warsaw and its environs. Three divisions of cavalry were posted above and below the city, on the left bank of the Vistula, whose duty it was to patrol the river, and to guard the communications between the fortress of Modlin and Kozienice. This chain of patrols, by watching the movements of the enemy, kept the Grand Army continually advised of his intentions, and in constant readiness to act against him, at any point which he might choose for attempting the passage of the Vistula.

The corps of General Dwernicki was at Pulawa. The plan of operations which had been assigned to him, and which, indeed, he had already put in execution, was to transfer the seat of hostilities to the right bank of the Vistula, to hang over and harass the left wing of the enemy, to relieve the Lublin Palatinate from his presence, and, in case of danger, to fall back to the fortress of Zamosc, and from that point to act on the neighboring region, according as circumstances might indicate.

Colonel Valentin was in the environs of Pultusk, with his small corps of partisans. In concert with the garrison of Modlin, he was to act on the right wing of the enemy, and hold in check all his maneuvers upon Plock. This concave line of operations,

131

of which the extremities were at Zamosc and Modlin, and the centre at Warsaw and Praga, was strengthened by the Vistula, which, although frozen, would not allow of a passage by the enemy in large bodies, or of the construction of a bridge, as the ice of the river was momentarily expected to breakup.

The position of the Russian army was as follows: The right wing was at Nowy-dwor, opposite to Modlin. At Jablonna, which is situated half way from Praga to Nowy-dwor, was placed a strong detachment. At Praga were two divisions, one of infantry, and the other of cavalry, with twelve pieces of cannon, under the command of General Giesmar. The greater body of the Russian forces was between Wawr and Milosna; and with them was the headquarters of Diebitsch and Constantine. Their left wing occupied Earczewo, and their patrols extended themselves along the right bank of the river, as far as Macieowice.

NOTES

42. The regulation led to an occasion for the exhibition of the firmness of General Skrzynecki's character. On the very day of the issuing of the order, the General of Division Szembek brought in a report, in which he presented for decorations the names of several officers. General Skrzynecki refused his application. General Szembek, thinking himself injured by this refusal, addressed a letter to the General-in-Chief, renewing his application, and adding that if it should not be granted, he would feel obliged to surrender his commission. General Skrzynecki, far from being moved from the resolution which he had adopted, again promptly refused the request. Szembek surrendered his commission. The whole nation regretted the loss of the valuable services of this officer, and under such circumstances. But in regretting their loss they applauded the firmness of General Skrzynecki. The latter indeed felt this regret strongly, but on the other hand he was satisfied that he had done his duty. The opinion of most of the patriots was decidedly expressed against General Szembek, who, upon such a point of personal feeling, could forget his duties to his country, and abandon the ranks of his fellow-soldiers, by whom he was held in high estimation. Szembek indeed more than once reproached himself for the sacrifice which he had thus made. The following anecdote will show the degree to which general Skrzynecki was beloved by the army, and the influence which his appointment to the chief command had on the minds of the soldiers. A soldier named Golembiewski, of the 7th Infantry Regiment, who had been wounded in the battle of Boimfe, had, on the 1st day of March, left the hospital convalescent, although his wounds were not entirely healed. Skrzynecki, while inspecting, the regiment, noticed him with his head still bandaged, and said to him, "My dear comrade, why have you left the hospital in such a state? You had better return immediately." The soldier answered, "General, I have heard of your courage and your achievements, and how much you are beloved by the nation, and I could not refuse myself the satisfaction of being present at the first fire under your command, and in which I hope that the Polish Army will be victorious." Skrzynecki, embracing him, exclaimed, "with such soldiers to command, I have no fear that I shall fail to support the honor of my country."

43. The Polish women, wishing to share the dangers and sufferings, and to witness the triumphs of their brethren, proposed to follow the example of the daughters of Sparta, and to form three companies under the command of several ladies of the most distinguished families. They proposed to march upon the rear of the army, and when an action occurred, they were to advance to the aid of their countrymen. The first company, to be composed of the young and active, were to receive and carry off the wounded from the field of battle, thus at the same time animating the soldiers by their presence. The second company was to be placed near the vehicles in which the wounded were transported, there to receive and place them, and to dress their wounds. The third was to take charge of the provisions, the preparation of lint and bandages, and even of the washing of the clothing of the soldiers. These patriotic propositions, however, neither the nation nor the General-in-Chief were willing to accept, considering that the fatigues of a campaign would be too trying to the female constitution. But to satisfy in some degree the noble impulses of these ladies, the three companies were distributed among the hospitals, to take care of the sick and wounded there.

44. To satisfy the reader that Marshal Diebitsch had begun to be conscious of his weakness, the following trifling circumstances will suffice. On the first day of March, two of our soldiers who had been made prisoners by the Russians, returned to Warsaw, and presented themselves to the General-in-Chief. One of them, who was a Galician volunteer, on the question being asked in what way they escaped, answered, that General Diebitsch himself dismissed them with a present of four ducats each, enjoining them to make it known in the army, and to say that each soldier who should go over to the Russians, would receive a like sum, and in addition to it

a portion of land sufficient for his maintenance; and that moreover they should not be forced to enter the service of the army. He also assured them that if they should return with many of their comrades, to accept these terms, they should be made officers. "Dear General," the Galician added, "we have sought your presence, in order to apprize you of these circumstances, and to place you upon your guard. The money which we have received, we request you to take as a contribution to the service of our country. We have no need of it, your care will provide for our wants, and our desires are limited to the satisfaction of fighting for the cause of our beloved country." These brave soldiers were hailed with enthusiastic expressions of respect and affection by their comrades, and the circumstance was published in an order of the day, to the whole army. This adoption of such a system of intrigue and espionage indicated sufficiently the sense of weakness which Marshal Diebitsch began to feel, in the situation in which he was then placed.

One of our generals published in the Gazette some remarks upon this conduct of General Diebitsch, from which the following is a passage. "Marshal! Such conduct is reproachful to you; and by it, you have strengthened the current suspicions of the world that the passage of the Balkan, which has given you such a name in history, was made upon a bridge of gold. But if such measures might have been successful in Turkey, they will not do in Poland. If you do not by this time know it, I can assure you that every Pole is willing to sacrifice his all in the cause of his country, and your offers can therefore avail little. I repeat to you, that the words of our motto are, 'to die or conquer.' Come then, Marshal, with the saber, and not with ducats, to the contest!"

45. *Extract from the proclamation of Yermolov.* "Brave sons of Russia! An old man of seventy, who, the contemporary of four reigns, knows well his nation and its sovereigns, lifts his voice towards you, with a heart devoted to the good of his country. He wishes, in the decline of a life which has been agitated by the storms of despotism, to infuse into your hearts the sentiments of liberty, and to die a freeman. Our complaints have .been uttered in vain: our blood has been shed in vain. Are these complaints the only arms worthy of the Russian people? No! It is with the sword in hand, in the capital itself, on the field of battle, in the north and in the south, that you should claim your national liberty. The idols of despotism will fall before you. The books of the divine law will be opened. The Czars will become the fathers of their people: we shall be no longer orphans and strangers upon our native soil. As the French and English have done, and even as the Greeks, our brethren in Jesus Christ, have done, we will swear to conquer our liberty, and that achievement will immortalize us. Nations less celebrated, and less populous than ours, surrounded by monarchs who have combined to destroy them, have arisen. Their brave men have joined together. They hasten, at the call of their country, to defend their national liberty, by their arms and their acts of valor. The hour is come. God, who holds in his hands the fate of kings and people, will bless us. Russians! break the chains of despotism! You have sworn fidelity to the Czar, but he also has sworn to be our father. He has perjured himself, and we are therefore released from our oaths. Respect nevertheless the person of the Czar, for he is the anointed of the Lord, and our sovereign. Limit yourselves to a change of the form of the government, and demand a constitution. Rise up, and the throne will tremble. But if the despot should attempt to arrest your enterprise by the aid of the accomplices upon whom he lavishes all his favors, forgetting that he is our monarch, and not theirs, and that he is the father of the great family of Russians; it is then that it will be seen that the autocracy must cease to exist, that the Russians long for liberty, that they can and will be free. YERMOLOV, Samara, 29th of January, 1831."

46. In the construction of these works in the city and the environs, all the citizens engaged, without distinction of age or sex. One of the outworks received the name of the "lunette of the women," having been constructed wholly by the hands of the fair sex

CHAPTER XII.

Operations of the corps of General Dwernicki against the Russian corps under the Prince Württemberg, in the Lublin Palatinate. - Battle of Pulawa, and defeat of Württemberg —Atrocities of that Prince at Pulawa. - Pursuit of the enemy. - Battle of Kurow, and annihilation of Württemberg's corps. - Operations of Colonel Valentin, between Modlin and Poltaak. - A detachment of the enemy is surprised at Nasielsk. - Transports of provisions for the enemy from Prussia taken. - Successful skirmishes. - Marshal Diebitsch demands the capitulation of the fortress of Modlin. Reply of Colonel Leduchowski. - A detachment from the garrison of Modlin attacks and defeats a Russian force at Serock. - General Skrzynecki makes an offer of pacification on the basis of the concessions originally demanded by the Poles. - This proposition is rejected and hostilities are recommenced - Reconnaissance upon the right bank of the Vistula under Jankowski and Gielgud. - A Russian corps under General Witt is sent against Dwernicki. - General Uminski is sent against the Russian Guard. - First encounter. - The Russian Guard is compelled to leave their position for Ostrolenkju - The guard evacuates Ostrolenka to join the Grand Army.

ON the day after the battle of Grochow, Colonel Lagowski fought with success at Pulawa, at the head of a detachment from the corps of General Dwernicki. The details of that combat are as follows:

COMBAT OF PULAWA.   [See Plan XIII.]

Prince Württemberg, having been beaten, as the reader has seen, by General Dwernicki at Swierza and Nowawies, was forced to retreat rapidly in the direction of Pulawa, and to repass the Vistula, opposite that place. The ice of the river was, fortunately for him, still strong enough to admit of a passage upon its surface; but notwithstanding this advantage, he had been pursued by Dwernicki so closely, through the whole of his line of retreat, that he daily lost great numbers of prisoners. It was on the night of the 23rd of February, that this passage was made by the Russians, and Pulawa occupied by them. As the position of that place was strong and commanding, General Dwernicki did not think it expedient to attack the enemy in front, who, although beaten, were still superior in force. He conceived the plan of passing the Vistula, at a point at some distance below Pulawa, and of making an attack upon the Russian right wing. On the evening of the 26th, the brave Colonel Lagowski, with 500 infantry and two squadrons of cavalry, passed the Vistula (f). On reaching the opposite side of the river, he threw himself into the forests which surround Pulawa. The position of Lagowski would have been critical, if the Russians had obtained intelligence of this maneuver; but they had no suspicions of it. Colonel Lagowski, expecting

137

that General Dwernicki would soon make a demonstration in front, left the forest, and approached the town, keeping up a brisk fire of skirmishers (a). The Russians, surprised by this attack, directed against it as strong a fire of artillery (f) and infantry (d) as its suddenness would allow; but our light troops succeeded in approaching the town, and getting possession of several houses, keeping up a continued fire. The two squadrons of cavalry (b) which had been sent to attack the enemy in his rear, threw themselves upon him at the same time, with great impetuosity. The consternation of the Russians became general, the greatest disorder soon followed, and a retreat was commenced, which was attended with the loss of several hundred men and horses, and four pieces of artillery. The enemy, in evacuating the town, set it on fire, to complete the barbarities which they bad been practicing. Pulawa, a spot one of the most favored of nature, and perhaps presenting one of the finest scenes in Europe, was soon a mass of ruins, the sight of which filled the bosom of every Pole with regret and horror. Those ruins, such indeed as the whole country is now filled with, evidences of the horrible barbarity of the Russians, in recalling to the minds of the Poles the lost beauty and mag-nificence of their country, will be a pledge of their eternal hatred of the despotism which authorized those ravages.

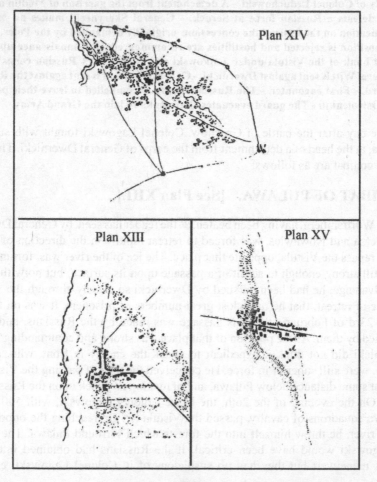

The Russians had gained already a considerable distance from Pulawa, before the corps of General Dwernicki approached it, and, of course, the whole glory of that defeat is due to Colonel Lagowski.[47]

The corps of General Dwernicki, after a short repose at Pulawa, renewed the pursuit of the enemy on that night. In every part of their route the enemy's stragglers were continually falling into their hands. This corps overtook the enemy so soon, that in order to save himself from total destruction, he was forced to give battle.

BATTLE OF KUROW.   (See Plans XIV. and XV.)

General Dwernicki, in his pursuit of Württemberg, had the intention of effecting the destruction of this corps before they could reach Lublin. To accomplish this object, he took advantage of the two roads, which lead from Pulawa to Lublin (1). Remaining himself with the greater part of his forces (a) upon the causeway which leads to Lublin by Konskawola (2), Kurow (3), and Marjtuszew (4), he sent a small detachment (6) with two pieces of cannon by the other and smaller road, which, traversing the forest between Belzyc and Pulawa, presents a shorter and more direct route to Lublin. This road had not been occupied by the enemy. Colonel Lagowski, who commanded this detachment, had instructions to follow out this road, and to keep up a constant communication with the superior force under General Dwernicki. He was ordered to keep himself constantly abreast of the enemy. At the moment that he should hear the fire of our cannon, he was directed to hasten to the attack of the enemy on his left wing, or on his rear, as circumstances might direct. This maneuver was executed with the utmost punctuality. The enemy pressed in upon the causeway by the larger body under Dwernicki, and thus forced to give battle, took a position upon the heights of the town of Kurow, in doing which, his consternation or his inconsiderateness was such, that he neglected the ordinary means of security, and did not occupy the roads which centre at that place, not even that which it was of the utmost importance for him to occupy, —the one which leads from Belzyc to Pulawa; in fact, he had even neglected to send out reconnaissances on any side, supposing that our entire force was before him on the causeway. This battle commenced on the afternoon of the 2nd of March, and continued only a few hours.

General Dwernicki, after reconnoitering the enemy's position, which was commanding, and strengthened in its front by sixteen pieces of cannon [(f) PL XV.] thought it expedient to commence with a fire of skirmishers only (a), under cover of which he maneuvered his cavalry (b) upon the Russian wings, with the sole purpose of occupying the attention of the enemy until the detachment of Colonel Lagowski should make its appearance. The enemy, on the other hand, commenced a warm fire from his artillery, and threw forward his light troops (d) in every direction. Some hours passed in this manner, the' enemy attempting from time to time to force our position. But the hour of his destruction was approaching. General Dwernicki perceiving, from an elevation of ground, the detachment of Lagowski (A) advancing upon the enemy's rear, instantaneously gave orders for the cavalry to concentrate themselves. The signal for advance was then given, and the cavalry having formed on each side of the main road, pressed forward and fell upon the centre of the enemy. At the same moment, a charge was made by the cavalry of Lagowski upon the enemy's rear. The disorder and consternation of the Russian forces was indescribable. In a moment ten pieces of cannon, a thousand prisoners, some hundreds of horses, with many wagons of ammunition and baggage, fell into our hands. The route was general. The enemy fled pell-mell, and his loss was much increased by a fire of grape from the two pieces of artillery of Colonel Lagowski, which he placed by the side of the road from Kurow to Lub-lin, over which the Russians retreated. This road was literally covered with dead. Nothing but the coming on of night saved the enemy from entire destruction. After this battle, the forces of the Prince Württemberg ceased to act as a corps. What remained of them, took the direction of Lublin, where the corps of General Dwernicki arrived the next day, having taken prisoners during the whole rout. The Prince Württemberg barely escaped from our hands, for he was in quarters in that city when our advanced detachments entered it, and was just able to save himself by flight. Such was the end of this Russian corps, which, when it began to act against Dwernicki with his small force of 3,000 men, and ten pieces of cannon, consisted of 15,000 infantry and 24 pieces of cannon. In the course of eleven days, General Dwernicki gave battle to this corps four separate times, viz, at Swierza, Nowawies, Pulawa, and Kurow; and besides the loss he caused them in killed and wounded, he took 8,000 prisoners, 19 pieces of cannon, besides 1,000 horses, with a great quantity of ammunition, baggage, &c. In all these actions the corps of General Dwernicki lost but 500 men, in killed and wounded. The panic which had begun to prevail in the Russian forces, in consequence of these disasters, reached such a degree that, at times, the mere sight of our troops was sufficient to put them to flight. The Russian Commander-in-Chief deprived the Prince Württemberg of his post, and his name was not heard of during the rest of the war.

General Dwernicki, by his victories over this corps, had completely freed the department of Lublin from the presence of the enemy. On arriving at Lublin, he restored the authority of the National Government in that place, and the region about. He made the necessary arrangements for reinforcing his corps, and left for Krasnystaw, in the environs of Zamosc.

While these successful operations of General Dwernicki, in the southern part of the kingdom, were in progress, and by this series of victories, he was approaching the frontiers of Wolhynia and Podolia, our arms were not loss successful in the \north.

The brave Colonel Valentin, with a small detachment of partisans, fought the enemy with success between Modlin and Pultusk. This detachment was thrown into that region, (acting, however, more particularly between the Rivers Wkra and Orsyca), in order to hold in check the operations of the enemy upon Plock. This detachment was to obtain succor, in case of necessity, from the garrisons of Modlin. It was especially destined to intercept the transports which were to come from Prussia upon the road to Mlara, for the relief of the Russian army.

Colonel Valentin was occupying with his detachment the forest near the town of Nasielsk, when he was apprised that a small body of Russian troops, under the orders of Colonel Schindler, consisting of two regiments of cavalry, a battalion of infantry, and two pieces of cannon, had arrived on the 3rd of March, at that town. This detachment had been sent to protect a transport which was to pass there. Colonel Valentin immediately formed a plan to attack it. During the night of the 3rd and 4th of March, he approached the town, invested it, and ordered an attack, in which the detachment surprised the enemy, and forced him to quit the city, leaving his two pieces of artillery, and a number of prisoners. Colonel Valentin, thinking that the Russians might possibly return with a superior force, evacuated the city, and took his prisoners to Modlin, in order, by disembarrassing himself of them, to hasten his march and reach the environs of Pultusk, in time to intercept the transport. On the 5th, he took this transport, consisting of eighty vehicles loaded with various kinds of provision, together with twelve loads of equipage, &c. for the Russian generals, which he sent to Warsaw. The detachment of Colonel Valentin continued to maneuver for a long while in those environs without any support.

In the vicinity of Warsaw, along the banks of the Vistula, both above and below the city, small skirmishes almost daily occurred. On the fourth of March, the brave Lieutenant Berowski, passing the Vistula opposite Jablonna with his platoon, surprised a squadron of Cossacks, and took a hundred prisoners and as many horses. The battalion of volunteer chasseurs of Colonel Grotus, posted in the environs of the villages Siekierki and Wilanow, brought in, almost every day, parties of Russian prisoners, by surprising the different de-tachments of the enemy placed upon the island of Saxe, opposite to the above-mentioned places. This same battalion burnt two bateaux, in which were a party of Russian troops, who were sent during the night with combustibles to burn the bridge between Warsaw and Praga. These boats were sunk, and the Russians who escaped drowning were taken prisoners. In the environs of the small town of Gora, about twenty miles from Warsaw, a considerable body of workmen who were sent by the enemy to prepare the materials for building a bridge, were surprised by a battalion of the 2nd Regiment of Light Infantry. A hundred pioneers and sappers were taken prisoners, and many hundred male and female peasants set at liberty, who had been forced to work for the enemy.

At about the 8th of March, Marshal Diebitsch demanded the capitulation of the fortress of Modlin, for which object he dispatched Colonel Kil. This officer was entrusted with a letter to the Count Leduchowski, written by the Marshal's own hand. His proposition was rejected.[48]

Some days after this answer, a part of the garrison of this fortress, sent as a reinforcement to Colonel Valentin, surprised the Russians in the town of Serock. They had passed the Bug River, and the Narew opposite that town, to make requisitions of forage in the country around. By a prompt arrangement, the bateaux of the enemy were taken by our troops; and his forces, suddenly attacked and defeated, were compelled to evacuate their position, leaving a thousand prisoners in our hands, which were immediately carried to Modlin, and thence to Warsaw.

In this state of things, and while circumstances were continually occurring with uniform advantage to the Polish arms, General Skrzynecki, with the sincerest wish to finish a bloody struggle, and anxious to show that the Poles were always ready

141

to hold out the hand of reconciliation, wrote, with the permission of the Provisional Government, a communication to Marshal Diebitsch, with propositions of that purport. But as these offers of conciliation were rejected by the Marshal, the contest was recommenced.[49]

On the 10th of March, the operations of the campaign were recommenced. The 2nd Division, the command of which, after the death of General Zimirski, was given to General Gielgud, and a division of cavalry, under the command of General Jankowski", received orders to make a strong reconnaissance upon the right bank of the Vistula. This division was ordered to pass the bridge, in the night, and at break of day to commence the attack upon whatever force of the enemy they might find on the plains of Grochow or Kawenzyn, and, by this maneuver, to harass the right wing of the enemy. But General Jankowski arrived late. It was near eight o'clock, A. M. before he approached with his division, at which time the two divisions united left Praga to commence their attack, but this operation being thus retarded, could not be made effective. The enemy, seeing our movement, had time to prepare themselves to counteract it. Our forces having advanced a mile or two upon the main road, commenced a fire of tirailleurs, and the enemy began to retire. As it was designed to act upon Kawenzyn, a battalion was sent to attempt an attack on the forest of elders, well known to the reader; but as the enemy was quite strong at that point, and particularly in artillery, a fire from which was immediately opened upon our force, the attack was not made, and our battalion was ordered to withdraw. The Russians, at about mid-day, began to show a stronger force upon the plains of Wawr. Their artillery, also, opened a fire upon the main road. This fire had continued an hour, when our generals, not perceiving that the artillery was protected by cavalry, decided to make a charge upon them with the Mazurs Regiment, and the 3rd Light Cavalry Regiment. This brigade of cavalry, under the command of the brave Colonels Blendowski and Miller, threw themselves with courage upon that artillery, when, at the moment of the charge, two regiments of Ataman Cossacks, which were posted in a wood adjoining, displayed their front, and advanced to charge our cavalry upon the flank and rear. Our attack therefore failed, and it was owing to good fortune alone that by a rapid bending of our flank,' this body of cavalry was saved from total ruin. This unfortunate affair cost us a heavy loss of men, and of both of the brave colonels who commanded the attack. At about 2 P. M. as the enemy began to debouch from the great forest with increased forces, it was decided to return to Warsaw, and thus ended this reconnaissance, which, had it been executed by more skilful generals, might have had the best success, for all the Russian regiments which had advanced towards Praga, at a considerable distance from their main forces, might have been taken. A reprimand was publicly given to the two generals, Gielgud and Jankowski, for their remissness in executing their instructions. The only advantage which was gained by this reconnaissance was the taking of a great quantity of fascines and other materials prepared for a storm of Praga, and the collection from off the field of a considerable quantity of arms, which had been left there by the enemy, after the battle of the 25th.[50]

The Russian commander having, as the reader is aware, lost nearly the whole of the corps of the Prince Württemberg, the remnants of which was dispersed and had wholly ceased active operations, sent against General Dwernicki the corps of General

Witt, composed of 8,000 infantry, 2,000 cavalry, and 16 pieces of cannon. This corps ar-rived on the 11th at Lublin, in which town was a small detachment of Dwernicki's corps, commanded by the Colonel Russyian. This small detachment, having only barricaded a few streets, de-feuded with much firmness the passage of the small Bystrzyca River, and left the city at nightfall to rejoin its corps, which was in the environs of Zamosc.

Again the corps of the Russian Guard, which had recently arrived, under the command of Prince Michael, consisting of 16,000 infantry, 4,000 cavalry, and 36 pieces of cannon, a division of cavalry, with eight pieces of cannon, was sent into the environs of Pultusk, commanded by General Uminski, who was to take under his command the detachment of Colonel Valentin, and acting in concert with the garrison of Modlin, he was to occupy the attention of the enemy, in order that our main body should not be disturbed in the offensive operations which General Skrzynecki had decided to adopt.

General Uminski arriving with his corps, met an advanced detachment of the Russian Guard in the environs of Makow, composed of two regiments of hussars and eight pieces of cannon, who were sent forward as a party of observation in that vicinity. This was the first encounter with this celebrated guard. Our cavalry waited impatiently for the moment to try their strength with them. Two young regiments, one the Podlasia Krakus Regiment, and the other the 5th Uhlans, entreated their general to be permitted to make the charge. General Uminski, observing that there was no stronger force near, ordered an immediate attack.

Our cavalry, on receiving the order, did not even give the enemy time to display his front, or to make use of his artillery; but rushed upon him with an impetuous charge, under which he was at once borne down. Of one regiment of those hussars nearly a squadron was taken prisoners. This Russian cavalry, which were in full rout, were pursued as far as the environs of Magnieszewo. The enemy was not permitted to take position, and the pursuit was pressed with such rapidity, that they had not time to destroy the bridge which crosses the River Orsyca, but were followed even to the environs of Rozany, where they reached the position of their main body. General Uminski, in order not to expose his force to the observation of the enemy, halted in an advantageous position in the forests near Rozany, and from this position he continued to hold the enemy in check. In fact, by harassing and wearying the enemy with continual attacks, he at length forced the Prince Michael to quit Rozany, taking the direction of Ostrolenka. General Uminski sent in pursuit of the enemy the brigade of cavalry under the command of Colonel Dembinski. This brigade, opposite Ostrolenka upon the Narew, had on the 26th of March an advantageous affair with the advanced guard of the enemy, in which forty prisoners were taken. By closely observing the enemy in this manner, it was ascertained that the Russian Guard, after destroying the bridge, had completely evacuated Ostrolenka. It was evident that the design of Prince Michael, in this sudden evacuation of Ostrolenka, was to join himself to the Grand Army. General Uminski immediately sent an officer to inform the Commander-in-Chief of this movement, continuing in the meantime in the position which he had taken before Ostrolenka.

NOTES

47. General Dwernicki, on arriving at Pulawa, regarded it as his first duty to repair to the palace of the Princess Czartoriski, the estimable lady of the President of the National Senate, to offer his services to her, and to assure her of safety. On entering the court, the venerable Dwernicki and the officers who accompanied him, could not restrain their tears at the sight of the ruins of that edifice, so uselessly destroyed, to gratify the brutality of the Prince Württemberg, who pushed his fury to such a degree, as to have directed a fire of artillery against the central division of the palace, occupied at that moment by the Princess and her attendants. General Dwernicki and his officers, struck by the melancholy scene before them, feared to advance another step, in the dread of meeting even more horrible traces of barbarity, to find perhaps the Princess and her suite the victims of Russian cruelty. But what was their astonishment, when, on entering the porch of the edifice, they were accosted by the Princess, who with a cheerful air exclaimed: "Brave general, and officers! how happy am I, that God has allowed me to greet my brave countrymen once more, before my death." Then giving her hand to General Dwernicki, and presenting to him and his officers the ladies who were her attendants during the whole of these horrible scenes, she con-tinued, "General, do not be astonished to see us accoutered in the best garments which the Russians have left to us; we have arrayed ourselves in our funeral attire,"—and pointing to the holes with which the enemy's artillery had pierced the walls, she added, "Those marks will explain my language." General Dwernicki, struck with the heroism of the Princess and her companions, addressed her in the following terms: - " Madam, permit me, in the name of the whole nation, to make to you the homage of my high admiration. Brave indeed ought Poles to be, with mothers and sisters such as these!" He then urged upon the Princess the expediency of leaving Pulawa, which might still be the scene of distressing events, and upon this suggestion she departed under an escort furnished by General Dwernicki, for her estates in Galicia.

48. The reader will perhaps be gratified with a short topographical description of this fortress, and some details of this affair. The fortress of Modlin, which is in a pentagonal form, is situated sixteen miles from Warsaw, upon the right bank of the Vistula, at the junction of the Narew with the former river. Not far from this fortress, the small Wkra River also joins the Narew. The fortress is thus situated between three rivers. In addition to this peculiarity of its situation in regard to the rivers, its commanding elevation makes it a point of great strength. Opposite to it is the small town of Nowydwor, but this tower is so low that it is commanded by the fortress, and it is besides too distant for the erection of batteries by which the latter could be bombarded with success. This post is very important in regard to tactics, and it is a key of position, to protect, or to act upon, all operations between the Narew and the Vistula. Marshal Diebitsch considering these circumstances, and seeing that an open attack was scarcely possible; was led to attempt negotiation. The letter sent by the Marshal, was full of flattering language in regard to the heroism of the Polish Army. He permitted himself, however, to say that it was to be regretted that such a degree of heroism was not exhibited in a better cause—that the brave Polish Army was made a sacrifice of, by some ambitious and opinionated men, who had forgotten their duties to their monarch, and their oaths of fidelity. From such men as those, he wished to distinguish Count Leduchowski, for whom he had the highest esteem, and who, he was convinced, had no desire to continue a useless expenditure of blood, and would willingly surrender the fortress to the troops of his legitimate monarch. To all this, Marshal Diebitsch added the assurance that the fortress should be garrisoned by equal bodies of Russian and Polish troops. Colonel Leduchowski made a reply to this complimentary communication in nearly the following terms: "Marshal, to your letter, in which you have chosen to flatter the valor of my countrymen, and in which you have honored me, in particular, with your attentions, I have the honor to answer, that I cannot better deserve your good opinion, than in defending,

with my compatriots, our beloved country to the last drop of my blood. This is the course which the honor of each brave Pole dictates to him."

49. This letter, written at the moment when our army was victorious, and when a revolution, ready to break out in all the Polish provinces attached to Russia, made the position of the Russian army extremely dangerous, was couched in most conciliatory terms, having for its sole object the termination of a fraternal struggle. In this letter, the Generalissimo sought to convince Marshal Diebitsch, that this was not a war undertaken on our part at the instigation of a few individuals, but that it was espoused by the whole nation, and that the people were forced to take up arms by the enormity of those acts of tyranny, which were not perhaps even to which the monarch. He urged him to consider the amount of blood which had been already shed, and the indefinite prolongation to which such a struggle might be extended. He urged him also, to make known these representations to the monarch, and to invite him to lay aside all enmity, to visit and hear in person the complaints of the nation, who would receive him with sincerity, and who demanded of him only the confirmation and observance of the rights granted by the constitution, and the extension of the same rights to our brethren in the Russo-Polish provinces. What an opportunity was here presented to the Emperor Nicholas to act with magnanimity, and to extend a conciliatory hand to the Polish nation! Those letters will be an eternal testimony, that the Poles attempted every amicable means, to establish upon an equal basis their own happiness and civilization, and that of the whole north, and that all the responsibility of the bloody struggle which was continued, rests on the side of despotism.

50. The following particulars will demonstrate to the reader how much even the enemy appreciated Polish courage and devotedness. After this affair, our Generalissimo, regretting much the loss of the brave Colonel Blendowski, who had fallen in his wounded state into the enemy's hands, sent a flag to General Giesmar, the commander of the Russian advanced guard, to propose an exchange, if Colonel Blendowski was still living, and if dead, to request that his body might be given up. At the moment that the officer bearing the flag, with a party of lancers, arrived at the Russian quarters, he saw a body of Russians with General Giesmar, and his suite at their side, bearing a wounded officer, and advancing towards them. Our officer, as they approached, recognized Colonel Blendowski in the wounded officer, and announced to General Giesmar that it was to obtain him that he had been sent. On receiving this communication, General Giesmar replied, "You see, sir, that I had anticipated your object. Make my intentions known to your commander, and let him know how much I honor Polish heroism." This general took part, with his own hand, in all the arrangements for transferring the wounded officer, and two of his suite were among those who bore his body.

CHAPTER XIII.

Plan of General Skrzynecki to act upon the isolated corps of Rosen and Giesmar. - Battle of Wawr. - Various detachments of the enemy are taken after that battle, and a great number of prisoners. - Battle of Dcmbe-Wielke. - Destructive pursuit of the enemy by our cavalry. - View of the Russian losses in the preceding days. - Marshal Diebitsch abandons his plan of crossing the Vistula, and marches to the rescue of the remains of the corps of Rosen and Giesmar, and the Imperial Guard. - View of the position of the two armies, after the second repulse of the enemy from before Warsaw. - Operations of General Dwernicki. - Successes of a reconnaissance under Colonel Russyian at Usciulog. - Effect of Dwernicki's victories on the inhabitants of the provinces. - Acknowledgement of General Dwernicki's services by the National Government - The instructions for his future operations.

THE news of this prompt and sudden evacuation of Ostrolenka by the Russian Guard, and the evident intention of the Grand Duke Michael to discontinue his operations in the Plock Palatinate, and to make a junction with the Grand Army, as well as other certain intelligence that Marshal Diebitsch had withdrawn the main body of his forces, [See (A) Plan XVI.] and had left only a corps of observation composed of the two corps of Rosen and Giesmar (B), in the environs of Wawr and Milosna, determined our Generalissimo to hasten to the execution of the plan, for a long time decided upon, which was to throw himself with his whole force upon the nearest Russian corps, and to crush them before Marshal Diebitsch could come to their succor.

On the 29th and 30th, our Commander-in-Chief made a review of the greater part of the army. All the troops received him with expressions of the greatest enthusiasm. He could not but be delighted at the sight of that fine and energetic force, and be confident of the most brilliant successes. All the troops defiled before the general, carrying with them the trophies which they had taken from the enemy; and each platoon, as they passed) hailed him with some patriotic exclamation, and pledged themselves that they would never return without having satisfied his orders to the utmost. On the night of that day, the commanders of the several divisions received the order to hold themselves in readiness to march at a moment's warning.

BATTLE OF WAWR. [See Plan XVII.]

On the evening of the 30th, the two divisions of infantry under Rybinski and Gielgud, and the brigade of cavalry under Kicki, received orders to pass from Warsaw to Praga. That force quitted Warsaw at 10 P. M.

147

Whilst the division of Gielgud and the cavalry of Kicki were to occupy the great road (g) leading to Grochow, the 1st Division under Rybinski was to march upon the right wing of the enemy at Kawenzyn (K). This last division was to drive the enemy from his position in as short a time as possible. If the enemy's forces at Kawenzyn were found to be greatly superior to his own, General Rybinski was directed to continue his fire, and await a reinforcement, which should be immediately sent to him. If he should be so fortunate as to take Kawenzyn, General Rybinski was to send, by a small road (f) leading from this place, through the forest, to Milosna, a few battalions (m) to that village. Other battalions (d) were to be dispersed in the forest, between that small road and the main road. Having made those arrangements, the position of Kawenzyn was to be vigorously defended, in order to baffle every effort of the enemy to retake it. The accurate and prompt execution of this plan was expected to affect the cutting off of all the enemy's forces, which were to be found upon the field of Wawr. 'In regard to the division of Gielgud upon the main road, the instructions given were that it should not commence its fire until appraised of General Rybinski's having gained possession of Kawenzyn. This division was till then to limit its attention to the object of retaining the enemy in his position near Praga, long enough to give time for the corps of General Rybinski to occupy the above mentioned forest, and to operate in the enemy's rear. The moment for the advance of the 2nd Division was to be when the fire of the light troops of Rybinski should be heard in the forest.

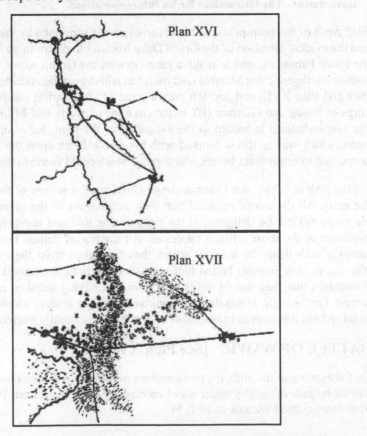

Plan XVI

Plan XVII

148

All these dispositions were executed with the greatest exactitude under the protection of a thick fog. The division of General Rybinski having quitted Praga at midnight, arrived as far as the environs of Kawenzyn, without being in the least disturbed by the enemy. This skilful general had the precaution, not to attack the enemy until an hour before daybreak; in the interval, while resting in the woody ground near Kawenzyn, he sent forward a patrol, with directions to approach near enough to ascertain, as far as practicable, the position, the strength, and the nature of the force of the enemy, and sent another patrol in the direction of the forest of elders to reconnoiter the enemy there. Those patrols returned with the intelligence that the enemy's force could not be great, as they could perceive no large detachments placed as advanced posts. It was between five and six in the morning, when the first fire of General Rybinski, at Kawenzyn, gave notice to the 2nd Division of Gielgud, at Praga, that it was the time to advance. The brigade of cavalry, under Kicki (b), with the 2nd and 7th Regiments of Lancers, having with them three pieces of cannon, spread out their flankers, and advanced slowly, directed continually by the fire of General Rybinski, who in the meantime had pushed two battalions at the charge, supported by a few pieces of artillery, and had carried the enemy's position by storm, and taken possession of Kawenzyn. The enemy were instantly routed by this impetuous attack, and lost three pieces of cannon. The division passed through Kawenzyn, sent two battalions (m) to Milosna, occupied the forest (A) in the rear of the enemy's principal force, and commenced a fire. When this fire was heard by our forces (B) upon the main road, they pushed forward, and a general and rapid advance was commenced under cover of the thick fog. Two regiments of Cossack cavalry (A), who were posted in columns near the Obelisk of Iron, were borne down before them. A great number of prisoners were taken on the spot. Our brave lancers, under Kicki, animated by this success, did not halt in their attack. They fell upon an advanced post of Russian artillery of three pieces (f) near Grochow, and took them before they had time to fire. By seven or eight o'clock, the enemy was entirely surrounded, and his retreat by Milosna was wholly cut off. It was with the dissipation of the fog that we witnessed the confusion into which had been thrown the whole advanced guard of Giesmar, composed of four regi-ments or sixteen battalions of infantry (a), eight squadrons of cavalry (A), and twenty-four pieces of cannon (f). The disorder of this advanced guard was such, that the Russian battalions had actually been firing against each other, and that fire ceased only with the clearing up of the fog. The 95th and 96th Russian Regiments, amounting to 5,000 men, with all their officers and colors, were taken in a body and with them the Brigadier General Lewandowski. If the fog had continued half an hour longer, so that we could have occupied the road to Karczewo, the whole of this advanced guard would have been taken; for what remained of them saved themselves only by flying along that road.

This attack, which was the business of a few hours, forced the enemy to quit his advantageous position in the commanding forest, between Wawr and Milosna, which be had occupied for a month, and on which he had constructed considerable fortifications. Driven from this important position, he could only expect to be subjected to still greater losses. At Milosna (3), three battalions of the enemy, with four pieces of cannon, placed as an isolated detachment, were dispersed, and their

149

cannon taken. Another isolated detachment of cavalry of hussars and Cossacks of Czarno-morskie, posted at Janowek, met the same fate, and prisoners were taken in every direction. Our two divisions pursued the enemy with unremitted celerity, and, followed by our main forces, reached Dembe-Wielke, at which place was the corps of General Rosen, composed of about 30,000 men and 40 pieces of cannon.

BATTLE OF DEMBE-WIELKE.   [See Plan XVIII.]

As the enemy occupied the heights (D) of Dembe-Wielke, on the side of the marsh opposite to our forces, which, to attack him, would have had to traverse the dyke (k) constructed over this marsh, the commanders of the two divisions considered it expedient to await the arrival of our whole force, which approached some hours after. General Skrzynecki, satisfied that an attack made, over the dyke, upon the commanding position of the enemy on the other side, in broad day, would cost too great a sacrifice of men, determined to amuse him by a constant fire of our skirmishers (a), who advanced as far as the marshy ground which divided the two armies would permit. A little before night, the Commander-in-Chief ordered ail the cavalry (6) to be brought together, and formed in columns of attack, with the two squadrons of carabiniers, under the brave Colonel Sneyder, at their head. At the approach of twilight, he ordered these columns to pass the dyke at a trot, and to throw themselves upon the enemy on the right and left, attacking with the saber.

While the cavalry was passing the dyke, the artillery (c) was to open a general fire, ceasing, however, when the passage of the dyke should be affected.

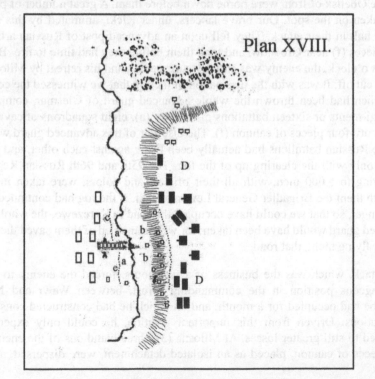

The order was given, and this mass of cavalry, under the fire of the artillery, raised the hurrah, and passed the dyke with the rapidity of lightning, followed by our infantry, having at their head the brave 4th Regiment. The enemy was in such consternation that he was not in a state to make a defense, and his whole battery was overthrown. Full three thousand prisoners were taken, together with the entire battery, consisting of twelve pieces of cannon of large caliber, some fifty wagons of different kinds, as well as caissons of ammunition, baggage-wagons, &c, and a great number of horses.[51]

In a word, the corps of General Rosen was completely broken up; the coming on of night, and the forests, alone saved them from total ruin. General Rosen himself, with his suite, was pursued and was near being taken. All his equipage, consisting of three wagons, fell into our hands. Thus, ended the glorious 30th of March. The Generalissimo, who was always in the advance, and who had personally arranged all the details of that day's operations, particularly at Dembe, justified well the high opinion which the general officers and the army had entertained of him. The 80th 6f March placed his name high on the roll of distinguished leaders. On that memorable day, two Russian corps, those of Giesmaf and Rosen, were completely broken up. It cost the enemy, in dead, wounded and prisoners, full 10,000 men and 22 pieces of cannon. On our side the loss was not more than 500 killed and wounded. For the successes of that day General Skrzynecki received from the government the order of the great Cross of Military Merit. The Commander-in-Chief was accompanied, during the actions, by Prince Adam Czartoriski, and the members of the National Government, Berzykowski, and Malakowski.

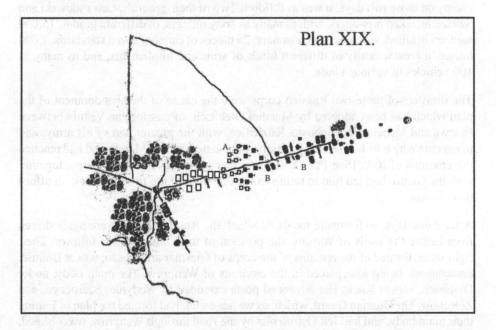

Plan XIX.

To follow up the pursuit [See Plan XIX.] of the fragments of the two Russian corps, General Skrzynecki designated the division of cavalry (A) under General Lubinski, with a battery of light artillery. This detachment set out during the night, sending reconnaissances to the right and left, to see that the enemy did not prepare ambuscades. The army followed this advanced guard, which soon overtook the enemy (B), who was still in great disorder. Infantry, cavalry, artillery, and vehicles, were mingled together, pressing their retreat. At each step, our cavalry took up prisoners. Upon some positions the enemy attempted to make a stand, but every such attempt was thwarted, and he was carried along before our troops. This was the case in the position of Minsk and of Jendrzeiow, where two regiments of Russian cavalry were routed by the second regiment, of chasseurs. It was the same case in the forest of Kaluszyn, where our artillery approached the Russian rearguard, and poured upon them a fire of grape, which scattered death among their ranks. The Russians, being no longer in a state to make any stand whatever, fell into a panic, and commenced a general flight. They were pursued by General Lubinski as far as Kaluszyn, where night closed upon the scene of destruction.

This day cost the enemy nearly as much as the preceding. Besides their loss in dead and wounded, 3,000 prisoners fell into our hands, with three standards, four pieces of cannon, and a hundred vehicles of baggage, ammunition, &c,—in fact, the whole baggage of the corps. But the most agreeable success of our army, on that day, was the taking possession of the hospitals of Minsk and Jendrzeiow, in which as many as two hundred of our comrades were lying wounded. To witness the joy of those brave sufferers was recompense enough for all our fatigues. The impetuosity of our attack was such that the enemy had not time to burn the magazines of Milosna, Minsk, and Kaluszyn, which fell into our hands. To make a recapitulation of the loss of the enemy on those two days, it was as follows: Two of their generals, Lewandowski and Szuszerin, taken pris-oners, with as many as sixty officers, of different grades, 15,000 soldiers in killed, wounded and prisoners; 26 pieces of cannon, seven standards, 1,600 horses, a great quantity of different kinds of arms and implements, and as many as 100 vehicles of various kinds.

The disasters of these two Russian corps were the cause of the abandonment of the plan which had been adopted by Marshal Diebitsch, of passing the Vistula between Pulawa and Maceiowice, opposite Kozienice, with the greater part of his army; and to execute which he had left his position on the latter days of March, and had reached the environs of Ryk. [See Plan XVI.] The fear of losing those two corps, together with the Guard, had led him to return in the direction of the town of Kock, to afford them succor.

After these days, so fortunate for us, in which the Russian forces were again driven from before the walls of Warsaw, the position of their army was as follows: Their right wing, formed of the remains of the corps of Giesmar and Rosen, was at Boimie; detachments being also placed in the environs of Wengrow. The main body, under Diebitsch, was at Kock. His advanced posts extended to Wodynie, Szeroczyu, and Zelechow. The Russian Guard, which, as we have said, had formed the plan of joining their main body, and had left Ostrolenka by the road through Wengrow, was obliged, in consequence of the successes of our army, to abandon that plan, and to retire again to the environs of Ostrolenka, where they now were posted. In the Lublin Palatinate was the Russian corps under General Witt.

The position of our army was as follows: Our left wing was opposite Boimie. It sent out its reconnaissances along the Kostrzyn River, as far as Grombkow, Zimoa-woda, and even beyond. The headquarters of the Commander-in-Chief were with the main body, at Latowicz. Our right wing was at Siennica. Its reconnaissances were sent out as far as Zelechow, at which place was a detached corps, under the command of General Pac. In this manner, the marshy Kostrzyn and Swider Rivers, covered our front. [Refer to Plan VI.] General Uminski, with his detached corps, was at Rozany, in the Plock Palatinate, opposed to the Russian Guard. In the environs of the fortress of Zamosc in the Lublin Palatinate, opposed to the Russian corps of General Witt, was the corps of General Dwernicki. Besides this, a small corps was placed in the environs of the town of Granica, upon the left bank of the Vistula, under the command of General Sierawski.

While the main forces were acting with such success, the two detached corps, under Generals Uminski and Dwernicki, had also fought gloriously, and gained important advantages. The corps of General Dwernicki spread terror in its vicinity, and the Russians were compelled to send a new corps against him, under the command of General Kreutz; so that the combined Russian forces opposed to him amounted to 20,000 men. Greatly superior as this force was, they did not dare to attack General Dwernicki, who, reinforced every day by volunteers coming from Galicia and Volhynia, soon found himself at the head of 4,500 men, and 20 pieces of cannon. This corps, in concert with the garrison of Zamosc, was sufficient to hold in check all the operations of the enemy in that quarter.

On the 25th of March, General Dwernicki sent a reconnaissance as far as the environs of Usciulug, at which place a new Russian corps, coming from Turkey, was expected to arrive. This reconnaissance was composed of two battalions of infantry, one company of Galician volunteers, three squadrons of cavalry, and four pieces of cannon. The commander of this force was the brave Colonel Russyian. The detachment arrived at the above place, and received intelligence of the approach of an advanced guard of the corps of General Rudiger, composed of two regiments or six battalions of infantry, one Cossack regiment, and eight pieces of cannon. Colonel Russyian did not stay for the approach of this guard. He took possession of the different bateaux which were prepared for, and were waiting the arrival of the Russian force at the distance of a league from the town. Passing the Bug River, with his corps, in these boats, he suddenly attacked the Russian advanced guard with such success, that he took two thousand prisoners, and six pieces of cannon, and several hundred horses. With these trophies he returned and joined the corps, to their astonishment, for they had received but a single report from him, and had no expectation of such results. The rumor of the continual successes of this corps of General Dwernicki spread along the borders of the Dnieper, reached the distant regions of our brethren in the Ukraine, and awakened in them an ardent desire to unite themselves to our cause.

For the continued and glorious advantages of this corps, which commenced its operations with 3,000 infantry, 800 cavalry, and three pieces of cannon, and had nearly destroyed two Russian corps, those of Kreutz and Württemberg, taking 10,000 prisoners, and thirty pieces of cannon, the National Government promoted its brave commander to the rank of full general of cavalry, and honored him with the surname of the famous Czarnecki, the ancient Polish chief.[52]

The Commander-in-Chief communicated to General Dwernicki his promotion, with the sincere thanks of the National Government; and at the same time sent him instructions and advice in regard to the operations which he was then to follow. The corps of General Dwernicki was to maneuver in such a manner as to menace continually the left wing of the Russian Grand Army. Keeping this object in view, he was not, unless with the expectation of some very extraordinary advantages, to remove himself very far from the fortress of Ra-mose. This place was to serve as a point d'appui in every case of sudden danger. About this point he was to maneuver, and from thence he was to push himself, as circumstances might allow, into the environs of Lublin and Wlodawa, to trouble incessantly the above mentioned wing, and even the rear of the Russian Grand Army. In this instruction of keeping himself near the fortress of Zamosc, and in the Lublin Palatinate generally, another advantage was contemplated: Viz. that he might receive daily accessions of volunteers from Volhynia and Podolia. Our brethren, in those provinces, would hasten to join themselves to his victorious eagles, (of which disposition, indeed, he received continual evidence), and, in this manner his corps would be gradually increased by such aid from those provinces, without attracting the attention of the enemy. As the provinces of Volhynia and Podolia, from their geographical character, having no large forests, were not in a state to carry on a partisan warfare, as was quite practicable in Lithuania and Samogitia, and also as the Russians had several corps upon the frontiers of Turkey, which, by being concentrated in that open country, might be dangerous to our small forces, General Skrzynecki was of the opinion that General Dwernicki, by keeping near the frontiers of the above mentioned provinces, should rather act by a moral influence upon their inhabitants, than hazard certain advantages by entering them. The Wieprz River was to be the leaning point of his left wing, and the Bug River on his right. Between those two rivers, in a woody and marshy region, he would find many strong natural positions. Of such he would take advantage, and endeavor to strengthen them by different fortifications. General Dwernicki, in receiving these instructions, was also invested with full powers, by the National Government, to institute a provisional administration over the above provinces, (in case that circumstances should lead him to establish a footing there), similar to that of the kingdom in general, and to bring them into a state to act with effect in concert with the rest of the kingdom.

NOTES

51. The horses taken on that day, and at the battle of Wawr, were employed to mount the entire new regiment of Lancers of Augustov.

52. General Wernicki, who received, among other titles, that also of the "Provider of Cannon," used his cavalry so constantly in the charge upon artillery, that if the artillery of the enemy began its fire, and the charge was not ordered, our cavalry were always disappointed. This was the case at the battle of Kurow, on the 3rd was awaiting the arrival of detachments under Colonel Lagowski, in the direction of Belzge, he was not disposed then to give the order for a charge, but preferred to amuse the enemy by various maneuvers of his cavalry. Passing down the front of his lancers, he observed that they wore a look of dissatisfaction. On noticing this, he was astonished, and demanded an explanation. "What does this mean, my dear comrades?" said he "you are sad at a moment when, after so many victories, you ought to be joyful." The lancers replied, "Dear general, it is an hour since the enemy's artillery commenced their fire, and you do pot allow us to charge upon them." The General, smiling, answered, "Make yourselves content; you shall soon have that satisfaction;" and in a short time, as the reader will remember, general Dwernicki, seeing the detachment of Colonel Lagowski approaching, gave the order for an attack upon the enemy's artillery, and in a moment they were driven from their position, sabered, and ten pieces of their cannon taken. The Russians, to whom the name of Dwernicki was a terror, would speak of him in the following manner: "What can we make of such a general? He performs no maneuvers, and never permits our artillery to fire. His generalship appears to lie only in taking possession at once of our cannon!"

CHAPTER XIV.

The insurrection in Lithuania. - Dispositions of the Lithuanians at the breaking out of our revolution. - Their offers of co-operation were rejected by the Dictator. - View of the condition of Lithuania under the Russian sway. - Scheme of the Russian Government to destroy all Polish national feeling in that province. - The insurrection is brought about by the massacre of the patriots at Osmiany. - Capture of numerous towns by the insurgents, and dispersion of their garrisons. - Storm of Wilna, and delivery of prisoners. - Several partisan corps are formed. - Their destination and successes.

IT had pleased Providence thus far to make the success of our arms, in every point, a just chastisement of our enemy, and encouraged by this success, the nation had begun to cherish the brightest hopes for the future. Their confidence and exultation were complete, when the report was received, that our brethren in Lithuania and Samogitia had risen to break the yoke of despotism, and had openly commenced a revolution. The certain confirmation of this happy intelligence was brought to the kingdom by one of the students of the University of Wilna. This brave young man belonged to the Patriotic Club which had been secretly formed there, and that club had sent him to Warsaw to carry the authentic intelligence of the insurrection.[53]

Then it was, at last, that the voice of liberty was heard upon the shores of the Baltic, and at the sources of the Dwina and the Niemen; and with this voice, was heard that of union with ancient Poland. The brave inhabitants of this immense region, animated with an attachment for us, the strength of which ages had proved, regarded themselves only as a part of one great family with ourselves. Almost within hearing of the bloody combats which had been fought, the could not restrain themselves from joining in the struggle, and acting side by side with us, for our common Poland.

Before I enter upon the details of this revolution in Lithuania, the reader will permit me to refer him, in the Appendix, to a short description of that country and a view of its connection with Poland, which is, in general, so imperfectly understood.

The Lithuanians of Wilna knew, four days after the 29th of November that Warsaw had given the signal of a new Polish insurrection. A deputation was immediately sent by them to the Dictator Chlopicki, announcing to him *that all Lithuania, and particularly the Lithuanian Corps d'armee, of* 60,000 *strong, was ready to pass to the side of the Poles*. But that inexplicable and lamentable dictatorship *rejected this offer*, so great and so generous. The Lithuanians, however, not despairing, waited for a more propitious moment; and scarcely was the Dictatorship abolished, when the National Government, thanks to the thoughtful care of Joachim Lelewell, - addressed itself officially to the Lithuanian committee. Every disposition was made for a rising at an appointed time, which at length arrived.

It would not be in my power to give the reader a just idea of the tyranny and persecution to which the Polish provinces united to Russia were subjected. If the kingdom was oppressed, it has always had some glimmer of constitutional right, but in the provinces the only constitution was absolute power. Those provinces, abounding in resources, and which, had they been protected by free laws, would have been, as they formerly were, the granary of Europe, presented everywhere traces of misery, being exposed to the abuses of the Russian administration and its agents, who wrung them to the last drop, to enrich themselves. Justice was unknown. Sometimes the governors, or sprawnaks, men of most depraved conduct, changed the laws at their own will, and not to obey that will was to be subject to be sent into Siberia. All those provinces were submerged by the Russian military, who were quartered in every village; and those soldiers, receiving only the small compensation of a groat a day, which was altogether insufficient for their subsistence, levied upon the inhabitants the means of their support. But the cause of the greatest suffering in Lithuania was, that, in order to prevent all sympathy between the soldiers and peasantry, and all national feeling in the Lithuanian soldiers, most of the levies from that province were sent to serve on the barbarian frontiers of Asia, while Russian soldiers were substituted for them, who were without any sympathy with the inhabitants, and who would be regardless of their feelings in their deportment towards them, and merciless in their exactions. It was not so under Alexander, - the arrangement was made by Nicholas. No idea can be given of the distress which it caused. Many a family was obliged to deny themselves their necessary food, to supply the demands of the military tyrant who was quartered upon them. The peasantry of those provinces were treated like brutes. No civilization, not the least glimmer of light, not a school was permitted. That poor race was kept in a state so degraded, that the elements of civilization seemed to be lost in them, and the possibility of their being recovered seemed almost hopeless.

One of the greatest evils was the systematic endeavor to destroy all national sympathy with Poland. The Russians carried their oppression, indeed, so far, as to change the religion of the country, and to introduce the Greek schism. But through all these persecutions, Providence saved that people from losing their national sentiments as Poles. On the contrary, they have proved that neither time nor persecutions will ever destroy that attachment, but will, indeed, rather strengthen it. The late insurrections in Lithuania and Samogitia, which have been so" long under the Russian Government, and the inhabitants of which hastened to take up their arms, at the signal of our revolution, afford a sufficient evidence of this attachment. What deserves especially to be noticed, is, that in Lithuania, it was the peasants and the priests, joined by the youths of the academies, who first began the revolt, and who were the most zealous defenders of the common cause. That heroic people commenced the revolution without any munitions, and without any arms but the implements of husbandry. Armed in most cases with clubs alone, they abandoned all to unite in our aid, and fought with courage and success for nearly two months, against the different

Russian corps, before the corps of Geilgud and Chlapowski arrived, which, ^instead of succoring them, by the misconduct of their generals, sacrificed the Lithuanians, as well as themselves, and gave the first downward impulse to our cause.

The insurrection of Lithuania and Samogitia was propagated with rapidity through all the departments of those provinces. The commencement was made in the departments of Osmiany and Troki, accelerated by the following circumstance:

Many of the patriots, for the purpose of consulting upon the different arrangements for the revolt, had secretly assembled on the last of March at Osmiany, and held their secret conferences in the church of the place. While occupied in this manner, a loud shouting was heard in the town. A Cossack regiment had entered the place, and a great part of the regiment surrounded the church. The doors were broken down, and the Cossacks entered and sabered the unfortunate men within these sacred walls. Wounded as they were, those who survived the attack were thrown into wagons to be carried to Wilna. But in this the barbarians did not succeed. A few escaped from their bloody hands, ran into the suburbs of the town and collected the peasantry, and on that very night, some hundreds of the inhabitants having been got together, Osmiany was attacked with the greatest fury by the patriots. Several hundreds of Cossacks were massacred. The others took flight, and the poor prisoners were delivered. From that moment, the flame spread to the departments of Wilna, Wilkomierz, Hosseyny, and Szawla. In a few weeks, more than twelve towns were taken by storm, and the Russian garrisons driven out and dispersed. The principal of these towns were Jarbourg, Szawla, Keydany, Willcomierz, Kowno, Troki, Swien-ciany, Rossienice, and Beysagola. In a short time, more than a thousand Russians fell under the blows of the Lithuanians, and another thousand were taken prisoners. The Lithuanians accoutred themselves with their arms. Some hundred horses and several pieces of cannon were also taken. The bloodiest affair was the storm of Wilna, on the night of the 4th of April. Two hundred Lithuanians attacked this town, and fought with 4,000 Russian infantry (nearly two regiments), six squadrons of cavalry, and twelve pieces of cannon. For the whole night, the Lithuanians pressed their attack with fury. They took the powder magazine, and arsenal, where they found many arms. But the most consolatory success was the rescuing of some hundred patriotic students, and proprietors, who had been confined in prison there for years. The battles of Keydany and Szerwinty was also severe, and the valor of the brave Lithuanians was equally displayed there. At Keydany, twenty of the brave youths of the academy defended the bridge over the Niewiaza, against two squadrons of cavalry, while, on the other side, some hundreds of those brave youths made a storm upon the city, and routed the garrison, which consisted of three squadrons of hussars. In a word, not quite 2,000 Lithuanians, armed in the most defective manner, commenced the struggle, and drove out garrisons to the amount of eight or ten thousand Russian regular troops, spreading consternation throughout the whole of the enormous space between the Dwina and the Niemen. Their numbers were soon augmented, and armed with weap-ons taken from the Russians. Their forces were afterwards divided into several small detached partisan corps, which received the following destination. 1st, the corps under the command of B***, consisting of about 1,500 infantry and 100 horse, was to observe the territory upon the Russian frontier, between Jarbourg, upon the Niemen, as far as the frontier of Courland. This corps was to interrupt the transport of provisions from the Russian territory, and also to keep a communication between the ports of the Baltic Sea, Lipawa and Polonga, so as to secure a correspondence with foreign vessels which might arrive with ammunition and other aid for Poland. The 2nd Corps consisted of about 2,000 infantry, under the command of P***, and Z***, and were to act between Uceamy and Dawgeliszki. There this corps of partisans was to profit by the strong positions which the nature of the country offers, among its lakes and forests. This corps was to observe the great road which leads through that country from St. Petersburg to Warsaw, and to surprise and attack all the Russian detachments which might pass that road, on their way to Poland.

To act in communication with this corps, and against the garrison of Wilna, was designated a 3rd Corps, under the command of M***, composed of nearly 2,000 infantry and 100 cavalry. This corps made itself severely felt. A fourth small detachment, under the command of B***, of about 300 strong, acted in the Grodno Department, and occupied a part of the Bialowiez Forest.

Besides these, was a detachment of 400 horse, under the command of V***. This detachment was constantly in movement, and kept open the communications between the other corps, and acted as occasion required. It was especially to attempt to surprise the enemy's artillery, which was often sent in an unprotected state. This detachment of cavalry, with the first named corps under the command of B***, attacked so sudden and vigorously the Russian corps under the command of General Szyrman, that they were forced to take refuge upon the Prussian territory at Metnel. The Prussians received them, and afterwards permitted them to leave with their arms and ammunition. This was not the first nor the last example of such relief afforded to our enemy by Prussia.

The insurrections of Lithuania and Samogitia, which had begun so successfully and promised to extend even to the borders of the Dnieper and the Black Sea, could not but threaten the utmost danger to the Russian forces which had entered the kingdom, and it was from this moment that the situation of the enemy became in a high degree critical, as every military judge will perceive. The danger of their position was still more to be augmented by our success in the battle of Igani, on the 9th of April.

CHAPTER XV.

Plan of operation against the two corps of Rosen and Kreutz. - Battle of Tgani. - Reflections on the state of the Polish cause after the victory of I gam. - Review of the course of the campaign. - Condition of the Russian army. - Discontents in Russia. - Representations of the Senate at St Petersburg to the Emperor. - Comparative view of the forces of the two armies at the present stage of the conflict.

MARSHAL DIEBITSCH, as is known to the reader, was forced, by our victories of the 31st of March and the 1st of April, to abandon his plan of passing the Vistula opposite to Kozienice, and to think of nothing further at present, than of saving the two corps of Rosen and Giesmar, and the guard. He was so far separated from them while between Kock and Ryk, where he then was, that by a prompt diversion on our part, by Lukow, he might have lost those corps, and it was in fear of this, that he hastened to arrive as soon as possible to their succor at Siedlce. Our Commander-in-Chief thought to anticipate this movement, and to throw himself upon the combined corps of Giesmar and Rosen, before Diebitsch should reach them.[54]

BATTLE OF IGANI.   [See Plans XX. and XXI.]

On the 9th of April, the Russian army was nearly in the same position as we have last described them. The main body, under Marshal Diebitsch, were in the environs of Kock, and the combined corps of Rosen and Giesmar [Plan XX. (a)], were upon the small Kostrzyn River (6), at Boimie. Our army also had not changed its position.

The following were the dispositions for the attack: The reader, on examining the plan, will see that the two-corps opposed to our forces, which were at Latowicz (c), were too far advanced, which exposed them to be turned on their left wing, and even taken in the rear, if our forces there should succeed in driving back the forces-(e) of the enemy on the road (d) from Latowicz by Wodynia to Siedlce. To execute this movement the order was given that when the 1st Infantry Division (f), supported by twenty-four pieces of cannon, should commence the attack upon the great road opposite Boimie, the 3rd Division (g), having with them the brigade of cavalry of Kicki, should leave the position at Latowicz before daybreak, and take the direction of Wodynia, to attack the forces which it might find there; but if those forces should be found greatly superior, the division was to remain in a strong position at Jeruzalem (A). If it should succeed in driving back the enemy's forces, it was to take the road on the left, leading from Wodynia through Igani (i) to Siedlce. Every effort was to be directed to the point of arriving as soon as possible upon the dyke (k) at Igani, which leads over the marshes of the river Sucha (f). By a prompt maneuver of this kind, the enemy could not, as we have said, escape being turned. For the better execution of this plan, the enemy was to be harassed on the main road, in order that General Prondzynski, who was to command the expedition to Wodynia, might have time to maneuver upon the enemy's flank.

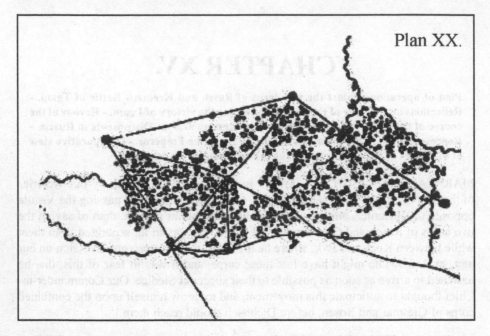

Plan XX.

A division of cavalry (m) under the command of General Stryinski, was to leave Boimie, and take a direction on the left, towards the village of Gruski, to pass there the fords of the Kostrzyn River, and in case of the retreat of the enemy, to fall upon his right wing.

Having issued these instructions, and confided the command of the little corps which was to act upon the enemy's left wing at Wodynia, to General Prondzynski, the Commander-in-Chief left himself for Boimie, to lead the attack in person upon the main road. As was the case in the position at Boimie, [Refer to Plan II.], we were separated from the enemy by the marshes of the Kostrzyn River. The two ruined bridges upon the dyke not permitting either ourselves or the enemy to pass, General Skrzynecki contented himself with opening a fire of artillery upon the Russian position, in order to occupy the attention of the enemy, while preparations were making to repair the bridges sufficiently to admit a passage.

The moment that the work of reconstructing the bridges was to be put in execution, was to be decided by the time and the direction in which the fire of General Prondzynski should be heard. If the latter general should succeed on the enemy's flank, then, of course, the bridges were to be reconstructed, if not, they were to remain in their present state to obstruct the passage of the enemy. Several hours were occupied by this fire of artil-lery, and slight maneuvers of the light troops, when at last, between eight and nine o'clock, the fire of General Prondzynski was heard, who had evidently passed Wodynia, and had begun acting on the enemy's flank. This was the signal to commence repairing the bridges. General Skrzynecki, with his suite, superintended the work, and several battalions were employed in bringing together the materials. A degree of consternation was observed in the enemy's forces, in consequence of the attack on his flank, and his columns began a movement; but his artillery continued in their position, and commenced a terrible fire upon our men who were engaged in reconstructing the bridges. The presence of mind, however, of the Commander-in-Chief, who exposed himself at the most dangerous points, encouraged the men to persevere in their labors under this destructive fire of artillery.[55] When the fire on his flank was at its height, the enemy began to withdraw his artillery, and commenced a retreat. By between 10 and 11 o'clock no part of the enemy's forces remained upon the plain of Boimie; but, although the work of repairing the bridges was pressed to the utmost, it was near two o'clock before they could be brought to such a state as to admit the passage of artillery; and although several battalions of the infantry had passed over before this, they were not able, without too much exposure, to overtake the enemy, who was in rapid retreat, leaving his cavalry as a rearguard. It was not until the last mentioned hour, that the whole division passed the bridges, and pressed forward at a rapid pace in the pursuit, the cavalry advancing upon the trot. While this was taking place upon the great road to Boimie, General Prondzynski (A), who, according to his instructions, advanced to Wodynia, found there a division of sixteen squadrons of Russian cavalry, whom he drove from their position; he pursued them in the direction of Siedlce, and reached the environs of Igani [See Plan XXI.] where he saw the corps of Rosen and Giemar (B) in full retreat. At this moment the position of General Prondzynski was also critical; for, as the reader is already aware, our main army was not in a condition to follow the enemy, on account of the obstruction from the broken bridges. If the enemy had thrown himself upon Prondzynski, they could have crushed him, and with their other forces could have safely passed the dyke (o) at Igani, before our main forces, retarded as they were, could have arrived. This danger was perceived by Prondzynski, and he therefore contented himself with driving the division of Russian cavalry (C) from a position they had taken upon the heights of Igani (a task which was bravely executed by the cavalry of Kicki, and in which the Colonel Mycielski was wounded, and occupying that position himself, placing there the brigade of Romarino to defend it.

It was between four and five o'clock that Prondzynski first perceived our lancers (D) advancing upon the main road. A great part of the enemy, particularly of their cavalry, had not yet passed the dyke (a), being obstructed by their artillery. Generals Prondzynski and Romarino, dismounting from their horses, with carbines in their hands, placed themselves at the head of their columns, and commenced a fire of artillery, to apprize our advancing cavalry of their position. At the sound of this fire, the cavalry of Lubinski raised the hurrah, rushed forward, and as they approached near the brigade of Romarino, threw themselves at the charge upon that portion of the enemy's rearguard which had not yet passed the dyke. Our infantry and cavalry thus fell simultaneously upon them, the enemy was terribly cut up, and the battle was gained. Nearly five Russian battalions, amounting to 4,000 men, with their officers, amounting to near one hundred, their standards, and eight pieces of cannon of large caliber, were taken. Six regiments of cavalry were dispersed, many of them were lost in the marshes of the river into which they were driven, and several hundred men and horse were taken prisoners there. In this battle, which may be counted one of the finest in the campaign, the circumstance that our main force was retarded by the state of the bridges, alone saved the enemy from total ruin. It is to be re-marked that the 2nd Cavalry Division of General Stryinski, did not improve its time, and effected nothing upon the right flank of the enemy, as the instructions contemplated. The negligence of that general was inexcusable, and the Commander-in-Chief deprived him of his command. We lost in this battle about five hundred men, in killed and wounded. The brave General Prondzynski was slightly wounded. Before night the two armies were not at the distance of a cannon-shot from each other, but all was tranquil. The disorder and consternation of the enemy may be imagined, when it is stated that our columns took position before their eyes, on the field of Igani, without being in the least disturbed by them.

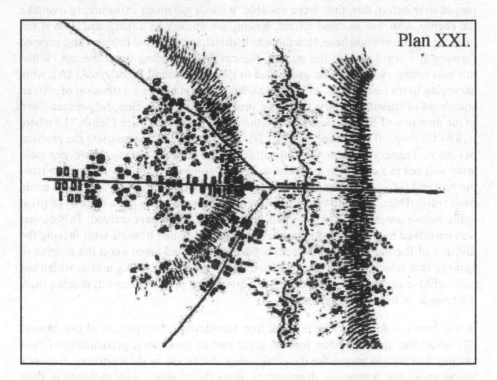

Plan XXI.

The reader will permit me to fix his attention upon the epoch of the battle of Igani, which was indeed the brightest moment of our war, the moment of the highest success of the Polish arms, the moment of the most confident hopes, when every Pole in imagination saw his country already restored to her ancient glory. Let us then, from this point, cast a look backwards to the commencement of this terrible contest. Two months before, an enormous Russian force had invaded our country, defended as it was by a mere handful of her sons; and anyone who had seen that immense army enter upon our soil, could not but have looked on Poland with commiseration, as about to be instantaneously annihilated. In this expectation, in fact, all Europe looked on, and at every moment the world expected to hear of the terrible catastrophe, to see Poland again in chains, and the Russian arms reposing on the borders of the Rhine. Such, in fact, were the expectations and even the promises of Marshal Diebitsch. Providence, however, willed otherwise. The first shock of the Polish arms with the Russians taught the latter what was the moral strength of patriotism, - what a nation can do for love of country and of liberty.

The fields of Siedlce, Dobre, and Stoczek, the first witnesses of our triumphs, and the grave of so many of our enemies, taught them to respect the nation which they expected to subdue, made them repent the audacity of having passed our frontiers, and gave them a terrible presage of how dearly they would have to pay for this unjust invasion of our soil. Battle upon battle was given, in which the enemy were uniformly subjected to the severest losses. The two great roads leading from different directions to Warsaw, on which they had followed the Poles, were covered with their dead. Thus subjected to loss at every step, the enemy reached at last the field of Praga, and there collecting all his forces in one body, under a tremendous fire of artillery, he thought to overpower our small forces. But he failed to do it. The immortal day of the 25th of February was nearly the destruction of his enormous force, and, after fifteen days of severe fighting, that great army, which was designed to destroy Poland and to make Europe tremble, was brought to a state of extremity. The autocrat and his general blushed by the menaces which they had uttered. Poland believed that the former would reflect upon those bloody struggles and the immense losses which he had suffered, and would be unwilling to continue such sacrifices. Nearly 50,000 Russians were already sacrificed. How many more lives might he not still lose? The Poles, although conquerors held out the hand of reconciliation, as the letters that Skrzynecki addressed Diebitsch have proved. In those letters, written with the utmost cordiality, frankness, and directness, he invited the Russian commander to present the real state of things to the monarch, and to assist him that the Poles longed to put an end to this fraternal struggle. A word of justice, of goodwill, indicative of a disposition to act for the happiness of the nation, and to observe the privileges which the constitution granted, -- a word of this nature, from the lips of the monarch, would have disarmed the Poles, blood would have ceased to flow, and those arms outstretched for the fight would have extended towards him as a father, to him, the author of a happy reconciliation. He would have been immortalized in history, and would have taken a place by the side of Titus.

Far, however, from that true and noble course, that proud autocrat, as well as his servant, Diebitsch, thought little of the thousands of human beings he was sacrificing: Far from such magnanimous conduct, he sent for other thousands to be sacrificed, to gratify his arrogance and ambition. He contrived new plans to pass the Vistula. It was not enough to have covered four palatinates with ruin on one side of that river. He determined to spread devastation and ruin upon the other side also: In fine, to attack Warsaw, and to bury in its own ruins that beautiful capital, the residence of the successors of Piast and Jagellow, and where he could have reigned in tranquility by only having been just and good. In the execution of this plan of destruction, he was arrested and justly punished upon the glorious days of the 1st of March and the 1st of April, which, in conjunction with the recent revolutions in Lithuania and Samogitia, and the recent battle of Igani, seemed to threaten the ruin of his army.

The Russian army was now in a state of the greatest disaffection, being posted in a devastated country, and having their resources for subsistence entirely cut off by the state of Lithuania and Samogitia. In addition to their immense losses in action, fatigue, sickness, and other inconveniences had reduced them to a state of extreme distress. Besides the influence of physical evils, there was a moral influence which impaired their strength, arising from a conviction which they could not avoid feeling, of the justice of the Polish cause. The Russian soldiers began also to reflect, that by thus serving the ends of despotism, they were only securing the continuance of their own servitude. These reflections were not made by the army alone, but, as we were secretly advised by persons coming from the interior of Russia, they were made there also, and were accompanied with the same sentiments of discontent. At St. Petersburg, as well as at Moscow, various discontents were manifested, and notices of such must have met the eye of the reader in the journals of the day. The St. Petersburg Senate presented to the consideration of the monarch the continual severe losses of the preceding years, in the wars with Persia and Turkey, and those of this campaign (though much underrated by them), which they had reason to fear would be still increased, and which might encourage revolutions in all provinces. For these reasons the Senate took upon themselves to advise some measures, and some attempt by concessions to satisfy the demands of the Poles. The party most zealous in favor of such a course was composed of those who had relations and friends exiled to Siberia, on account of the revolutionary movement of 1825. The Russian patriots in general, not only thought it a favorable moment to attempt to effect an ame-lioration of the fate of those individuals, but they hoped that the restoration of their ancient constitutional privileges and nationality to the Polish provinces attached to Russia, would authorize a claim for equal privileges to the people of the whole Russian Empire.

To these circumstances, is to be added that at this time the other cabinets began to feel dissatisfied at the course of Russia, and decidedly refused the requests of aid in men and money which she made on the pretext of former treaties. Everything, in fine, seemed to promise a near end of the present difficulties. The Polish Army, to whom this state of things was well known, waited impatiently for the moment of a decisive contest. One victory more and the Russians would not be in a state to push their attempts further. Nothing could then stop the progress of our arms, which would rest on the borders of the Dnieper, the only frontier known to our ancestors. One struggle more, and the darkness of ages, which had hung over the Polish norther provinces, would be dispersed. The light of civilization would then spread its rays as far as the Ural Mountains, and with that civilization a new happiness would cheer those immense regions. Upon the borders of the Dnieper fraternal nations would hold out their hands towards us, and there would be made the great appeal: "Russians! Why all this misery? The Poles wish to deprive you of nothing. Nay, they have even sacrificed their children for your good. Russians! Awake to a sense of your condition! You, like us, are only the unhappy victims of the relentless will of those who find their account in oppressing you and us. Let us end this struggle, caused by despotism alone. Let it be our common aim to rid ourselves of its cruel power. It is despotism alone that we have any interest in fighting against. Let us mark these frontiers, which so much fraternal blood has been shed to regain, by monuments, that shall tell posterity, that here ended forever the contest between brothers, which shall recall the disasters that despotism has caused, and be a memorial of eternal friendship between us, and of eternal warning to tyranny."

A COMPARATIVE VIEW OF THE FORCES OF THE TWO ARMIES AFTER THE BATTLE OF IGANI.

The Russian forces, which commenced the contest on the 10th of December, amounted, as has been before stated, to about 200,000 men and 300 pieces of cannon. That army received two reinforcements, viz. the corps of General Prince Szachowski, consisting of 20,000 men, and 36 pieces of cannon and the corps of the Imperial Guard, consisting also of 20,000 men and 36 pieces of cannon. The whole Russian force, then, which had fought against us, amounted to 240,000 men, and 372 pieces of cannon.

To act against this force, our army, counting the reinforcements of 6,000 men which it received before the battle of Grochow, had in service about 50,000 men, and about 100 pieces of cannon. Up to the battle of Igani, fifteen principal battles had been given, viz. those of Stoczek, Dobre, Milosna, Swierza and Nowawies, Bialolenka (on the 20th and 24th), Grochow (on the 20th and 25th), Nasielsk, Pulawa, Kurow, Wawr (on the 18th and 31st), Dembe-Wielkie and Igani. To these are to be added a great number of small skirmishes, in not one of which could it have been said that the Russians were successful. By their own official reports, - after the battle of Grochow, more than fifty thousand Russians were *hors du combat*. It will not, then, be an exaggeration to say, that their whole loss, taking into the account prisoners and those who fell under the ravages of the cholera, which had begun to extend itself in their army, must have amounted to between 80,000 and 100,000 men.[56] From the enormous park of artillery which the Russians had brought against us, they lost as many as sixty pieces. It may then be presumed that the Russian army remained at between 130,000 and 150,000 men, and about 240 pieces of cannon, not estimating, however, which it would be impossible to do, the number of cannon which might have been dismounted. Our army, which was reorganized at Warsaw, after its losses, was brought to about the same state as at the commencement of the war, that is, about 40,000 strong. The artillery was now augmented to 140 pieces.

Although the enemy's force was still sufficiently imposing, the reader will permit me to say (and in fact we did reasonably calculate thus) that as we had fought with such success against the enemy in his unimpaired strength, we might with confidence promise ourselves a certain issue of the conflict in our favor, when, with his forces thus diminished in numbers, sick, discouraged, and discontented, we could meet him with the same and even a stronger force than that with which we had already been victorious, animated too, as we now were, by the inspiriting influence of our past success, and aided by the terror with which our arms had inspired in the enemy.

NOTES

54. Every military reader, who shall follow, with strict attention the plans of our general in strategy and tactics, will be astonished, perhaps, that after such victories as those of the 31st of March and the 1st of April, he should have abandoned the advantages which he might have gained, in following up, immediately, his operations upon the two corps of Rosen and Giesmar, and then throwing himself rapidly upon the superior forces of Diebitsch, which, after those corps were cut off, could, by a simultaneous diversion upon Zelechow and Lukow, [See Plan], have been attacked on both sides, and thrown into confusion. Although I cannot give a satisfactory explanation of this apparent fault, it must be considered, that those subsequent events which give a color to the imputation, could not, perhaps, have then been reasonably anticipated by the general; and the talent so uniformly displayed by Skrzynecki should force us to suppose that there were some conclusive objections to such a course, occurring to his mind, which are not now apparent to the observer.

55. During the re-construction of these bridges, under such a fire, no terms can express the admirable conduct of our commander and his suite, who directed the work of reconstructing these bridges, in person. The general and his officers all labored with their own hands at this important task. Some of them were wounded. Our brave soldiers, witnessing the fine example of their chief, shouted their patriotic songs, as they worked, under this destructive fire. While a party were placing some trunks of trees, a shell fell among them. To have left their labor in order to avoid the danger, would have delayed the work, they therefore remained in their places, and with the noise of the explosion was mingled the shout of "Poland forever!" Providence granted that in that exposed labor our loss was very inconsiderable.

56. I cannot pretend to give the reader an accurate idea of the number of prisoners which were taken during the first days of April. From the battle of Wawr to that of Igani, not a day passed in which great numbers of them, with baggage and effects of all kinds, were not brought in. They must have amounted in that interval to a full 16,000. Those prisoners arrived generally without escort, and it was often the case that old men and even women of the peasantry were seen leading them, or rather showing them the way,—two or three peasants, perhaps, with twenty prisoners. This continual influx of prisoners gave a name in fact to that interval of time, which was referred to, as "the Period of the Prisoners." The inhabitants of Warsaw found an amusement in witnessing this continual arrival of the captured Russians. "Let us go to Praga, to see the prisoners brought in," was a proposition often made, as referring to an ordinary recreation which might be counted on with perfect certainty. If, for a half day, no prisoners appeared, the complaint would be sportively made, "What is Mr. John about (referring to Skrzynecki) that he sends us no prisoners to-day?"

The great number of the prisoners engaged the attention of the National Government. It was impossible to leave them all at Warsaw; and they were at first divided into three parts, one of which remained in Warsaw to work upon the fortifications, and every soldier was paid for his labor. The second part being also employed upon wages, labored on the great roads leading from Warsaw, in a direction opposite to the seat of the war. The third part were dispersed among the farmers in the proportion of one Russian for three farmers; and these were also paid for their labor. At stated times, an assemblage of the prisoners was held, in which they were addressed in such a manner as to produce a moral effect upon them. They were instructed in the true nature of their political rights, the real causes of the contest were exhibited to them, and they were made to be convinced that it was for their advantage at well as our own that we were fighting.

The greatest harmony reigned between the Poles and their prisoners; and I am sure that those Russians will remember the days they passed as prisoners, as the happiest in their lives. With us their prison was a state of freedom and tranquility, in which they received a liberal reward for their labor, while in their own country they were the slaves of despots, great and little, to whom obedience was enforced by the knout.

CHAPTER XVI.

Position of the two armies after the battle of Igaoi. - Plan of a simultaneous attack upon the Russian forces upon opposite sides. - Instruction to the different corps. - Operations on the enemy's front - Unfortunate operations of General Sierawski, and the first defeat. - Details of those operations. - Operations of General Dwemicki. - He defeats Rudiger; but by a false operation exposes himself to be attacked disadvantageous. by two Russian corps. - In the course of the action the Austrian frontier is passed by the combatants. - An Austrian force interposes, and General Dwernicki consents to go into camp. - His arms and prisoners are taken from him, while the enemy is permitted to leave the territory freely. - Reflections on the conduct of Austria. - Consequences of the loss of Dwernicki's corps. - The cholera makes its appearance in the two armies.

THE positions of the two armies, [See Plan XXII.] were now as follows: The Russian army was divided into four principal bodies, having no communication with each other. First, their main body (a), consisting of about 60,000 men and 130 pieces of cannon, were between Lukow (1) and Kock (2). Secondly, the remains of the corps of Rosen and Giesmar (6) were at Siedlce (3). They could be counted at about 20,000 men and perhaps 50 pieces of cannon. Thirdly, at Ostrolenka (4) was the Imperial Guard (c), consisting of 18,000 men and 36 cannon. Fourthly, in the Lublin Palatinate, were the combined corps of Witt and Kreutz (d), consisting of 30,000 men and 60 pieces of cannon. Their different scattered detachments might be counted at 10,000 men. This separation of their different corps invited a sudden attack on either, before it could receive succor from the others.

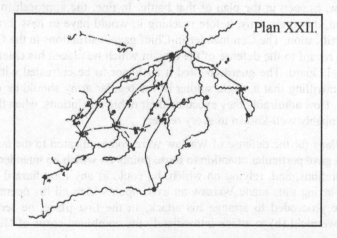

Plan XXII.

173

Our main body (c), composed of four divisions of infantry, and three of cavalry, making in all about 30,000 men and 80 pieces of cannon, was placed between Igani (5) and Siennica (6). Our reconnaissances were pushed along the left bank of the river Liwiec (L), as far as its junction with the Bug River (B). On the right, those reconnaissances reached Zelechow (7). This was nearly the same as our first position, and it was strong. Besides this main force, was the division of cavalry of General Uminski (f) upon the right bank of the Narew, at Nasielsk (8), amounting to 3,200 horse and 24 pieces of artillery, placed there to observe the Russian Guard. In the environs of Pulawa (9) was a small partisan corps, under the command of General Sierawski (g), with 3,000 men and four pieces of cannon. The corps of General Dwernicki (A) was in the environs of Zamosc, (10) and consisted of 4500 men, and 30 pieces of cannon. This corps, though at a distance from the rest of our forces, could not be cut off, having the fortress of Zamosc as a point d'appui. If the reader will examine a map of the country, or even the small plan in the preceding pages [Chapter VI. or XXII.] he will be satisfied that by our forces, small as they were, the Russian army was already surrounded, and that on the least advantage which Dwernicki, in conjunction with Sierawski, might gain over Witt and Kreutz, that army could have been taken in the rear, by means of a diversion upon Kock (2) and Radzyn (11). In a word, the moment approached at which our commander had determined to give the enemy a last decisive blow, by attacking him at the same time on every side; and for this object, the following instructions and orders were given: First, the Generalissimo renewed the order for strengthening the fortifications of Warsaw and Praga, as well as those on the whole plain of Grochow. From the first day of April, as many as 5000 Russian prisoners were continually employed upon those fortifications. Warsaw, which was already, as the reader is informed, defended by a girdle of lunettes and redoubts, communicating with each other, received the additional defense in some places of blockhouses. To strengthen the fortifications of Praga, besides the bridge-head, there were constructed, within the distance of an English mile, a line of circumvallation, which could hold more than twelve thousand men. Still further, at a distance of two miles beyond, or nearly upon the field of Grochow, was constructed a third line of lunettes and redoubts, which occupied the whole distance from Kawenzyn to the marshes of Goclaw, or the entire field of battle of Grochow, as seen in the plan of that battle. In fine, the approach to Praga was so defended, that the enemy, before reaching it, would have to pass three different lines of fortification. The Commander-in-Chief gave instructions to the Governor of Warsaw in regard to the defense of the city, in which he placed his chief trust upon the National Guard. The guard counted it an honor to be entrusted with this duty, and were unwilling that a single soldier of the regular army should be detailed for the service. How admirably they executed their noble resolutions, when the occasion came, is probably well-known to every reader.

After his plans for the defense of Warsaw were communicated to the authorities of the city, he gave particular attention to those points on which he intended to support all his operations, and, relying on which, he could at any time hazard the boldest attempts. Having thus made Warsaw an axis, upon which all his operations could revolve, he proceeded to arrange his attack. In the first place, he sent orders to General Dwernicki (h) to attack immediately the combined corps of Generals Witt and Kreutz (d). In this attack, the small corps of General Sierawski (g) was to aid, and the two corps were to preserve a constant communication with each other. For that object, General Sierawski was to pass the Vistula at Kaziemierz (12), and, avoiding an engagement with the enemy, to endeavor to join, as soon as possible, the corps of General Dwernicki, who received orders to leave Zamosc and approach Lublin (13). These two corps were to take such a position, that they could at any time retire upon Zamosc or Kaziemierz. General Dwernicki was also informed that a third small corps would be sent in the direction of Zelechow (7) and Kock (2), to act in concert with him on the enemy's rear. If they should succeed in the attack, General Dwernicki was to endeavor to force the enemy to take the direction of Pulawa (9), to drive him into the angle formed by the Vistula (V) and the Wieprz (P); in fine, so to act as to cut off those two corps from all communication whatever with their main body. Leaving the corps of General Sierawski to continue to observe them, and to push his advantages over them, Dwernicki himself was to pass the Wieprz at Kock, and from thence by forced marches to leave in the direction of Radzyn (11) for Lukow (1) or Seroczyn (14), as circumstances might direct, and according as he should ascertain the position of the enemy to be. Arrived at Lukow or Seroczyn, as the case might be, he was to await there the orders of the Commander-in-Chief, to join in the attack upon the main force of the enemy under Diebitsch (e), in which attack he was to act on the enemy's left wing. The main body of the enemy, thus taken in front and in flank, simultaneously, could not but have been broken up. For all these operations the Commander-in-Chief had destined fourteen days only.

On the night of the battle of Igani, the General-in-Chief having decided upon the above plan, sent officers in every direction with orders and instructions. The officers sent to the corps of General Dwernicki were enjoined to communicate their orders to him with the utmost haste.

The Generalissimo, while making his preparations for this last blow, continued an unremitting observation upon all the movements of the enemy, even to the minutest details, and in order that the enemy might be constantly occupied, and diverted from suspecting our plans, he directed small attacks to be continually made upon his front. For this object the 2nd Division, posted at Siennica, received orders to advance to the small town of Jeruzalem. The division, in executing that order, fought the enemy for three successive days, the 12th, 13th and 14th of April, at Jedlina, Wodynia, and Plomieniece, and always with advantage. In one of those attacks, at Jedlina, a small detachment of sixteen Krakus attacked a squadron of Russian hussars, coming from Wodynia, dispersed them, and took some twenty prisoners. This division received also the order to communicate constantly with the corps of General Pac at Zelechow. This last general was to send continual reconnaissances toward Kock, to keep a constant observation upon the Russian corps of Kreutz and Witt. Of the movements of those two corps, the Generalissimo was each day to receive the most accurate information, in order to be prepared to prevent, at any moment, a junction which might be attempted between those corps and their main body.

General Skrzynecki, seeing that the enemy had fallen into his plan, of which, indeed, he could not have had the least suspicion, and full of the brightest hopes, waited impatiently in his strong position for intelligence from General Dwernicki, and the approach of the moment for his attack upon Diebitsch. Almost sure of the successful execution of his admirable arrangements, what can express his disappointment on hearing of the unfortunate operations of the corps of General Sierawski, and of the defeat of that corps at Kazieoiierz in the Lublin Palatinate, the first defeat in the whole war? That general, in neglecting the instructions of the Commander-in-Chief, not to engage with the enemy, on account of the inferiority of his own forces (with which forces in fact he could not expect to act but in partisan warfare), approached Lublin, where the two corps of Kreutz and Witt were supposed to be posted, while his orders were, by avoiding those corps, and taking the most circuitous roads, to endeavor to join as secretly and as soon as possible, the corps of Dwernicki. He was probably deceived by false information as to the direction of the enemy's corps, and led to believe that those two corps had quitted Lublin, to attack General Dwernicki at Zamosc. He therefore probably took the direction of Lublin, with the idea of acting upon the rear of the enemy at the moment of his attack upon Dwernicki. In this manner, General Sierawski, quitting Kaziemierz, arrived on the 16th of April at Belzyca. To his great astonishment, he found there a strong advanced guard of the above mentioned corps. To avoid compromising himself, he engaged with this advanced guard, when, observing the very superior force and the advantageous position of the enemy, he ordered a retreat, which retreat was well executed and without much loss. This general should have continued his march the whole night, with as little delay as possible, in order to repass quietly the Vistula, and thus be protected from all molestation by the enemy. But, for what cause it is almost impossible to conjecture, he awaited the enemy in order of battle the next day, at Serauow. Perhaps, finding himself in rather a strong position, he thought that the corps of General Dwernicki might arrive to his aid. The enemy approached the next day with his whole force against Sierawski, and as warm an action commenced as the nature of the ground would admit, it being covered by woods with patches of open ground intervening. Some squadrons of young Kalispian cavalry, led by the general himself, advanced to the attack of the enemy's artillery, which being disadvantageously posted, was exposed to be captured. That cavalry, however, by a false direction of their charge, fell among the concealed masses of the enemy's infantry, and their attack failed.

This unsuccessful attack had unfortunate results. The corps of General Sierawski was obliged to evacuate its position, and along its whole retrograde march continual attacks of the enemy were pressed upon it. The peculiar nature of the ground, and the extreme bravery of General Sierawski, a veteran of between sixty and seventy, who, at the head of the detachments of his rearguard always led the charges against the enemy, and held him in check, was all that saved the corps from destruction. At length the corps reached Kazimierz, the point which it had left; and here again, instead of passing the Vistula, Sierwaski awaited another attack from the overwhelming force of the enemy, and that too with only the half of his corps, for the other half was to pass the Vistula. This course was inexplicable, and excited much remark in the army. On the 18th, the Russians reached Kaziemierz. The town was vigorously attacked by them, and their assaults were repeatedly repulsed by the new Kaziemierz infantry, under Colonel Malachcowski, who, with a scythe in his hand, marched at their head. But the death of that brave patriot spread among the ranks of those new soldiers a degree of disorder, and the city was taken by the enemy. We must again thank General Sierawski for having saved the rest of the corps from ruin; having executed the evacuation of the town with such order that he passed the Vistula at the point of Borowa, not far from Kaziermierz, without being molested in the attempt. He then took a position on the left bank.

Although the unfortunate affairs of those two days were not attended by severe losses, yet they were deeply afflictive to the Commander-in-Chief. They threatened the entire disarrangement of this plans, and were followed by the more important disasters of General Dwernicki. The latter, who, as is known to the reader, commenced his career so gloriously; whose very name, indeed, was a terror to the Russians, and who, by his successive victories of the three corps of Kreutz, Württemberg, and Rudiger, had established the strongest claims upon the gratitude of his country, this general, I must repeat it with pain, finished his great career in the most unfortunate manner. His case should serve as a strong example, that it is not bravery alone, which is required in a great general, for in that it would be difficult to find his equal, but that this bravery loses its value when not united with circumspection.

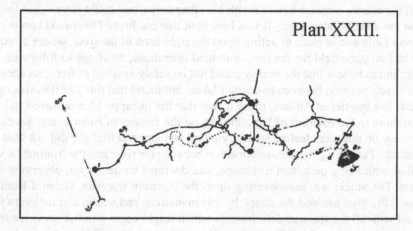

Plan XXIII.

The following are the details of the operations of General Dwernicki [See Plan No. XXIII.]. We cannot well imagine the cause which induced that general to quite Zamosc (I), and the important operations of the Lublin Palatinate, and, neglecting all his instructions and orders, to have crossed the Bug (B) and entered the province of Volhynia, unless it were the reception of some certain news of a fresh insurrection in that province, and the collection of insurgent forces there, who might be waiting for his approach, and who needed his protection. He might, perhaps, have thought to be able so to accelerate his movement as to avail himself of such new strength before a superior Russian force should arrive in that province to crush such insurrection, and disperse the insurgents at the moment when Dwernicki night have conceived such a plan, there was in fact, only a corps of about 12,000 men and some 20 pieces of cannon, under Rudiger, in that province. This corps, Dwernicki perhaps intended to attack, in his way, and crush them, and then attaching the insurgents to his corps, to return to the palatinate, or if circumstances might make it expedient, to follow up his blow into the heart of Volhynia. In fine, on the 15th of April, this general

177

quitted the environs of Zamosc, taking the direction of Uscialug (2), where, on the evening of the 16th, he passed the Bug River. On the 17th he continued his march in the direction of Dubno (3), where the insurgents were perhaps supposed to be awaiting him. On the road to that town he received information that the corps of Rudiger had marched from Radzivilov (4) and was now in the direction of Milatya (5). General Dwernicki turned immediately from the direction in which he was marching, to throw himself upon this corps, which he found on its march, at the village of Boromel (6), where, without giving the enemy time to take position, he attacked and overthrew him. The enemy was routed, and lost several hundred in killed and prisoners, with eight pieces of cannon. That in this fine, and the last fine battle of Dwernicki, the Russian corps was not wholly destroyed, was owing to the circumstance that the branch of the River Styr (s), over which the bridge had been destroyed, stopped our pursuit. The Russians, during the night of the 18th, evacuated their position, and took the road to Beresteczko (7), where they took a new position. In regard to tactics, the corps of General Rudiger could not have chosen a worse direction than that of the angle formed by the River Styr, and the frontier of Austria (F). General Dwernicki, by a passage to the right bank of the Styr, could have cut off all the enemy communications with his other corps, and could have again fought him at the greatest advantage. It was here then that our brave Dwernicki committed his great fault, and in place of acting upon the right bank of the river, where he could have had an open field for the most enlarged operations, he chose to follow up the attack; and as he saw that the enemy could not be safely assailed in front, on account of his strong position between two small lakes, but found that this position was open towards the frontier of Austria, there it was that the unhappy idea occurred to him, of marching to the environs of Kolodno (8), on the frontier of Austria, and attacking the enemy on that side, feeling sure of victory. But General Rudiger did not wait for this attack. Perceiving his exposed position between the river and the frontier, he was satisfied with being permitted to escape, and declined battle. Upon observing that General Dwernicki was maneuvering upon the Austrian frontiers, General Rudiger repassed the Styr, avoided the attack by this maneuver, and was in a situation to join himself with all the Russian detachments which might come into the province from the heart of Russia, by the different directions of Krzemieniec, Ostrog, &c., and to act with them in surround Dwernicki, who was confined in this above described angle. This is what in fact took place.

Dwernicki remained, for what reason we cannot conceive, at Kolodno until the 23rd of April, whence, following along the frontiers of Austria, he took the direction of Wereszczaki (9). There dispersing a Russian detachment, he arrived on the 26th at Knieloe and Wielkie (10). Knowing that the Russians were observing him, he determined to remain there and take advantage of a strong natural position. He wished in this position to await the enemy and give him battle, hoping by a victory to free himself from the contracted space in which he was confined. In fact, on the next day, the corps of General Rudiger (b) made its appearance, having come from the direction of the Krzemienic (11). The battle commenced, and in the midst of the action another Russian corps (c) was seen approaching from the direction of Proskirow (12) and Stary-Kostantynow (13) under the command of General Rott, acting thus upon the right wing and even the rear of General Dwernicki's corps. To avoid being turned, General Dwernicki retired in such a manner as to lean his right wing upon the Austrian frontier. The Russians, not regarding this, passed that frontier, and proceeded to push their attack upon his flank. This obliged General Dwernicki to withdraw his left wing, and indeed his whole front, upon the Austrian territory, where, in fact, the line was not distinctly marked, all the while being engaged with the enemy. The action having continued thus for some hours, a detachment of Austrian cavalry, under Colonel Fac, approached and threw themselves between the combatants, calling upon them to respect the neutrality of the territory. In this manner, the combat ceased. General Dwernicki gave his parole to discontinue hostilities, and consented to advance farther into the interior, and, placing himself in camp, waited the result of the Austrian Government upon what had occurred. The Russian corps, which had just passed the frontier, and which had, in fact, entered it with its whole force, was permitted to leave freely. The first duty which General Dwernicki thought imposed upon him in his present situation was to make a full and true report of what had occurred to the National Government and the Commander-in-Chief, which he was permitted to do. He also sent a letter to the Commander-in-Chief of the Austrian forces in Galicia, explaining how it was that, in the necessary maneuver, he had passed over a point of land on the Austrian territory without the intention of occupying it. Having done this, he supposed that he would be permitted to remain in camp, retaining his own arms, those taken from the enemy, and his prisoners, until conferences between the governments should decide in respect to the course to be taken. But the Austrian Government, far from giving such a reasonable permission, collected a strong corps in the environs of Tarnopol, and the Austrian Commander-in-Chief demanded of General Dwernicki to surrender both his own arms and those taken from the enemy. General Dwernicki, not wishing to make a resistance, although the Austrian corps was not formidable to him, being anxious to avoid the serious political consequences which might possibly follow such resistance, submitted to this unjust demand, which will be an eternal reproach to the Austrian Government. The Austrians returned their arms to the Russian prisoners, whom they liberated, and retained the arms of the Polish troops. The whole corps was transported to the interior, and thus ended the important body of our forces.[57]

The conduct of Austria, in regard to the corps of Dwernicki, I am sure will excite the indignation of the reader. If General Dwernicki had entered on the Austrian territory, he was forced to do it by the Russian corps, which had already passed the frontier; and that cannot be regarded as an intentional invasion of the frontiers which was done without design, and was a mere transition over an indistinct line, made necessary by the position which the enemy had taken: such a case certainly should have formed an exception to a general rule. To the Russian corps all the prisoners were returned, without any consent obtained from our government, to whom they, in fact, belonged and should have been considered as belonging, until the end of the war.

It was in this manner that those intriguing cabinets repaid the debt of gratitude which they owed to Poland. They had forgotten the times of John Sobieski, who, in 1683, delivered their capital, and their whole territory, from destruction at the hands of the Turks. They had forgotten that they thus owed their very existence to Poland.

At present, putting aside all obligations of justice, they concert with our enemy for our ruin. But if by this unjust treatment of their benefactors, they have gained some temporary advantages, the reader will acknowledge that in reference to their ultimate good, the Austrians have acted with a most short-sighted and mistaken policy. The aggrandizement of Russia can never be an advantage to Austria.

There were few more melancholy events in our war than this. The disaster of this corps grievously paralyzed all the fine plans of the Commander-in-Chief. It reinforced the Russian superior force by 40,000 men; for the different corps of Kreutz, Witt, Rudiger and Rott would now rejoin their main army without obstruction.

To these disasters of the two corps of Dwernicki and Sierwski, which were deeply felt by the nation, was now to be added the appearance of that horrible malady, the cholera, which after the battle of Igani commenced its devastations in our ranks. On the night of that battle several hundreds of our troops fell sick. This terrible disease caused us, on the first few days, the loss of nearly 1,000 men; but if it was terrible for us, nothing can express the suffering it produced in the Russian camp, aided by the want of comfort in the arrangements of that camp, and the acid food upon which the Russian soldiers were habitually fed. Thousands of those wretched sufferers were exposed to the open air, and died upon the field. The Poles took more care of them than of themselves. They were brought together, and transported to Menie, where was a large convent, which was turned into a hospital for their use. The number of those sufferers may be imagined, when it was stated, that, in that hospital and village, 2,000 Russian sick were reported.

NOTES

57. This unfortunate and painful event should serve as an impressive example, which cannot be too often brought to mind, of what disastrous consequences may follow from the neglect of observing a constant communication between corps acting together, and above all, of the consequences of departing from orders which are given upon a general plan, the absolute control of which should belong to the General-in-Chief. If General Dwernicki, conforming to his instructions, had acted only against the corps of Kreutz and Witt, and in concert with the corps of Sierawski, he would have been apprised of that general's quitting Kaziemiers, and both of those two corps could have joined in the attack, in which they would have been aided by another corps which was to be sent, as the reader is aware, to act against the enemy's rear. If those corps of Kreutz and Witt had been defeated, immense advantages would have followed; indeed the war would have been over for the Russian main army would have been taken in the flank and rear, and, in fact, completely cut off.

[Editor: In fact, the Austrian action is not surprising and most logical. The Kingdom of Poland had been divided by the Russians, Prussians and Austrians in 1794. The Grand Duchy of Warsaw had been restored in 1808 by Napoleon from territory taken by the Prussians in 1794, but it was erased from the map in 1813. If the Poles had succeeded in restoring a Polish state in Russian territory, the Poles in Austrian territory (taken in 1794) might have been provoked to rise and break away from Austria. So, Austria sought to maintain its conquered territories by quietly aiding the Russians suppress this rebellion.]

CHAPTER XVII.

The Russian commander resumes offensive operations. - Object of the attack of the 25th of April. - Combat of Kuflew. - General Dembinski evacuates the position of Kuflew and awaits the enemy at Bady. - Battle of Minsk. - The enemy suddenly evacuates his position. - Reflections on this stage of the conflict - Positions of the two armies.

THE Russian main army, which, since the last of March had been on the defensive, from weakness or from indecision, on the 23rd of April began to change its position, and to take the offensive. Having received intelligence, as we may suppose, of the disasters of Sierawski, and also of the passage of General Dwernicki into Volhynia, General Diebitsch gave orders to the corps of Witt and Kreutz to pass the Wieprz at Kock, and to attack our detachment at Zelechow, which was forced to retire. On the same day (23rd) the brigade of Colonel Dembinski was attacked at Jeruzalem, without any decisive result. Those small attacks by the enemy served, however, as an indication of the intention of General Diebitsch to take the offensive on a larger scale. To meet this intention, all our detachments received orders to hold themselves in readiness. Firstly, these detachments were to concentrate themselves upon a line of operations between Kaluszyn, Siennica, and Zelechow. [The reader can refer to Plan VI.] The whole line, in case of attack, on whatever quarter it might be, was to make a retrograde movement, upon the same plan as heretofore, as far as the field of Wawr. General Pac, in particular, who was the farthest removed from Zelechow, was to use the utmost vigilance, and to make this retrograde movement in the promptest manner, when occasion required.

On the 25th of April, in fact, Marshal Diebitsch commenced his attack at two principal points, Boimie and Kuflew. Upon the last of these two points, he threw his greatest force, intending to pierce our line there, and by a diversion at Minsk to divide our forces. Besides the prevention of this design, the defense of Kuflew was of the greatest importance to us from the circumstance that along the whole course of the Swider River, at Latowicz, Starygrod, &c. were posted various small detachments, which would have been cut off, if we should be forced to make a sudden evacuation of that point.

COMBAT OF KUFLEW. [See Plan XXIV.]

This combat deserved to be forever held up as an example in tactics, to show how much can be done with a small force, managed with prudence and skill. Colonel Dembinski, who, in this battle, commanded the inconsiderable forces that met the attack of the masses of Diebitsch, well merited the rank of general, to which he was then advanced. Our position was covered by the Swider River (S) and its marshes, which secured it from in flank. The enemy had one debouchment (a), consisting of a kind of dyke, which led from Kolacze (1). He could pass this dyke easily, for the bridge was entire. On our side, not far from this dyke, were small forests, or rather brush-wood, occupied by two battalions (6) of our infantry. Upon the plain between Kuflew and the Swider River, ten squadrons of our cavalry (c) maneuvered. Near the village (II) upon a little hill, on which was a windmill, our artillery (d), consisting of only four pieces, were posted, and directed their fire upon the passage over which the enemy were to debouch. The position of the enemy was commanding, for his artillery could sweep the whole plain on each side of the Swider. The details of this battle were as follow: At sunrise, on the 25th, several Cossack regiments (e) appeared upon the heights of Jeruzalem. They even several times attempted to pass the dyke, but were repulsed by the fire of our tirailleurs from the brushwood. It was mid-day when strong columns of infantry (f) began to show themselves in the direction of Lukowiec and Plomieniec. In a short time, all the heights of Jeruzalem were covered with columns of infantry, and they began their descent to Kolacze. The Russian light troops (g) began their debouchment, and a warm fire commenced between the Russian infantry upon the dyke, and our own tirailleurs in the brush-wood. The Russian artillery (A) which remained upon the heights on the other side, consisting of twenty and more pieces of large caliber, poured for several hours a heavy fire upon Kuflew, where they supposed a large force to be placed, but where, in fact, besides the four pieces of artillery, we had but one company of infantry. Under this terrible fire, that village was burnt to the ground. Those attacks of the Russian artillery and infantry continued for three successive hours, when Colonel Dembinski, being informed that the small detachments at Latowicz, &c. above referred to, had evacuated their position and were safe from being cut off, commenced his retreat, as his instructions directed. By accelerating his retreat he had another object in view, namely, to lead the enemy in the direction of the 2nd Division, which was posted at Ceglow, and was prepared to receive him. Our infantry and artillery had left their position and were on the road, when Colonel Dembinski, placing himself at the head of his cavalry, threw himself with great boldness upon the columns of the enemy which had debouched over the dyke, and by repeated attacks kept them off from our rear. After having passed the first forest without molestation, between Ceglow and Kuflew, Colonel Dembinski took a position, between forests, in the environs of Bady, where a part of the 2nd Division was placed in expectation of the enemy, in a kind of ambuscade. Here our forces waited in vain until night for the enemy, who had contented himself with having taken Kuflew. Two squadrons of Cossacks, whom he ventured to send towards our position, to reconnoiter, were, as soon as they were seen, fallen upon by our cavalry, and either cut down or made prisoners, to the amount of more than a hundred men and horses, with two officers. As the enemy attempted nothing more, our forces, during the night, evacuated their position, agreeably to instructions, and reached Minsk at 3, A. M. of the next day. At Kuflew, full 40,000 men, with some twenty pieces of artillery, and commanded by Diebitsch in person, were opposed to General Dembinski, who had not quite 4,000 men and four pieces of artillery, with which force he stood against the enemy for that whole day. The loss of the Russians was about a thousand men, and on our own side it was not fifty.

The actions which took place on the same day at Boimie were without any decisive result, consisting only of a continued fire of artillery. During the night of that day, our forces at every point made a retrograde movement. The Commander-in-Chief arranged his preparations to receive the enemy on the 26th, dividing his forces into two parts. The 2nd Division, under Gielgud, and the Cavalry Division, under Skarzynski, was to await the enemy at Minsk; while the Commander-in-Chief, with the main body, awaited him in person at Dembe-Wielke.

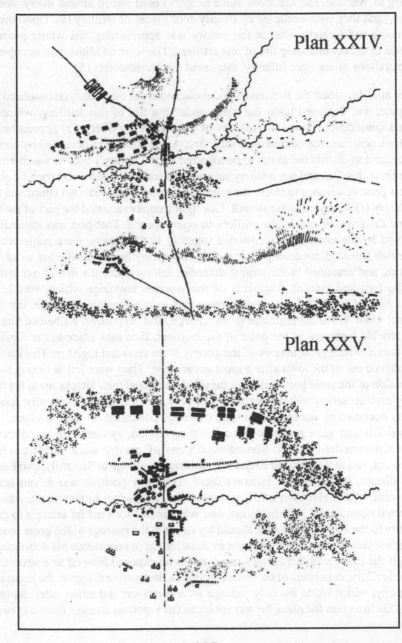

Plan XXIV.

Plan XXV.

BATTLE OF MINSK. [See Plan XXV.]

The position of Minsk may be considered as one of the strongest upon the great road from Siedlce to Warsaw. That town is situated in a plain, surrounded by an impenetrable forest, and traversed by a small river, which falls into the Swider. Upon the side of Warsaw, where our forces were placed, are heights which overlook the whole town, and they were particularly commanding upon the right of the roads leading to Warsaw. The fire from those heights could sweep almost every street of the city, and they were occupied by twenty-four pieces of artillery (a). Upon the side of Siedlce and Ceglaw, whence the enemy was approaching, the whole plain was exposed to the commanding fire of this artillery. The town of Minsk was occupied by two battalions of our light-infantry, dispersed as sharpshooters (6).

It was mid-day when the Russians (c) debouched from the forest, commenced their ad-vance, and deployed upon the plain under the fire of our artillery, which was opened immediately. Some fifty pieces of the enemy's artillery, (c) approached the city, took position, and commenced their fire. As the town was occupied by so small a force, and so distributed as not to be affected by the enemy's fire, he was permitted to continue this fire, and our artillery reserved theirs for the moment when he should make a general advance to storm the town. This soon took place. An enormous mass of infantry (f) advanced to the assault. Our light troops evacuated the part of the town beyond the river, to enable our artillery to open upon it. That part was immediately occupied by the enemy, who, crowded together in the streets, were subjected to a fire which spread death among their ranks. The enemy hesitated whether to advance or retire, and remained in the utmost disorder, falling under the fire of our artillery and the torn and burning fragments of the wooden buildings which were rent in pieces by that fire. While the enemy remained in this horrible suspense, the brave Colonel Oborski led his regiment to the charge, and bore down all before him. 'A, most terrible massacre, at the point of the bayonet, then took place in the Square of the Church, where great masses of the enemy were crowded together. The Russians were driven out of the town after a most severe loss. They were left at liberty to take possession of the same part again, but they did not repeat their attacks upon the town, satisfying themselves with concentrating a heavy fire of artillery principally upon the heights occupied by our own. This state of things continued till three o'clock, when General Gielgud gave orders to evacuate the position, agreeably to the directions of the Commander-in-Chief. Sixteen squadrons of cavalry were left to cover the movement, and in this way our division, reaching the village of Stoiardly, two English miles distant, took a second position there. This new position was advantageous, on account of the elevation of the ground. Our right wing, in particular, was well supported upon a thick marshy forest, and was pushed forward far enough to give a crossfire to the enemy, in case he should try to force the passage of the great road. As the enemy was so imprudent, after our evacuation, as to commence his debouchment through the town, with his cavalry in advance, he exposed himself to a severe loss; for our artillery, consisting of six pieces, poured a destructive fire upon the main street of the city, which led to the only passage over the river; and again, after deploying under this fire upon the plain, he was subjected to vigorous charges from our cavalry under Skarzynski, which cost him a severe loss, and delayed his advance for more than half an hour. As the space between Stoiardly and Minsk was a plain gently descending from our side, moist in the lower parts, and in every way favorable for attacks by our cavalry, their charges were continually repeated, and the combat on this plain deserved the name of the combat of cavalry. To give the reader an idea of these effective charges against a cavalry of much superior force, I will merely state that each squadron of the sixteen was engaged some three or four successive times with the enemy. Their horses were continually in foam. The Zamoyski Regiment, the Krakus, and the 5th Uhlans greatly distinguished themselves. The loss of the enemy's cavalry, of which the greater part consisted of regiments of heavy dragoons, was very great. Their horses' hoofs sunk into the humid ground, and our Krakus, on their light animals, assaulted them in the very midst of their ranks. Many staff and other officers of the enemy were left dead upon the field. Our advanced guard having, in this way, fought with such advantages, against the whole Russian army, at Minsk and Stoiardly, from mid-day until 5 P. M.; the Commander-in-Chief ordered them to evacuate their position as promptly as possible, and retire to Dembie-Wielke, where he awaited the enemy in order of battle, and where he was desirous of meeting his attack before night. This movement was executed without molestation from the Russians. Our advanced guard passed the forests between Dembe-Wielke and Stoiardly, and arrived at the position of Dembe-Wielke, where fifty pieces of our artillery were posted to receive the enemy, and our whole force took the order of battle. The enemy, however, did not debouch from the forests, but remained on the other side. This finishes the details of that day and of the battle of Minsk, in which the early cessation of the attacks of the enemy proved how much he had suffered. He had two generals mortally wounded, General Pahlen and the Prince Galiszyn, and lost nearly 4,000 men. On our side the loss was four or five hundred only.

For their conduct in this battle, the National Government and the Commander-in-Chief presented their thanks to the 2nd Division under Gielgud and the division of cavalry under Skarzynski. General Gielgud was advanced to the rank of general of division, and it was perhaps owing to his skilful dispositions and brave conduct on that day, that it was not feared to entrust him with the command of the all important expedition to Lithuania.

On the 27th and 28th, no events took place. During the night of the 28th, the enemy, to our astonishment, evacuated his position and retired as far as Kaluszyn, twenty-four English miles distant. We cannot give the true cause of this sudden and unexpected retreat. Perhaps it was on account of a failure of provisions. Another cause might have been the rumors, which had begun to take an aspect of importance, of the revolutions in Lithuania and Samogitia.

The reader will allow me to dwell for a moment upon this extraordinary movement of the enemy, which must be considered an indication, either of the extreme physical and moral weakness to which the Russian army was reduced, or of a great want of generalship on the part of Marshal Diebitsch. Such a course, voluntarily taken, in the eyes of the military critic, is enough to destroy all claims to military talent on the part of that com-mander. Such great objects attempted, followed up with so little perseverance, and abandoned without an adequate cause, would seem to indicate either the absence of any fixed plan, or a degree of indecision inconsistent with any sound military pretensions.

Our Commander-in-Chief felt sure that when. General Diebitsch attacked, on the 25th and 26th, it was with the view, having no longer any fear of the corps of generals Dwernicki and Sierawski, and being reinforced by the corps which had been opposed to the former, to follow up his attack and compel us to a general battle. Whatever might have been the result of that battle, it was the only course which a true general could have followed, especially when his army was in such superiority of strength. To one who considers these circumstances, two questions will arise: First, what was the object of commencing the attack? Secondly, what was, in regard to tactics, the cause of its cessation, and of that sudden retreat? It will be very difficult to find a satisfactory answer to either of those questions.[58]

Our army, after this retreat of the enemy, commenced anew its advance, and, on the 30th, it occupied again its former position at Boimie, on the River Kostzyn. At this time, our left wing under Uminski, which, as the reader is aware, was on the right bank of the Narew, at the environs of Pultusk, received orders to join the main army, leaving a detachment at Zagroby, where the Generalissimo ordered a strong bridgehead to be erected.

The position of the two armies on the 30th was as follows: [Plans VI. and XXIX.] Our army was again concentrated between Wengrow and Ceglow, and indeed Wengrow was occupied by a small detachment. The centre or the greater force was on the main road at Kaluszyn. Its advanced posts were along the banks of the Kostrzyn River at Grombkowo, Strzebucza, and Boimie. Our right wing was again posted upon the Swider River, between Karczewo and Ceglow. The Russian army was concentrated in the environs of Mordy and Sucha, where Marshal Diebitsch entrenched himself in a fortified camp, and took again a defensive attitude. The corps of Kreutz and Witt were in the environs of Pulawa, and the Russian Imperial Guard advanced to the environs of Pultusk.

NOTES

58. In the whole of this war, the vedettes of the two armies were at no time so near as they were after this last battle. On the 97th and 28th, those of the Russian cavalry, Cossacks and hussars, occupying the main road, were within fifty paces of the vedettes of our lancers, so near in fact that they could have conversed together. On having this circumstance reported to him, the General-in-Chief did not take advantage of any attack, but ordered the utmost forbearance to be observed, and the friendliest demonstrations to be made by our outposts. On changing of the guard, our sentinels, as they quitted their post, bade a friendly adieu to the opposite sentinel of the enemy; and under the cover of night, the enemy's sentinels, and even some of their officers, approached our vedettes, gave their hands, and entered into friendly conversation. It was touching to see those brave soldiers deeply affected at such meetings. With tears in their eyes, the Russians could only repeat that they had been forced to this contest, and confessed that, even if we should be conquerors, they would be the gainers in other respects. They also uttered their complaints of the tyranny and the privations to which they were subjected, and our lancers gave them all the relief which their own means could furnish.

CHAPTER XVIII.

**General Skrzynecki resumes the offensive. - He decides to adopt an enlarged plan
of operations, and to make the revolutionised provinces supply the place of a corps
d'armée. - The corps of Chrzsnowski is sent to occupy the Russian corps of Witt
and Kreuta. - Admirable execution of this enterprise. - Attack on Kock. - Attack of
Rudiger's camp. - Plan of operations by the main army against the Russian Guards
- Forced march from Kaluszyn by Praga to Serock. - Advanced post of the guard
attacked and defeated. - The corps of Sacken is cutoff. - The 2nd Division under
Gielgud sent into Lithuania. - The Imperial Guard are driven with great loss beyond
the frontier. - Retrograde movement.**

As several days passed away, without anything having been attempted on the part
of the enemy, our Commander-in-Chief decided to recommence hostilities by small
attacks, which were designed to mask the great plan he intended to put into execution.
The general view which occupied our commander was to continue the offensive, to
follow-up the enemy constantly, and not to leave him unless some very important
occasion should call for a different course. Let us reflect upon the difficulties of
such a plan, and let us then examine how it was in fact executed by the Commander-
in-Chief.

General Skrzynecki, regarding all the existing circumstances, the actual position of
the enemy, and his strength, found a great difference between the present state of
things and that which existed after the battle of Igani. The misfortunes of the corps
of Dwernicki and Sierawski had made a vast change in the relative strength of the
two parties. The fate of those two corps gave a great advantage to the enemy, leaving
him free to concentrate all his forces and to act in one mass. This advantage of the
enemy was to be met, and means were to be taken to keep his forces in detached
bodies, by giving occupation to each. To provide such means, it was next an object
to give an important character to the revolution in Lithuania, and in fact to make
that revolution supply the place of a corps dame, to send a body of troops to aid it,
and to direct and lead the partisan forces which might be there enrolled. If then by
such operation, Lithuania and Samogitia could be kept in constant communication
with the main army; the line of operations would be enlarged, and would be based
upon Wilna and Warsaw. This line of operations would embrace also the towns of
Grodnow and Lomza. To occupy the corps of Witt and Kreutz, which were still in
the Lublin Palatinate, the Commander-in-Chief detached a small corps under the
command of General Chrzanowski, which were furnished with the same instructions
as its predecessor, that of General Dwernicki, which were, in general, to act in the
environs of Zamosc.

191

To facilitate the execution of these plans, the Commander-in-Chief determined to give daily occupation to the enemy. On the 2nd of May, the fire was renewed along our whole line. Each following day presented sanguinary scenes at different points. In the midst of one of these actions, on the 7th, the small corps above mentioned, consisting of 4,000 men and eight pieces of cannon, under General Chrzanowski, left the main body [See Plan XXVI.], took the direction of Stoczek (1), Zelechow (2), and Kock (3), to reach the environs of Zamosc (4. The reader, on examining the plan, and looking at the space which this corps (a) was to pass over, in the midst of the enemy's detached corps (4), and in which it was exposed every moment to be surrounded and cut off, will acknowledge that this expedition, which was most successfully executed, is to be ranked among the finest operations in the campaign. It demanded a general of talent, and a soldier of determination.

When I allow myself thus to detain the attention of the reader upon the extraordinary efforts of this war, it is only with the view to convince him that nothing is difficult of execution which is prompted by a resolute determination based upon high principles, and that what would be deemed almost impossible in an ordinary war, in which despots, to gratify their ambition or their caprices, force their subjects to battle—an involuntary sacrifice, is far from being so, in a war like ours. In such a war, moral impulse becomes an element, the importance of which cannot be over-estimated.

General Chrzanowski, quitting, as we have mentioned, the main body, took the direction of Ceglow, and threw himself into the great forest of Plomieniec. Leaving that forest, he met, near Wodynia, a strong detachment of the enemy, composed of infantry, cavalry, and several pieces of artillery, belonging to their main body, and probably detached to make a reconnaissance. By a sudden attack that detachment was at once overthrown. The cavalry ordered for their pursuit were instructed to return in another direction, in order to deceive the enemy. In this manner General Chrzanowski, frequently meeting with small detachments of the enemy and deceiving them continually, traversed the woody plain between Stoczek and Zelechow, and arrived, on the night of the 9th, at the environs of Kock, where he had to pass the Wieprz River.

ATTACK OF KOCK. [See Plan XXVII.]

At the moment of the arrival of the corps of General Chrzanowski, this town was occupied by a part of the corps of General Witt, composed of 6,000 men and 20 pieces of artillery. Besides this considerable garrison, the place had been strengthened by several fortifications (1) on each side of the river, to defend the passage of the bridge (2), and without taking those fortifications it would be impossible for us to pass the bridge. In such circumstances there was no alternative, and it was necessary to attempt to take the town by storm. General Chrzanowski announced his intention to the corps, and addressed a few animating words to them. Having divided his corps into small parties (a, a), he surrounded the town. He placed especial importance upon the forcing of the avenue (3) leading to the palace, and getting possession of the garden (4) which surrounded the palace, and bordered on the river. If all this could be rapidly executed, the enemy would be taken in the rear.

The signal for the attack being given, a warm fire from our skirmishers was commenced at all points round the city, and, while the cavalry (b), divided into detachments, threw themselves continually upon the Russian infantry (c), our infantry, at the charge, forced the entrance to the palace and garden, which was immediately occupied by our tirailleurs, who opened their fire upon the fortifications (1) and on the Russian columns in the square (d). In this manner the enemy was surrounded, and forced to evacuate the city with great loss, and to take the direction of Radzyn. General Chrzanowski passed the river and took the direction of Lubartov. Leaving the town of Lublin on the right, and following the banks of the Wieprz River, he reached on the 11th the envi-rons of Piaski. In the latter place he was apprized that a Russian corps under Rudiger was at Krasnystaw. Chrzanowski decided to attack them.

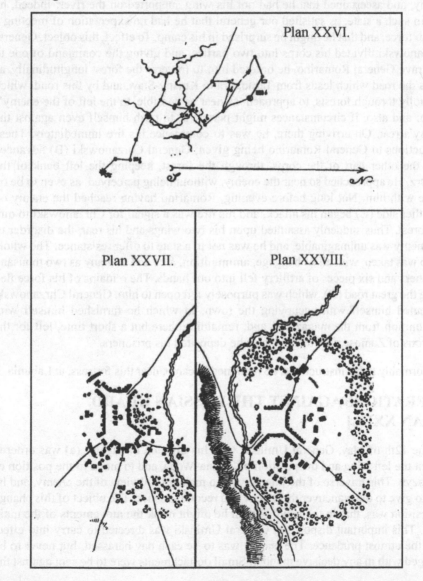

Plan XXVI.

Plan XXVII.

Plan XXVIII.

ATTACK OF RUDIGER'S CAMP. [See Plan XXVIII.]

The corps of General Rudiger, after the unfortunate disaster of General Dwernicki, having traversed Volhynia, entered the frontiers of the kingdom, and took the direction of Lublin, being destined probably to reinforce the main army under Diebitsch. This corps, which was composed of about 12,000 men, and some twenty pieces of cannon, was in camp (A) near the town of Krasnystaw, having that town and the Wieprz River in its rear.

General Chrzanowski, who halted with his corps in the forest between Piaski and Krasnystaw, having sent out patrols, was perfectly informed of the position of the enemy, and ascertained that he had not his wing supported on the river; indeed, he was in such a state, as satisfied our general that he had no expectation of meeting a Polish force, and that he might be surprised in his camp. To effect, this object, General Chrzanowski divided his corps into two parties, and giving the command of one to the brave General Romarino, he ordered him to traverse the forest longitudinally, as far as the road which leads from Tarnogora to Krasny-Staw, and by this road, which is wholly through forests, to approach, as near as possible, to the left of the enemy's camp; and also, if circumstances might permit it, to push himself even against the enemy's rear. On arriving there, he was to commence his fire immediately. These instructions to General Romarino being given, General Chrzanowski (B) advanced with the other part of the corps, through the forest, keeping the left bank of the Wieprz. He approached so near the enemy, without being perceived, as even to be on a line with him. Not long before evening, Romarino having reached the enemy on the other side (C) began his attack, and his fire was a signal for Chrzanowski to quit the forest. Thus suddenly assaulted upon his two wings and his rear, the disorder of the enemy was unimaginable, and he was not in a state to offer resistance. The whole camp was taken, with all its baggage, ammunition, &c., and as many as two thousand prisoners and six pieces of artillery fell into our hands. The remains of his force fled along the great road (D), which was purposely left open to him. General Chrzanowski contented himself with occupying the town, in which he furnished himself with ammunition from the magazines, and, remaining there but a short time, left for the environs of Zamosc, in which fortress he deposited his prisoners.

Conformably to his instructions, he remained in camp, near this fortress, at Labunia. [59]

OPERATIONS AGAINST THE RUSSIAN GUARD. [PLAN XXIX.]

On the 12th of May, General Uminski with his division of cavalry (a) was ordered to quit the left wing and the position of Zimna-Woda, and to move to the position of Kaluszyn. This traverse of the line he was to make in full view of the enemy, and he was to give to the maneuver the aspect of a reconnaissance. The object of this change of position was, that in the new position he might mask the movements of the main body. This important disposition General Uminski was directed to carry into effect with the utmost prudence. The enemy was to be each day harassed, but never to be engaged with in any decisive manner. Small de-tachments were to be sent against the enemy, along his whole line, and especially on the first days of the movement. The Commander-in-Chief instructed General Uminski to watch every movement of the enemy, and give information of such at headquarters. If the main body of the Russian force should make an attack, he was to execute his retreat upon the main road, as far as the fortifications of Praga, and there he was to act in junction with the other detachments left there for the defense of those fortifications. If, on the contrary, the Russian army should make a retrograde movement, General Uipinski was to endeavor, by following them, to keep them constantly in view. If circumstances permitted, the rearguard of the Russians might be harassed during the night. Above all, General Uminski was to endeavor to keep up his communications with the neighboring corps of General Lubinski, and the detachments left at Siennica and Karczewo. In this moderate pursuit of the enemy, the general was to ascertain whether their retrograde movement was a retreat or a maneuver, in order to avoid every-hazard.

General Lubinski (6), with his division of cavalry, was to pass the right bank of the Bug (B), and leaving small detachments at Wyszkow (1) and Brook (2), he was to advance as far as the environs of Nar (3), not quitting the right bank of the river. All his care was to be devoted to the observing of the enemy, and to the preventing of any sudden passage of the river by him. In regard to his communications, the same instructions were given to him as to General Uminski.

Having given these orders to the above mentioned corps, General Skrzynecki, with the main force (d), left suddenly the position at Kaluszyn (4), making a retrograde movement upon the great road by Minsk (5), traversed Praga (6), and through Jablonna (7), and Zegrz (8), arrived on the 15th, at Serock (9). On the 16th, he passed the Narew (N), at this place, leaving a brigade of infantry and cavalry (i), under General Dembinski, upon the right bank, with orders to advance to Ostrolenka (10), through the towns of Pultusk, Magnies-Zewo and Rozany (11).   This detachment was not to commence the attack on meeting the enemy, but was only to harass him and keep him in check, and detain him as near as possible to Serock. If the enemy should commence the retreat, this corps was to pursue him with the greatest activity, in order that at Ostrolenka, where the Commander-in-Chief had determined to attack him, he might be exposed between two fires.

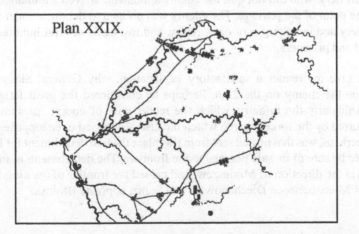

Plan XXIX.

195

On the 17th, this corps met the first advanced post (f) of the Russian Imperial Guard at Modzele, which, after a slight engagement, evacuated its position, and retired. Being pursued by the brigade of cavalry under General Dembinski, they, on the 18th, commenced the passage of the Narew, at Ostrolenka. In attempting this passage, the rearguard of the enemy was overthrown, and four regiments of the light infantry of Finland were taken prisoners. This pursuit by the brave Dembinski was executed with such rapidity, that the corps of General Sacken, which made a part of the grand corps of the guard, but was a little detached, was completely cut off from the main body and forced to take refuge in the palatinate of Augustov. It is much to be regretted that our main force (d) could not reach Ostrolenka; having to pass narrow roads, through forests, in which the artillery met with much obstruction. Otherwise, the whole of that Imperial Guard would have been surrounded.

With the arrival of our main body, on the night of the 18th, the Russians passed the Narew, but many wagons and stragglers fell into the hands of our cavalry in the Troszyn Forest (12). The Commander-in-Chief, having given the corps a short rest, and having dispatched a detachment, under the command of Colonel Sierawski, for the pursuit of the corps of Sacken, on the same night continued his march in pursuit of the Guard, in the direction of Troszyn (12). On the morning of the next day, arriving at Dluge-Siodlo (13), this village was found occupied by two regiments of infantry and two of cavalry, the latter covering the village. Our 1st Lancer Regiment, which were the leading force, leaving the forest and finding the Russian cavalry in line before that village, threw themselves upon them with the rapidity of lightning. The enemy's cavalry was borne down before them, and pursued by our lancers into the village; but his infantry, under cover of the village, opened a terrible fire upon our cavalry, which compelled them to retire and await the arrival of the artillery. At length, eight pieces of light artillery, commanded by Colonel Boehm, arrived, and commenced a vigorous fire of grape upon the village, which compelled the enemy's infantry to evacuate it, and they were pursued with such spirit, that one battalion was taken, and the rest were dispersed in the forest. On the same day, the enemy was again pressed upon in his retreat, in the environs of Zienzopol (14), especially on the passage of the river and marshes of Kamionka. The 1st Lancers, and the battery of light artillery, who did not quit the enemy a moment, arrived simultaneously with him at the point of the passage. The enemy was obliged to debouch under the fire of our artillery and the charges of our cavalry, and lost again several hundred in dead, wounded and prisoners.

I cannot give the reader a satisfactory explanation, why General Skrzynecki did not pursue the enemy on the 20th. Perhaps he considered the great fatigue of the army, particularly the infantry, which the reader will, of course, presume to have been incurred by the forced march which the distance passed over supposes. Another reason, perhaps, was that he had sent from this place the first detachment for Lithuania, wishing to be sure of its safe passage to the frontiers. The detachment, in fact, left on that day, in the direction of Minieszew, and passed the frontier of the kingdom at the village of Mien, between Diechanowiec and Suraz, opposite Brainsk.

Our army, having halted one day at Zienzopol, on the evening of the 20th, quitted this position to continue the pursuit of the guard, and overtook them in the Menzynin Forest (15). This forest, occupied by the Russian rearguard, was near the heights of the village, which command the whole vicinity, that it was exposed to a fire of artillery from these heights. Our Generalissimo placed his artillery on the heights, and directed a fire upon the forest; the infantry was ordered to take the enemy in front, in case he should quit the forest, and the cavalry was to advance in strong columns along the road, to cut off his escape from the forest into the road. In this, they were successful, and took many prisoners. Thus continually pursued, and subject to severe losses along the whole route, the guard (f) was again pressed at the passage of the Narew at Tykocin (16). The consternation and disorder of the enemy was such, that he did not take time to destroy the bridge. Our lancers, commanded by the brave Colonel Langerman, commenced an attack upon the Russian cuirassiers, on the bridge itself. The cuirassier regiment was almost annihilated, many being thrown from the bridge, and a great number taken prisoners.

Having thus driven the Russian Guard from the kingdom, (of which the Narew was the boundary), General Skrzynecki commenced a retrograde movement, to meet the demonstration which General Diebitsch might make upon his rear. On the night of the 22d, our army (m) began this movement, having destroyed the several bridges of the Narew.

These then are the details of the operations upon the Russian Guard, which will be admitted bring among the finest in the history of modern warfare. The operations of Napoleon, in the campaign of Italy—the brilliant commencement of his career, in 1796, - will be always cited as the highest examples of stratago-tactics, but I do not think that a finer and bolder plan of operations can be found even there. In both cases, success was owing, not more to the great military genius of the leaders, than to those high moral impulses which must animate armies in every contest for national existence.

Our army, evacuating on the 12th, the position at Kaluszyn, from that date to the 26th, when the battle of Ostrolenka took place, had passed over a distance of from 200 to 250 miles, which, deducting the six days occupied in action, was executed in eight days, making an average of twenty-eight English miles per day, an extraordinary and perhaps unexampled effort. The rapidity, in fact, with which this movement was performed, was such that our forces were on their return before Marshal Diebitsch commenced his march to intercept them. This object the Marshal thought himself in season to effect, but the reader will see in the sequel how completely he failed in it.

NOTES

59. The reader may be pleased with a short biographical sketch of General Chrzanowski, who distinguished himself here so much. This skilful officer commenced his military career in 1815, on leaving the military school at Warsaw, as officer of the Corps of Engineers, in which department he was distinguished for his skill and industry. In the year 1828, during the war of Turkey, the Emperor Nicholas was desirous of obtaining the aid of Polish officers of engineers, and Chrzanowski was among the number chosen. In this campaign, his talents made themselves remarked, and Marshal Diebitsch gave him great marks of confidence, and placed him near his person. He returned from the campaign as captain, and received several Russian decorations. In the revolution, like a worthy son of Poland, he offered his services to the common cause; but the Dictator Chlopicki, who, among his other faults, had that of either being unable to appreciate, or willing to overlook the merits of the officers from whom he was to make his appointments, did not give any important trust to General Chrzanowski; perhaps it was because Chrzanowski was among the number of those who were desirous of taking the field without delay. With the glorious commencement of the era of the command of our estimable Skrzynecki, this brave officer was advanced to the rank of Lieutenant Colonel, was placed in the post of the Chief of Staff. While in this post he was advanced to the rank of general. The Generalissimo, who in all his plans observed the greatest secrecy, and his example ought to be followed by every good general, initiated, however, Chrzanowski, and Prodzyneki, who succeeded the former as Chief of Staff, into all his plans: and indeed those two brave generals were valuable counselors to Skrzynecki. Among the other qualities necessary to a great general, Chrzanowsi was endowed with great coolness and presence of mind, and with a spirit of system, which he carried into everything which he undertook. He was seen in the midst of the hottest fire, with his plan of battle before him, referring the movements to the plan, and giving his orders with the most perfect sangfroid imaginable. The Generalissimo could not enough regret that he had not given him the command of the expedition to Lithuania, in place of Gielgud. If the skill and coolness of Chrzanowski, could have been united, in that expedition, with the bold and adventurous enterprise of Dwernicki, everything would have been affected there in a few weeks.

198

CHAPTER XIX.

The Lithuanians compel two Russian corps to evacuate Saroogitia. - Operations of General Chlapowaki in the department of Bialostok. - Capture of Bielsk. - Defeat of a Russian force at Narewka and expulsion of the enemy from the department. - Recapitulation of the forces which had been sent into Lithuania. - Operations of the main army. - Attempt of Marshal Diebitsch to intercept Skrzynecki on his retrograde march, by a diversion to Ostrolenka - General Lubinski surprises the Russian advanced guard at Czyzew. - Marshal Diebitsch attacks the Polish rearguard at Kleczkowo. - The rearguard quits its position at night, and joins the main army at Ostroienluu -Battle of Ostrolenka.

QUITTING the main army, which had thus successfully executed the important operation of driving the Russian Imperial Guard from the kingdom, and sending a corps into Lithuania, we will now turn to take a view of the state of affairs in that province.

The brave Lithuanians in a series of bloody encounters had made themselves severely felt by the enemy. In the departments of Roszyienie and Szawla, at about the middle of the month of May, a short time before the battle of Ostrolenka, the two Russian corps, under Malinowski and Szyrman, were almost annihilated by the Lithuanian insurgents, who, night and day, falling upon them from forest ambuscades, subjected them to immense losses. Those corps literally wandered about, for some time, and being unable to hold themselves in any position, were forced at last to evacuate Samogitia.

In the department of Bialostok, the little corps recently sent under the command of General Chlapowski began its operations with great success. In the environs of Bielsk, that small detachment, composed of four squadrons of the 1st Lancer Regiment, consisting of four hundred and eighty horsemen, a hundred and ninety light infantry volunteers mounted,[60] and two pieces of cannon, routed two Cossack regiments and two battalions of infantry, the latter being taken in a body and the former dispersed; and, what was of much importance to us, in Bielsk, as well as in Brainsk, several magazines of powder were found. In the environs of Bielsk, Colonel Mikotin, aide-de-camp of the Grand Duke Michael, and on his way with dispatches from him to the Grand Duke Constantine, was taken prisoner.[61]

The corps of General Chlapowski left Bielsk in the direction of the town of Orla, and entered the forest of Bialowiek, where he received reinforcements of Lithuanian insurgents.

201

On the same day that our main army fought at Ostrolenka, the 26th of May, this little corps had an engagement with the enemy in the environs of Narewka. A considerable Russian detachment, under the command of General Rengardt, composed of 6,000 infantry, 3,000 cavalry, and five pieces of cannon, in all, nearly 9,000 men—was posted near Nasielsk. This considerable force was attacked by our small corps, to which were added some hundreds of insurgents, making in all, a force of not more than a thousand men. The Russians were completely beaten in this action. Full a thousand prisoners were taken, and all their artillery. An important advantage of this affair was the taking of a great transport of some hundred vehicles with provisions, destined for the Russian Grand Army. By the dispersion and ruin of this corps, the department of Bialostok was entirely cleared of the Russians, and nothing interrupted the formation and organization of the insurgent forces. The taking of Bielsk, and the affair of Narewka, will be admitted by the reader to have been above the rank of ordinary achievements, and should immortalize the handful of brave men which formed this detachment. They may be pointed at, as examples, with many others, in this war, of how much can be effected by that prompt and energetic action which no ordinary motives will sustain.

While the affairs of Lithuania and Samogitia, and those in the department of Bialostok, wore this favorable aspect, a new corps was approaching to aid this propitious state of things, to protect the insurrections, and, as might be confidently hoped, to bring them to a sure and happy result. The new force destined for this object consisted of the 2nd Division, reinforced by a squadron of cavalry, which force quitted Lomza on the 27th for Lithuania. Before returning to the operations of the Grand Army, we will give a short recapitulation of the forces which had been sent into Lithuania and Samogitia, at successive periods, to support the insurrections in those provinces.

The 1st Corps under General Chlapowski, left, on the 20th of May, the village of Zienzopol, with this destination: To enter the department of Bialostok, to occupy the forest of Bialowiez, in which were collected the forces of the revolted Lithuanians, with the view to organize these forces, from that position to act on the Russian communi-cations, and, if circumstances might allow it, to make an approach upon Wilna. This little corps, as we have seen, was composed of 190 infantry volunteers mounted, the 1st Lancer Regiment, consisting of 480 horsemen, and two pieces of light artillery.

The second corps, under the command of Colonel Sierakowski, left, a few days before that of General Chlapowski, with the view, as we have also seen, to follow and observe the division of General Sacken, who had been cut off by General Skrzynecki from the Russian Guard, and compelled to remain on the right bank of the Narew. This corps consisted of two battalions of infantry of the 18th Regiment, recently formed, amounting to 1,500 men, two squadrons of horse, of Flock, also recently formed, 250 in all, and two' pieces of cannon. This corps, in the execution of its instructions, obtained several advantages over General Sacken, near Stavisk. Colonel Sierakowski then advanced to the environs of the little town of Graievo, where he took a strong position, and awaited the arrival of the corps of General Gielgud.

The third corps, under the command of General Gielgud, being the 2nd Division, left the town of Lomza on the 27th of May. It was composed of 9 battalions of infantry, consisting of 4,500 men, 5 squadrons of cavalry of 600 men, 160 sappers, and 24 pieces of cannon. The total force of these three corps was then as follows:

Artillery, 28 pieces. *Infantry*, 6,350 men. *Cavalry*, 1,300.

Besides these forces, which were detached from the Grand Army, there were formed in Lithuania, several regiments of infantry and cavalry, which we shall designate in the sequel, but which did not commence active service until the battle of Wilna.

To return to the main army. Such was the rapidity with which the operations of General Skrzynecki upon the Russian Guard were executed, that, as we have said, he was on his retrograde march, after having driven that guard beyond the frontiers, before Marshal Diebitsch received intelligence of his operations. It was then that the Russian commander, having no hope of saving the Guard, conceived the plan of attempting, by a prompt diversion towards Ostrolenka, to cut off the communication of our army with Warsaw. [See Plan XXIX.]

With this view, he evacuated his position at Sucha and Mordy (o), passed by Sokolow, crossed the Bug River at Granne (16), entered into the Russian province of Bialostok, passed through a comer of this department on the 24th of May, and crossing the little river Nurzec (R), at Ciechanowiec (17), entered again into the Polish territory, and occupied the road of Czyzew (18) and Zamhrowo (19). Without any delay he pushed his advanced guard as far as Czyzew.

General Lubinski was then at Nur. This little town was at the same distance from Ostrolenka as Czyzew, but the communications with Ostrolenka were more difficult, Czyzew being on a principal road. The enemy, observing this circumstance, and taking it for granted that Lubinski was cut off from the main army, sent an aide-de-camp with a flag of truce to summon him to surrender. This officer announced to General Lofeinski that the whole Russian army had occupied Ciechanowiec, that the advanced guard was already at Czyzew, and that those circumstances ought to satisfy him that his communications with his friends were entirely cut off, and that therefore he would do well to lay down his arms and throw himself upon the magnanimity of the Emperor. To this proposition General Lubinski replied, that although such might be his situation, he could not think of surrendering himself without a straggle; and to satisfy the aide-de-camp that this was not his individual feeling alone, but that it was partaken by the whole body of his soldiers, he would present him to them, and enable him to satisfy himself personally on this point. The aide-de-camp was then conducted to the front of the line, and he addressed himself to the troops, exhibiting the circumstances under which they were placed, assuring them that the bravest resistance would be hopeless, and inviting them to surrender. This address was interrupted by a universal shout of indignation from the soldiery,[62] and they commanded him to leave their presence. After the departure of the aide-de-camp, General Lubinski commenced his march, and, though it was practicable for him to reach Ostrolenka by a direct route, yet thinking it possible that Czyzew was not occupied by a very strong force, and that he might profit by the approach of night, he determined to march at once upon the latter place, and to attack the Russian advanced guard there. This bold thought was executed with perfect success. On reaching Czyzew he found two regiments of cavalry encamped, and wholly unprepared for an attack. They had not even an outer-guard upon the road to Nur. He made a charge which threw them into complete disorder, and compelled them to retreat with the loss of a great number in killed and wounded, and four to five hundred prisoners. It was to be regretted that the necessity under which General Lubinski was placed of reaching Ostrolenka as soon as possible, did not permit him to profit further by these advantages.

On the next day, (the 25th) the rearguard of our main army, consisting of the brigade of General Wengterski, was attacked at midday by the Russians, on the side of Zambrowo, near Kleczkowo (20), a village situated at the distance of three leagues from Ostrolenka, on the left bank of the Narew. General Diebitsch, being under the conviction that he had encountered the whole Polish force at Kleczkowo, consolidated his strength there, and determined to come to action, and, by so doing, give time for another corps to advance in the direction of Czyzew, and occupy Ostrolenka, by which movement he trusted that our army would be cut off from Warsaw, and forced to retire to Lomza. The Russian commander, presuming on the celerity of his movements, was so confident of meeting our whole army at this point, that nothing could exceed his surprise on learning that our army had already passed the town and that it was only the rearguard which was before him.[63] In order to lose no time, he commenced an immediate attack on the rearguard thus posted at Kleczkowo. Our Commander-in-Chief who was then at Troszyn, on hearing the fire of the Russians at Kleczkowo, immediately repaired thither, and profiting by the fine position of that place, which commanded the marshy plain on the side of the enemy, passable only by a dyke, the bridge over which had been demolished by our troops, ordered General Wengierski to sustain himself in that position until night. In vain the Russian cavalry and infantry attempted to pass this dyke. At each approach they were uniformly driven back by a destructive fire of grape from our artillery. In vain were sixteen pieces of their artillery employed to silence this fire; our position was too commanding to be affected by them.

The brigade of General Wengierski, having held out in this position, with the greatest determination against a vastly superior force, for nine hours, left the place at night in the greatest order, and followed the main army. On the next day, the 26th of May, our army (h) evacuated Ostrolenka, passed the Narew River, and took, upon the right bank of that river, opposite to Ostrolenka, a new position,[64] leaving the bridge partly destroyed, but in such a state that the Russian infantry might pass it slowly. Not long after we had occupied our -position, the enemy commenced debouching over this bridge.

BATTLE OF OSTROLENKA.   [See Plan XXX.]

The battle of Ostrolenka, which cost us the lives of two brave generals, Kicki, and Henry Kaminski, was, in point of tactics, simply the passage of the river. We may presume that the intention of General Diebitsch was, by passing the Narew at this point, to send at the same time a corps to Serock, in order to cut off our army, and place it between' two fires.   At 11 o'clock, the Russian infantry (a) under the protection of a most terrible fire from fifty-four pieces of artillery (b) placed in a very strong position on the left bank of the Narew, commenced, as we have said, the passage of the river. General Skrzynecki, not wishing absolutely to prevent this passage, placed but sixteen cannon in advantageous positions, on slight elevations of ground, (d) designed to prevent the repairing of the bridge, and the consequent rapid passage of the enemy's infantry. The powerful Russian artillery attempted, without success, to silence these few pieces. Their fire was equally harmless to the main army (A); for the latter was withdrawn to an advantageous position. Our artillery, on the other hand, was used with great effect, being brought to bear directly upon the bridge. During these operations, the advanced guard, with all the baggage and ammunition of the army, received the order to take up the march towards Warsaw.

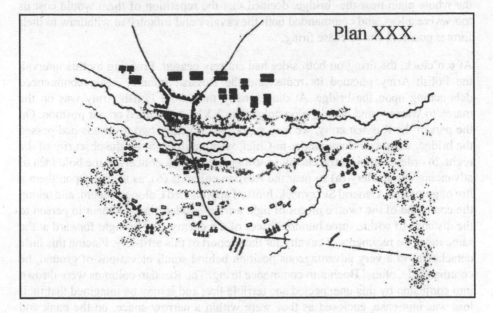

Plan XXX.

At 3 o'clock, our artillery received orders to evacuate their position, and the skirmishers (e) were ordered to advance. On the cessation of the fire of the artillery, the light troops commenced a warm fire upon the columns of Russian infantry, which had already passed the bridge. The enemy, profiting by the withdrawal of our artillery, commenced repairing the bridge, to afford a passage for large masses of infantry and artillery. A strong Russian column (f), after passing the bridge, took a direction to the left, to throw itself into the forest which borders on the Narew, at the distance of a quarter of a league from the bridge; and by occupying that forest and the communications which traverse it, they thought to commence an attack upon our right wing. To have permitted this would have much deranged our dispositions. The Polish commander, observing that a great body of the Russian infantry had already passed the bridge, and that this strong column had been sent to occupy the forest, ordered General Lubinski to send forward a brigade of cavalry (g) to charge upon this column, on its march, and at the same time ordered General Kaminski, with a division of infantry, to make a charge upon the Russian infantry near the bridge. These two attacks were executed with great promptness and spirit, and were successful. The column which the cavalry attacked on its march to the forest, was dispersed with the loss of more than a hundred men left on the field. The attack of the division of General Kaminski was equally fortunate. The Russian columns, on receiving his charge, fell back upon the bridge, or concealed themselves under the banks of the river. These two attacks cost us the lives of the two generals, Kaminski and Kicki, who threw themselves upon the enemy, at the head of their respective columns. Their loss was deeply regretted by the army and the nation.

Although the result of these attacks was favorable to us, yet, the Commander-in-Chief, considering the terribly destructive fire of the Russian artillery, which commanded the whole plain near the- bridge, decided that the repetition of them would cost us too severe a loss, and commanded both the cavalry and infantry to withdraw to their former position, and to cease firing.

At 6 o'clock, the firing on both sides had entirely ceased. Profiting by this interval, the Polish Army pursued its route, and the Russian infantry again commenced debouching upon the bridge. At dusk, nearly the whole Polish Army was on the march to Warsaw, and one division only [Plan XXXI.] remained on our position. On the part of the Russian army, we may suppose that nearly two divisions had passed the bridge, when our Commander-in-Chief, wishing to profit by the obscurity of the night, in order to subject the enemy to still greater losses, conceived the bold idea of advancing our artillery (a) so near the Russian columns (6), as to pour upon them a fire of grapeshot. General Skrzynecki himself approached Colonel Boehm, and taking the command of the twelve pieces of light artillery under him, led them in person to the distance of within three hundred paces of the enemy, and brought forward at the same time two regiments of cavalry for the support of this artil-lery. Placing this little detachment in a very advantageous position behind small elevations of ground, he commanded Colonel Boehm to commence firing. The Russian columns were thrown into confusion by this unexpected and terrible fire; and it may be imagined that their loss was immense, enclosed as they were within a narrow space, on the bank and on the bridge. Every discharge of the artillery was with effect, and by the testimony of the prisoners taken, their loss must have amounted to an entire brigade, without estimating those who left the field wounded, and those who fell into the river. On our side, this attack cost us only the loss of two officers of the artillery, although this detachment was exposed to the fire of the whole Russian artillery.[65] Our battery fired but three rounds, when the general gave the order to withdraw, and follow the main army (A) to Warsaw.[66]

These are the details of the battle of Ostrolenka, in which the loss on the enemy's side was from 10,000 to 15,000 men, and on our side, the two general officers above mentioned, with about 4,000 men.

On the afternoon of the day of the battle of Ostrolenka, the division of General Gielgud received orders to depart, from the town of Lomza. General Dembinski, on the night of the same day was ordered to join him with two squadrons of Poznam Lancers. The latter general left the field of battle with these squadrons, and on the next day joined the division of General Gielgud.[67]

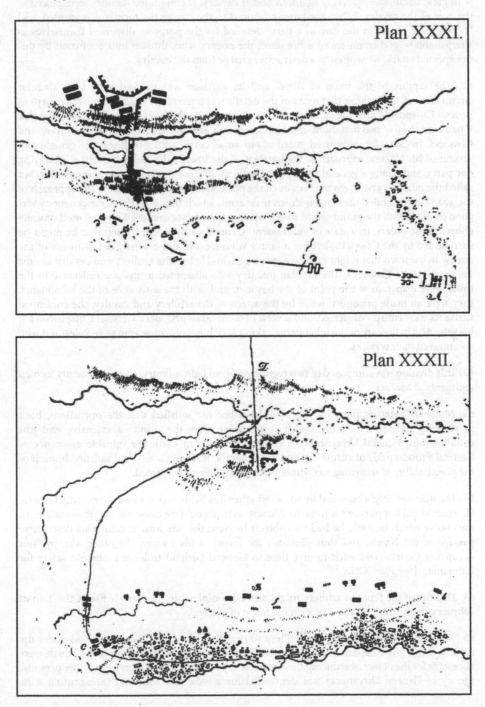

Plan XXXI.

Plan XXXII.

NOTES

60. The capture of the town of Bielsk and its garrison was conjunction with cavalry could be used with great advantage, especially against a hostile cavalry. The mounted infantry were placed in the rear of the cavalry. When the latter advanced to the charge the former dismounted, and leaving their horses in the care of a party detailed for the purpose, dispersed themselves as sharpshooters, and commenced a fire upon the enemy, who, thrown into confusion by this unexpected attack, were open to a destructive charge from the cavalry.

61. The capture of the town of Bielsk and its garrison was marked with such singular circumstances, that I think that some of the details will interest the reader. The small corps of general Chlapowski arriving suddenly before this town, on the 33d of May, was informed that it had a garrison of two battalions of infantry, and that near the town was a body of a thousand Cossacks, in camp. The advanced guard of our small corps, with which was the general and several of his officers, approached the barriers of the town. The Russian sentinel observing our party, and seeing a general officer among them, did not recognize them as enemies, but called the guard to give them the honors of the place. General Chlapowski, on the approach of the guard, commanded them to lay down their arms, which they did. The same ceremony was gone through with the grand-guard in the square of the town, and the Russians mechanically obeyed these orders, in a state of amazement. General Chlapowski, fearing that he might be surrounded by the Cossacks, left his infantry volunteers to disperse any detachments of the enemy in the town that might rally to oppose him, and led all the artillery and cavalry against the camp of the Cossacks. The Russian infantry who attempted to make a resistance in the town, were dispersed at the point of the bayonet, and, with the assistance of the inhabitants, they were all made prisoners; while by the attack of the artillery and cavalry, the encamped Cossacks were entirely dispersed, and several of them taken prisoners. General Chlapowski left his prisoners in the care of the inhabitants, taking with him only those who were Poles, and who volunteered their services.

62. This division was composed of two regiments of old light infantry, and two recently formed regiments of Mazurs.

63. Marshal Diebitsch must by this time have become satisfied that the operations, both in strategy and tactics, of the Polish commander, were the result of extensive and just combinations. General Skrzynecki, in contriving this plan (with the valuable assistance of General Prondzynski) of surprising and defeating the Russian Guard, had satisfied himself of the practicability of returning to Ostrolenka without being intercepted.

64. The question might be asked by some, whether this battle was necessary, and why General Skrzynecki did not pursue his route to Warsaw, as he could have done without molestation. In the course which he took, he had two objects in view; the one was, to cause this destructive passage of the Narew, and thus diminish the forces of his enemy; the other was, by thus occupying General Diebitsch to give time to General Gielgud to leave Lomza in safety for Lithuania. [See Plan XXIX.]

65. This fire of the Russian artillery might also be compared to the terrible fire of the 25th of February, at Grochow, in the attack on the forest of elders.

66. This maneuver, of bringing the artillery so near the columns of the enemy, and under the terrible fire of the Russian artillery, was one of those bold and hazardous steps which were necessary for the object of reducing the immense superiority of the enemy's force. The personal agency of General Skrzynecki was demanded for a blow like this; and in executing it he

displayed equally the qualities of the soldier and the general. The admiration of his soldiers was excited by seeing him dismount and place himself with the utmost coolness at the head of this battery of artillery, exposed to the incessant fire of that of the enemy. Neither the fear of the enemy, nor the entreaties of his officers who begged him, on their knees, to withdraw and to reserve his valuable life for his country, could induce him to move from his place, until he had seen the successful termination of this effort.

67. For those who have asserted that General Gielgud was cut off from the main body of the Polish forces and compelled to escape into Lithuania, the sending of these two squadrons of lancers to join him, will be a sufficient answer. The division of General Gielgud could have even remained at Lomza for as many as three days after this battle.

CHAPTER XX.

Operations of the Lithuanian Corps - Battle of Raygiod and defeat of the Russian corps of Sacken. - Importance of this first success in Lithuanian-General Gielgud neglects to follow up his advantages. - He loses time by passing the Niemen at Gielgudiski, and enables the enemy to concentrate his forces in Wilna - Entrance into Lithuania and reception by the inhabitants. - Position of the two main armies. - The Russian forces remain inactive and receive supplies from Prussia. - Death of Marshal Diebitsch.

ON the 27th of May, the corps of General Gielgud, attached to which were Generals Rohland, Szymanowski, Dembinski, and Colonel Pientka, left Lomza, and commenced their march into Lithuania. On the evening of that day, they arrived at Stawisk, passing through Szczuczyn and Graiewo. In the last town, they were joined by the little corps of general, then Colonel, Sierakowski, which, as we have already remarked, had been employed in observing General Sacken, and was here occupying an advantageous position. The force of this corps has been already stated.

I have divided this battle into two different periods, marked by the two different positions which the enemy successively took.

On examining the plan of the first position of the Russians, it will be at once seen that they had no knowledge of the arrival of our corps. They supposed that they were acting against the corps of Colonel Sierakowski alone, and they had conceived the design of out-flanking him. On the morning of the 29th, our whole corps, quitting the little town of Graiewo, met, at the distance of about a quarter of a league, the Russian flankers, against whom our own were immediately sent out. The Russian cavalry began to retire. Our columns continued their march slowly, having the forces of Colonel Sierakowski in front, as an advanced guard,[68] and we thus arrived at Lake Raygrod, the advanced guard meeting only small detachments of the Russian cavalry, which retired as we approached. On reaching the lake, our advanced guard was fired upon by the Russian skirmishers, concealed in the woods on the opposite side of the lake, which bordered upon the cause-way. Colonel Sierakowski received orders to engage with them. He sent forward his own light troops, and placed two cannons upon the causeway, with which he commenced a fire upon the woods. The Russian infantry instantly evacuated the woods, and allowed our skirmishers to occupy them. By this maneuver, the Russians intended to lead on our forces with the view to attack them on their flank, and even to surround them, by sending detachments (a, b) to the right and left, as will be seen on the plan. In a short time our larger force, under General Gielgud, commenced debouching between the two lakes. A strong column

211

(c) of our infantry took a direction towards the forest, to the left, and another column (d) to that on the right, to dislodge the enemy, if he should be found to have occupied either. At the same time our artillery (e), to the number of fourteen pieces, taking a position at the side of the causeway, opposite to that of the enemy (f), commenced firing. The whole of our cavalry, and the greater part of our infantry remained in the centre, and constituted a formidable front.

In a few moments after these dispositions were made, a brisk fire of tirailleurs was commenced on our left wing (A). The Russian centre (B), suffering from the fire of our artillery, and taken by surprise at the unexpected strength of our forces, began to waver. This was a signal for our advance. Colonel Pientka, who commanded the artillery, gave the order. A strong column of three battalions of infantry commenced the hurrah, and charged with the bayonet, upon the wavering columns of the enemy. At the same time, General Dembinski gave the order to our cavalry (g) to charge upon that of the enemy on the right and left. The 1st Squadron of the Pozman Lancers received the order to throw themselves forward, and fall upon the breaking columns of the enemy. The greatest consternation and disorder began to exist in the Russian ranks. It was no longer a retreat; it was a flight. This squadron of lancers, commanded by the brave Major Micielski, performed prodigies of valor. They entered the town simultaneously with the Russian columns, cutting down immense numbers of the enemy, and taking many prisoners. This squadron courageously remained in the streets of the city, exposed to the fire of the enemy's infantry, who had occupied the houses, until the arrival of our own infantry. In this exposed situation they lost their commander.[69]

These several attacks, which did not occupy two hours, caused an immense loss to the enemy. Three entire battalions, which formed their right wing (C), consisting of 2,000 men, were taken prisoners, with three superior officers, and fourteen of a lower grade. By the entry of our forces, the enemy was driven from the town, and took another position (O) upon elevated ground, on the opposite side of a small stream, near the town. This position was strong, and commanded the town and the whole of the other side of the stream. General Sacken would certainly have remained long in this position, if our right wing under Colonel Koss had not, as we shall see, succeeded in passing the stream at a higher point (i), and acting on his flank. The Russian general, as soon as he had established himself in his new position, commenced a fire upon the town, which was returned by our artillery. It was during this fire that Colonel Koss succeeded in passing the stream, at a quarter of a league above the city, on the right. This was affected by demolishing the buildings in the vicinity, and making a passage for the artillery from their materials. General Sacken, seeing his left wing thus menaced, evacuated his position, in which, as we have said, but for this attack on his flank, he could have well supported himself for some time.

At 3 o'clock the Russians commenced their retreat upon the road to Kowno, and thus terminated a battle of the most advantageous character for us, and with which begins an important era in our affairs.

By this battle the Polish forces had made the acquisition of great advantages, both in respect to strategy and tactics, and the highest hopes might reasonably be cherished in regard to the future.

It was, as it were, a return of the state of things brought about by the victory of Igani, and which menaced the enemy with total ruin. Our main army was then near to Warsaw, composed of a force of considerable strength, and which, under the command of Skrzynecki, had been victorious in every battle; new troops had been formed there. - Neither provisions nor forage had failed, for they were constantly sent from Warsaw to the army, in whatever quarter it might be.

The Russian army was, in the meanwhile, suffering under all the disadvantages which we have before described. Wearied and discouraged by the disasters of the campaign, posted in regions which they had devastated, and therefore suffering from scarcity; without hospitals for their sick and their wounded for the towns which contained them had been destroyed, - and with the cholera ravaging their ranks, that army was in the most precarious situation. The communications between the Russian provinces and the army were entirely cut off by the Polish Lithuanian Corps. They received -their provisions exclusively from Prussia; and, but for this assistance of Prussia, no one can doubt that Diebitsch would have been, before this, under the necessity of withdrawing from the country. The reader will also remember that at this time, the brave, and skilful General Chrzanowski had obtained repeated advantages over Rudiger, in the environs of Zamosc, and that the little corps of General Chlapowski which bad entered, on the 20th of May, the Russian department of Bialostok, was acting with great advantages. From the Baltic to the Black Sea, the provinces of Podolia, Volhyhia, Ukraine, as well as Lithuania and Samogitia, con-taining a population of twelve million inhabitants, were in a state of excitement, and would soon have risen in the holy cause. They were waiting only the arrival of our victorious troops. It cannot but be assumed, therefore, that if General Gielgud, at the head of the Polish corps in Lithuania, had acted with promptness and energy, the happiest results would have been achieved. It is, therefore, with the deepest chagrin, that I have to record that from the moment of the termination of the fortunate battle of Raygrod, all the opera-tions of General Gielgud were not only deficient in energy, but altogether wrongly planned. The first fault which he committed was not continuing to press the attack upon General Sacken, after he had retired from Raygrod. Under the pretext that the soldiers were fatigued, the corps was encamped. This pretext was groundless, for the soldiers themselves demanded to be led in pursuit of the enemy. In this camp we passed the whole night, and left it [Plan XXXIII] at the hour of nine the following morning; having given fifteen hours to the retreating enemy. We continued our march to Kowno, through the Duchy of Augustov. On the 30th of May, we arrived at Suwalki (1) its capital, and remained there a day and a night, without any conceivable reason. The enemy, profiting by the slowness of our movements, escaped the certain destruction with which he bad been threatened. On the 1st of June, we arrived at Kalwaryia (2), and at that town our corps was very uselessly di-vided into two parts, the larger (a), under General Gielgud, took the road to Gielgudiski (3), on the Niemen,[70] to pass the river at that point. General Dembinski, with the remainder of the corps (6), continued on the main road, and on the 3rd of June arrived at Alexota (4).

This separation of our forces into two bodies, to pass the Niemen at Gielgudiski, was not recommended by any conceivable advantage, and, indeed, operated much to our injury. This plan of operations was also in opposition to the instructions, not only of the Commander-in-Chief, but of the National Government, and obstructed the rapid execution of the great designs of the campaign.

In any plan for the occupation of a foreign country, the first object should be to get possession of the principal towns, for at those points are chiefly concentrated both the moral and physical resources of the country. Of Lithuania, the town of Wilna (5) is the capital. Against it all our plans should have been directed; and, in fact, the instructions of the government to General Gielgud were all to this effect. By a prompt occupation of that city, we should have unquestionably reaped the greatest advantages. As Wilna was the residence of the principal officers of the government of the province, it would have been there that all the arrangements could best be made for a provisional administration, and for the convocation of a conventional Diet of the people. In regard to the formation of new forces, Wilna was the place that presented the greatest facilities.

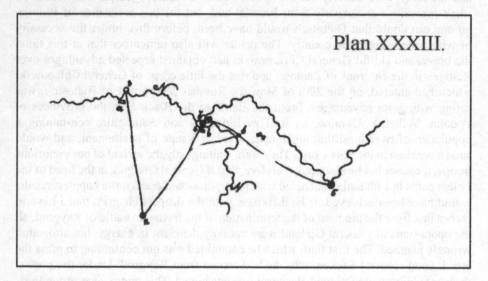

Plan XXXIII.

Taking all these circumstances into view, it must be conceded that after the battle of Raygrod, the first object of General Gielgud ought to have been to march upon and to occupy Wilna with the utmost promptness. With this view, his course should have been, after masking his movement at Kowno, to have passed the Niemen (N) at Rumszyski (6), a village which was about sixteen English miles above Kowno (7) and in the direction of Wilna, while Gielgudiski, on the other hand, was thirty-two miles below Kowno, and forty-eight from Rumszyski, and out of the direction of Wilna. With the exception of that of General Sacken, no other Russian force was interposed between us and Wilna. Indeed, the corps of General Chlapowski (c), with which he had traversed the department of Bialostok, was at that moment between Kowno and Wilna, and had we passed at Rumszyski, we should have been within but one day's march of him. It is evident, then, that Wilna would have fallen into our hands without a blow. All these advantages were sacrificed by making the passage at Gielgudiski. General Sacken, meeting with no interruption, thus escaped a second time, and marched from Kowno to Wilna. At the same time several other Russian corps began to concentrate themselves at Wilna.

The corps of General Dembinski, having maintained a moderate fire upon Kowno for two days, in order to mask our movements from the enemy, marched for Gielgudiski, to follow the other corps in the passage of the river, at that point, on the 7th of June. Our troops thus entered the Province of Lithuania, an interesting day for us, thus engaged in the effort to re-unite this dissevered portion of our country to its ancient parent. The manner in which the inhabitants of every village received us, expressive of the warmest satisfaction, showed that they regarded us as brothers. This reception deeply affected both soldiers and officers. They hailed us as their deliverers, and it is now a mournful reflection that, owing to the misconduct of our commanders, that enthusiasm, instead of leading to happy results, proved, in the end, only an aggravation of their misfortunes.

Leaving the corps of General Gielgud upon the Niemen, we will return again to the operations of the Grand Army, and of the different detached corp. Our main body, which, after the battle of Ostrolenka, retired towards Warsaw, was now at Praga, where the headquarters of the Commander-in-Chief were fixed. General Skrzynecki, during the re-pose of the army, occupied himself with its reorganization.

In the environs of Zamosc, the corps of General Chrzyanowski, in which the brave General Romarino commanded a brigade, was sufficient to keep the different Russian corps in check.

On the 3rd of June, the Russian army, which, up to the present time, continued in the environs of Ostrolenka, on the left bank of the Narew, commenced its operations upon the right bank of that river. A considerable corps, amounting to 20,000 men, passed that river in the neighborhood of Prasnysz. The principal object of this corps was not to recommence hostilities, but to protect the large transports of provisions which were sent daily from Prussia. In the environs of Brzesc was the corps of General Kreutz. The Russian army thus fed by Prussia, remained inactive in their position at Ostrolenka, during which interval, and while he was perhaps contriving new plans for our subjugation, occurred the sudden death of Marshal Diebitsch. He died at Kleczkowo, not far from Ostrolenka, on the 9th of June.[71]

The provisional command of the Russian army was taken by General Toll.

If the reader should examine closely the operations of the two armies after the battle of Ostrolenka, he will, perhaps, be astonished at their inactivity. He will, however, acknowledge that the blame of that inactivity cannot rest upon the Polish side. The retreat which we made was necessary; first, for the sake of the re-organizing of the army; secondly, for the object of leading the enemy to the environs of Praga, which were in a state of devastation, and generally into the region between the Bug and the Liewiec, where be would, not be able to support himself; and in this manner to force him either to attack the fortifications of Praga, to attempt a passage of the Vistula,

215

or to evacuate the country. That either of the two first would be attempted, while the insurrections in Lithuania and Samogitia, &c. were in progress, and after our success at Raygrod, was hardly to have been expected; for the one would cost too great a sacrifice of men, and the other would be attended with too much hazard. If, then, the Russian forces undertook nothing, it was a consequence of their critical situation. We can, in fact, safely assume that it was their intention to evacuate the country; for to have obtained sufficient supplies by their own means was almost impracticable. When, therefore, this army remained there, it was only because it was fed by Prussia, who did not scruple openly to succor the enemy in his per-ilous position, by sending enormous transports by the roads of Neydenburg and Mlawa. It was those transports which saved the Russian army from the utmost extremity. I leave to the reader to judge, then, whether it was with one enemy alone that the Poles had to contend. The PRussian Government, which arrested all the volunteers who were passing through its territory to augment our ranks, and which stopped all the aids of money and arms sent to us by the generous friends of liberty in other countries, took every occasion to aid and protect our enemy. If that government has satisfied its own inhuman will, by this interference to injure a cause so sacred as that of the Poles, they have unintentionally aided that cause by raising its merit in the eyes of the present and future ages, who will know with what difficulties we had to struggle. In return for these good offices of the PRussian Government, the Poles will only say, - "Przyidzie kryska na malyska," - "Everyone has his turn."

If the two main armies were at rest, it was not so with the corps in the Lublin Palatinate, where General Chrzanowski beat, on the 10th of June, General Rudiger, between Zamosc and Uchania, and took from him numerous prisoners. General Rudiger was forced, by this action, to retire to Lublin, and to cease offensive operations. General Chrzanowski then prepared to surprise this corps, with the aid of the garrison of Zamosc.

It was on the 12th of June, that after being apprized of the continual victories of General Chrzanowski, the Commander-in-Chief concluded to re-commence hostilities. His plan was, to act in concert with this corps, and to crush the enemy in all the southern parts of the kingdom. He would afterwards have to deal only with the Russian main army, which had commenced passing the Narew and entering into the Plock Palatinate, to keep its com-munications open with Prussia, and where it would have been in a manner cooped up between the Narew and the Vistula, with insurrectionized Lithuania in its rear, and our army in its front or flank, according as that army should operate, at Stanislawow, at Wyskow, or at Ostrolenka.

It was here again that our Commander-in-Chief felt his hopes renewed, confiding always in the fortunate result of the operations in Lithuania, which had so happily commenced; but he was to be again mournfully disappointed, by the pusillanimity of the generals to whom the all-important expedition to Lithuania had been entrusted.

NOTES

68. This disposition was made, expressly with the view of confirming the Russian general in the idea that he was opposed by Colonel Sierakowski alone.

69. The reader will allow me to give some details of this charge of cavalry, which was, indeed, of an extraordinary character. At the moment that the Russian centre began to waver; - with the view to continue and augment the disorder of the enemy, and to break their front, an order was given to the cavalry to push their attacks, without intermission, on the sides of the great road. With this force was the 1st Squadron of the Poznam Lancers, of between 80 and 100 men. This squadron threw themselves upon the Russian columns, and, simultaneously with them, entered the town, which was full of the enemy's infantry. Far from being discouraged by this overwhelming force, the brave Poznamians penetrated the different streets, and continued their attack on the enemy on every side. But the Russian infantry protected themselves within the houses, and behind the walls, and commenced a fire of musketry, which fell like hail upon this brave handful of lancers, so that it would have been thought that not a man would have escaped. It was impossible for our lancers either to advance or retire, for the streets before them were commanded by artillery, and the enemy's columns of infantry had closed in behind them, so there was only one outlet for them, which was by a small street, issuing out of the town to the left, and that was also occupied by the enemy. There was no alternative but to force their way through it. Our uhlans then, forming a phalanx of lances, opened a passage through the enemy, and quitted the town. It was here that the brave Micielski fell. The brave Poznamians, leaving the town, by the side of the lake, whither the Russian right wing had retreated and were about entering the city, presented to the Russians the impression that the city was in possession of our troops, and supposing themselves between two fires, they no longer hesitated to lay down their arms to the pursuing force.

70. Gielgediski was the paternal estate of the Polish general.

71. The reader may be curious to know some details of the career of Marshal Diebitsch. He was born in Silesia, not far from Wroclaw, the capital of that province. His father was a major in the Prussian service, and young Diebitsch was sent by him at an early age to the military school at Berlin. It was, perhaps, in about the year 1805, that he first entered the Russian military service as a cadet in one of the regiments of the Guard, from which he was, in 1807, transferred to the corps of engineers. In this service he advanced rapidly, not so much by real talent, as by a certain art which he had of exhibiting himself to the best advantage. In the place of aide-de-camp of the late Emperor Alexander, to which he was soon advanced, he was known to have intrigued in opposition to the interest of Poland. These intrigues, as well as those which he afterwards practised, to supersede Wittgenstein, in the command of the army against Turkey, degraded him in the esteem of all upright men. He was never regarded by us as a general of talent, and the truth of our estimate will be by this time conceded. One cannot but be impressed with the fate which has awaited the two greatest enemies of Poland, Diebitsch and Constantine. Arrested by Providence, amid the persecutions which they had inflicted, and were designing to inflict upon our country, they perished in disgrace. They died acting the part of the enemies of humanity, and their names thus rest, sealed with the eternal reproach of history. Here is a fate which ought to alarm despots. The thought that in the moment that they are most deeply engaged in contriving the oppression of their fellow-men, a sudden death may come upon them, and thus stigmatize their names forever, should teach them an impressive lesson.

CHAPTER XXI.

General Gielgud advances into Lithuania. - Allows a Russian corps to pass within a league of him unperceived. - Operations on Wilna. - -Enumeration of our present force. - Plan of a simultaneous attack upon Wilna on opposite sides by the corps in two divisions. - General Dembinski engages the enemy with the smaller part of the corps. - Being unsupported by Gielgud, is forced to retreat - General Gielgud attacks Wilna. - Battle of Wilna. - A retreat is commenced. - Prodigious efforts of the Polish cavalry in protecting this retreat - Consequences of the repulse from Wilna. - The removal of General Gielgud is called for. - General Chlapowski consents to take the virtual com-mand of the corps, in the post of chef d'etat major. - Consideration on the state of things consequent to the battle of Wilna. - Details of the admirable plan of operations proposed by Colonel Valentin.

THE forces of General Gielgud having thus crossed the Niemen, passed a night at Rewdany, and the next day [Plan XXXIV.] marched onto Czaykiszki (1), in the direction of Keydany. We cannot understand why General Gielgud did not attack Malinowski (6), who passed at the distance of half a league from us, at the head of 6,000 men, on his march to Wilna. It is, we believe, a thing unheard of in the history of military affairs, that an inferior force should be suffered to pass, unmolested, so near a hostile army. It discovered the very last degree of carelessness, to enter a country in the occupation of the enemy, without sending out even the ordinary reconnaissances. General Malinowski,[72] with his corps, which ought to have fallen into our hands, escaped, and made the second Russian force which had owed its safety to our negligence and contributed a new accession to the forces which we should have to contend with.

On the 10th of June, the corps arrived at Keydany (2), in which place it was joined by General Chlapowski with his corps, which had so successfully traversed the Departments of Bialostok and Grodno.

This force, which, on quitting Zienzopol, amounted to scarce 1,000 men, received reinforcements of cavalry and infantry, from the insurgents of the provinces, through which it had passed.[73] From the new forces, ten squadrons of cavalry, counting nearly 1,200 horse, and two battalions of infantry, amounting to nearly 1,800 men, were formed.

On the 11th of June, the united corps quitted Keydany, to march to Zeymy (3), where we arrived at night. In this little town we remained several days, we know not for what object. From this place General Chlapowski was sent with a detachment, consisting of the 1st Lancer Regiment and five pieces of light artillery, to make reconnaissances in the direction of Wilna. The new forces, of which we have just spoken, were attached to the main body, under General Gielgud. A few hundred of insurgent cavalry of Lithuania also arrived at Zeymy, which were joined to the Pozman Lancers and the 3rd Lancer Regiment.

On the day of our departure, General Szymanowski received orders to leave for Polonga with a small corps of insurgents (c) from the department of Szawla. This corps consisted of 1,500 infantry, 400 light cavalry, and two pieces of cannon.

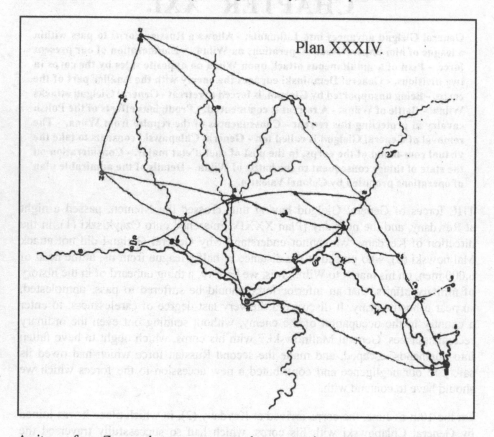

Plan XXXIV.

As it was from Zeymy that we commenced our operations upon Wilna, after having organized the new forces; and as from this point begins an era in the history of the expedition, it may be well to give a new enumeration of our forces. Our infantry consisted of 13 battalions of infantry, amounting, in all, to nearly 8,700 men, including a body of sappers; our cavalry of 24 squadrons, amounting to about 2,750; and our artillery of 29 pieces of cannon. To these forces we might add a detachment of 500 men and 100 horse, acting independently as a corps of partisans, under Colonel Zaliwski. This corps of Colonel Zaliwski was formed in the Duchy of Augustov, with the destination to operate there upon all the demonstrations the enemy, on his communications, his magazines, his baggage, his transportations of provisions, &c; and when it is considered that this officer remained for four months thus successfully employed, and exposed to the enemy's forces on all sides, a particular acknowledgment is due to him for his meritorious services. In the above enumeration we have, of course, excluded the force of General Szymanowski, which, as we have stated, received another destination.

With the forces which we have enumerated, General Gielgud left Zeymy on the 14th of June. The operations on Wilna were planned for an attack on two sides, and with that view General Dembinski was detached with a small corps (d) of 1,200 infantry, 900 cavalry, and 4 pieces of cannon. This general was to attack Wilna on the road from Willcomierz to that city, at the same time that the larger force (e) made the attack on the road from Kowno, on the left bank of the Wilyia River. This plan demanded the most exact communication be-tween the two attacking corps. That communication was not observed, and, in fact, as it will be seen, the plan itself was not executed.

The corps of General Dembinski reached Wieprz (4), on the River Swieta, on the 14th of June. On the next day it passed that river, and arrived at Szerwinty (5). From thence, after resting for a few hours, the corps marched to Myszegola (6), where it passed the night. On the 16th, leaving this village, after a march of two leagues, the corps began to meet with small detachments of the enemy's Circassian cavalry.[74] General Dembinski gave the order to throw forward the flankers. The Circassians commenced a retreating fire, and, thus engaged with them, we approached within a league of Wilna, taking a position at Karczma Biskupia (7), or The Tavern of the Bishop, a large public house, surrounded by small dwellings, and which was in rather a commanding situation.

On the 17th, General Dembinski sent parties of cavalry to the right as far as the Wilyia River (W), and to the left as far as Kalwaria (8), to make reconnaissances, and advanced with the body of the corps in the centre, for the same object. In these reconnaissances a constant fire of flankers was kept up, with which the whole day was occupied. It was a great fault in General Dembinski, to have commenced this fire, without having any intelligence of the situation of the corps of General Gielgud, with which he was to act in concert. On the morning of the same day, in fact, on which General Dembinski was thus employed, the corps of General Gielgud was at a distance of thirty-six English miles from him. By these imprudent reconnaissances, General Dembinski laid open all his forces to the knowledge of the enemy. Of this fault, the enemy took advantage on the next day.

On the 18th, at sunrise, clouds of Circassian cavalry made their appearance, and commenced attacks upon our flanks, endeavoring to turn them. Several columns of Russian infantry then approached, and maneuvered upon our centre, on which also 12 pieces of Russian artillery of large caliber commenced firing. Other columns of cavalry maneuvered upon our wings. As far as we could judge, the enemy's forces amounted to about 8,000 men. General Dembinski, seeing the strength of the enemy, and appreciating his own danger, gave orders for a retreat, which was commenced under a terrible fire from the enemy's artillery, and from his flankers, who harassed us on every side. The retreat was executed in the greatest order, as far as Myszegola, a distance of 12 miles from our po-sition, with the loss only of some fifty cavalry. On arriving at Myszegola, General Dembinski, concerned at receiving no intelligence from General Gielgud, sent an officer with a report of what had occurred. That officer found General Gielgud with his corps, at Oyrany, occupied in making the passage of the Wilyia, at that place. The report of General Dembinski, as we can assert from personal knowledge, gave a faithful description of the occurrences of the preceding days, and contained a request, that, in case he (Dembinski) was expected to maintain the position in which he then was, General Gielgud must send him reinforcements of infantry and artillery. The report finished with the suggestion, that it would be, under all circumstances, the course most expedient, to re-unite his forces with those of General Gielgud. Upon the receipt of this report, to which General Gielgud gave little attention, orders were sent to General Dembinski to depart for Podbrzeze (9), eight miles to the left of the road which leads from Willcomierz to Wilna. The pretext of this order was to attack Wilna on the side of Kalwargi, and to pass the Wilyia River at that point. Thus, instead of being allowed to unite his corps with that of General Gielgud, as he had proposed, General Dembinski was ordered to remove to a still greater distance, a disposition, for which we can conceive no possible motive. On the 19th of June, the day on which General Gielgud commenced his attack on Wilna, General Dembinski was thus employed on his march, without an object, to Podbrzeze.

BATTLE OF WILNA. [Plan XXXV.]

The battle of Wilna was, in point of tactics, simply a strong attack upon the Russian centre (A), with the view, by forcing it, to pass onto the occupation of the city. The adoption of such a plan supposes an ignorance of the nature of the position of the enemy, and of the strength of his forces.[75] Indeed any plan of attacking this city on its strongest side, that toward Kowno, was almost impossible of execution.

The battle commenced on the morning of the 19th of June. The enemy was dislodged from his first position, which was about one mile from the city. Their retreat was caused by a spirited charge, by the 1st Lancer Regiment, upon the Russian artillery, and the columns of infantry in the centre. The enemy, on quitting this position, took another of great strength on the heights called Gory-Konarski (B). This strong position was already covered with fortifications. The right wing of the enemy (C), composed of strong columns of infantry (a), rested on the Wilyia River; the centre, (A), embracing all their artillery, which consisted of 50 pieces of cannon (6), occupied the heights above mentioned; the declivity of those heights was covered with sharpshooters (d), concealed behind small heaps of earth, thrown up for this purpose. The left wing of the enemy (D) was entirely composed of cavalry (c).

After driving the Russians from their first position, our artillery (f) was brought forward and placed opposite the enemy's centre. This is to be regarded as a great fault. At the same time that our artillery was thus disposed, our left wing received orders to attack the right wing of the enemy. The columns of our infantry (g) composed in part from the new Lithuanian levies,[76] threw themselves with such fury upon the enemy, that they did not give them even time to fire, but fought them hand to hand: an immense slaughter ensued, and the Russians began to give way before this desperate assault; but at this very moment, our artillery, who could not sustain themselves under the overpowering fire of the enemy from his commanding position, began to fall back; and this gave time to the Russians to send fresh bodies of infantry to support their right wing. Our left wing, being unable to sustain a conflict with the reinforced strength of the enemy, and apprehensive of being cut off, to which hazard they were exposed by the retreat of our artillery, began to give way also, and upon that a retreat commenced along our whole line, under the protection of the cavalry (h). The cavalry, both old and new, performed prodigies of valor, in executing this duty. Single squadrons were obliged to make charges against whole regiments of the enemy, who constantly pressed upon us, with the object of throwing our forces into disorder. All the efforts of the enemy were thwarted, by this determined bravery. The Russians themselves have borne testimony to the unparalleled efforts of our cavalry on that occasion. Our lancers seemed to feel the imminent danger of permitting the Russian cavalry to fall upon our ranks, and they fought with the energy of desperation. They repelled the attacks of a cavalry three times superior in force, and which was in part composed of regiments of the Imperial Guard.

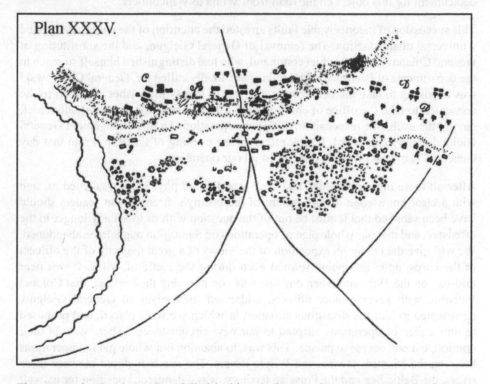

Plan XXXV.

The enemy having been thus foiled in his attacks, our forces repassed in safety the Oyrany Bridge, leaving it destroyed.

The battle of Wilna, so disastrous to us, was our greatest fault in the expedition to Lithuania; and it was the first of a series of disasters. The evil consequences of this battle did not rest with ourselves; they fell heavily upon the inhabitants of Wilna, whose hopes of acting in concert with us were disappointed. At the sound of our cannon, a revolt of the inhabitants was commenced, and after the repulse of our forces, arrests and imprisonments of course followed. This unfortunate battle, in fine, disorganized all the plans of the main army, and had a most discouraging effect upon the spirits both of the army and the nation. An attack upon Wilna, at a time when all the enemy's forces were concentrated there, should only have been made upon the basis of the most extensive and carefully adjusted combinations. A successful attack on Wilna would have been a difficult achievement, even by a force equal to that of the enemy, when the strong positions of the place are considered. What then shall we say of an attack, with a force amounting to but one third of that of the enemy, and made also, in broad day, upon the most defensible point of the enemy's position?

But, as if these disadvantages were not enough, General Dembinski, after having been compromised at Myszegola, instead of being enabled to aid in this attack, was, by the orders of General Gielgud, at the very moment of the attack, marching in the direction of Podbrzeze [See Plan XXXIV.] and was also by this separation exposed even to be cut off by the enemy, who could easily have done it, by sending a detachment for this object on the road from Wilna to Willcomierz.

This succession of inconceivable faults arrested the attention of the corps, and created a universal dissatisfaction. The removal of General Gielgud, and the substitution of General Chlapowski in the chief command, who had distinguished himself so much in the departments of Bialostok and Grodno, was loudly called for. General Chlapowski was unwilling to take the chief command, but, to satisfy the wishes of the corps, he consented to take the office of chief of staff, a post in which he was virtually chief, having the exclusive responsibility of every operation. To this arrangement General Gielgud readily consented. It took effect on the evening of the 20th. From that day General Chlapowski was the director of all our operations.

After all these disasters, which had both morally and physically weakened us, and with a clear knowledge of the amount of the enemy's strength, our leaders should have been satisfied that it must be out of the question with us to act any longer in the offensive, and that our whole plan of operations on Samogitia ought to be abandoned. We will give the reader an exposition of the views of a great majority of the officers of the corps, upon this point, formed even during the battle of Wilna. It was near mid-day on the 19th, and when our line was commencing their retreat, that Colonel Valentin, with several other officers, addressed themselves to General Gielgud, represented to him the disastrous situation in which we were placed, and proposed to him a plan of operations adapted to our new circumstances. There was, in their opinion, but one course to pursue. This was, to abandon our whole plan of operations between the Niemen, Dwina, and Wilyia Rivers. The space enclosed between these rivers, the Baltic Sea and the Prussian territory, was a dangerous position for us, as it contracted our movements, and at the same time exposed us to being surrounded by the superior forces of the enemy. Colonel Valentin designated, as the most eligible line of operations, the space between Kowno and Lida. From this oblique line, we could at any moment menace Wilna. He proposed to occupy Kowno, and to fortify that town as well as Alexota and Lida in the very strongest manner. On this line we should have been in a situation to profit by any advantageous opportunities which the negligence of the enemy might leave to us, of acting upon Wilna; and if we might not be fortunate enough to surprise that city, we should, at least, compel the Russians to keep a strong force within its walls, as a garrison. The town of Lida touches upon the great forest of Bialowiez. It is situated at the meeting of three great roads, viz. those from Poland, from Volhynia, and from the Province of Black Russia, a circumstance in its position which made it a place of great importance. The communications of the town with the neighboring forest were extremely easy, and this forest Colonel Valentin designated a place of concentration for all the insurgent forces of Lithuania and the other provinces. He proposed to fortify, in the strongest manner, all the roads which concentrated there, and thus to make the position difficult and dangerous of access to the enemy. This forest, which is more than one hundred and twenty English miles in length, and from thirty to sixty in breadth, reaches the great road which passes by Bielsk, from Warsaw to St. Petersburg and Moscow, and extends northwards to the environs of Wilna.

By means of prompt operations, according as circumstances might direct, our forces could act upon each of these roads, and could obstruct all the communications of the enemy with St. Petersburg and Moscow. Colonel Valentin, in proposing this plan, also gave much weight to the consideration that our main army under General Skrzynecki, was victorious in the vicinity of Warsaw, and that General Chrzanowski was with a corps in the environs of Zamosc, having been victorious over Rudiger, and on the point of entering into Volhynia; with this latter corps, a junction could easily be effected, and the two corps could act in concert, for the support of the insurrections which might occur in all the provinces between the Dnieper and the Black Sea; and even if all these great advantages, which we should have been justified in counting upon, had not been attained, we should, at least, have compelled the enemy to retain a great body of forces in Lithuania, and thus have hindered him from reinforcing his main army.[77]

NOTES

72. This general, Malinowski, was generally understood to be a native of Mohilev, or Little Russia, a province of ancient Poland, and had been long in the Russian service. The Lithuanians and Samogitians had much reason to complain of his conduct in those provinces.

73. Among the Lithuanians who hastened to join our ranks, and aid in the restoration of their beloved country, were several of the fair sex, generally from the principal families of the province. There were personally known to me the following, whose names I deem it an honor to record: Plater, Rasinowicz, Karwoska, Masusewicz, Zawadzka, and Lipinska. The Countess Plater, perhaps, should receive a more especial notice. This young heroine joined our corps with a regiment of from five to six hundred Lith-uanians, raised and equipped at her own expense, and she was uniformly at their head in the midst of fhe severest engagements. How strongly do such examples prove the sacred nature of our cause! What claims must not their country have presented to the minds of these females of the most exalted character, to have induced them thus to go out of their natural position in society, and to sacrifice domestic happiness, wealth, life itself, in the effort to rescue that country from her degradation?

74. This was a formidable force from the province of Circassia, consisting of two regiments, amounting to about 3,000 men, which had recently arrived at Wilna. It was a species of light cavalry, of the most efficient character. The fleetness of their horses was such that they would often throw themselves in the very midst of our flankers, and having discharged their arms, retreat in safety. They were armed with two pistols, a long fusil, a saber, a long knife, and a lance.

75. As we have been informed, Wilna was defended by five corps, consisting in all of about 30,000 men, under Generals Kurata, Tolstoy, Sacken, Malinowski and Szyrman.

76. This Lithuanian force consisted of the regiment of the Countess Plater, who accompanied them in the charge.

77. This valuable officer, Colonel Valentin, unfortunately lost his life on the day after the battle of Wilna, while bathing in the Wilyia. The regrets of his brother officers were aggravated by their sense of the value of those wise counsels, the suggestion of which was the last act of his life. He had every quality of heart and intellect for the highest military station.

CHAPTER XXII.

Operations of the main army. - Expedition under Jankowski. - General Chrzanowski having driven Rudiger from his position, crosses the Vistula, but returns to act in concert with General Jankowski against the enemy near Kock. - Details of General Jankowski's movement - He remains inactive within sight of the fire of the corps with which he was to co-operate. - Other evidences of treason. - Generals Jankowski and Bukowski are arrested and ordered for trial. - View of the advantages that were sacrificed by this misconduct. - Discovery of a plot to liberate and arm the Russian prisoners at Warsaw, and to deliver the city to the enemy - State of the public mind induced by these events.

FROM these melancholy occurrences in Lithuania, let us turn to follow the operations of the Grand Army.

On the 13th and 14th of June, a division of infantry, under the command of General Muhlberg, left Praga, and took the direction of the environs of Stanislavov and Jadow. In the latter place this division surprised a strong detachment of the enemy in camp, and took many prisoners. Thence they were instructed to follow the left bank of the Liwiec as far as the environs of Kaluszyn, and even to Zelechow, clearing each bank of the presence of the enemy. This division was then to join itself with the division of cavalry of General Jankowski, which on that day left for Kock. Those two divisions combined were to endeavor to act upon the different corps of the enemy which were pressed by the corps of General Chrzanowski.

The latter general had commenced the offensive on the 16th, and had driven the corps of General Rudiger from its position at Krasznystaw, and compelled it to retreat to Lublin, continually pursued by him. On the 23rd, he took that town by storm. The enemy was obliged to evacuate it in disorder, leaving a great number killed, wounded, and prisoners, and to take the direction of Kock. The corps of Rudiger would have been inevitably destroyed, if another Russian corps of 15,000 strong had not marched to its aid.

General Chrzanowski, apprized of the arrival of this reinforcement, quitted the pursuit, for a more favorable moment; and, to avoid an engagement with this combined force of the enemy, as well as to escort the prisoners, which he had taken at Lublin, to a place of safety, he repassed the Vistula, at Pulawa. He had scarce reached the opposite side of the river, when he received the intelligence that the division of General Jankowski, reinforced by a brigade of infantry, was approaching Kock, where was already the corps of General Rudiger, and whither the corps of General Keisarow, above mentioned, was hastening to join him. In order, therefore, to take between the two fires all the forces which might be collected at Kock, General Chrzanowski, promptly repassed the river, reached the environs of Kock, and waited impatiently for the attack of General Jankowski, in the opposite direction; but Jankowski delayed his movement, and allowed the corps of Keisarow to join Rudiger.

The following are the details of this expedition, as they were related by an officer of the division of Muhlberg, and which exhibit satisfactory evidence of treason on the part of General Jankowski.

 The result of this expedition, which could have had the most brilliant results, has filled us with grief and indignation. We were marching in the utmost haste upon Kock, with the hope of beating Rudiger. On our route, at Stoczek, for our misfortune, we were joined by the division of cavalry under General Jankowski, who then took the command. We ought to have passed the Wieprz, to meet Rudiger, and cut him off. Suddenly news was brought to us that the enemy had passed the Wieprz, at Lyssobyki, with 6,000 infantry, sixteen squadrons of cavalry, and ten pieces of cannon. General Jankowski then called a council of war, at which the following plans were adopted: General Turno was to attack the enemy, in the direction of Sorokomla, and General Jankowski was to come to his support at the first sound of his cannon. The brigade of General Romarino (detached from the corps of General Chrzanowski, and destined to act as an independent corps) was to act upon the left wing, and General Bukowski, with a brigade of cavalry, upon the right wing of the enemy by Bialobrzegi. This plan, which in the conviction of all our officers would have exterminated the corps of General Rudiger, and the execution of which was reserved to General Jankowski, came to nothing.

General Turno, trusting in the faithful execution of the plan, attacked the enemy with courage and vigor. He was sure of receiving support on three sides. He made head against the enemy for six hours, while Generals Jankowski and Bukowski, at the distance of about three miles from him, hearing and even seeing the fire of the action, remained in a state of complete inaction. Nay more, a Russian detachment took possession, almost before their eyes, of the ammunition and baggage of a whole regiment, and they did not stir to prevent it. General Turno fought with bravery and sangfroid, notwithstanding that none came to his support, and did not retire till he received orders to do so. The whole corps was indignant at the conduct of Jankowski, and his brother-in-law, Bukowski, who had evidently acted the part of traitors.

General Skrzynecki was deeply afflicted with the sad result of an expedition, which, based upon infallible calculations, had promised the very surest success. The event was of the most disastrous consequence to us. If the corps of General Rudiger had been crushed, as it certainly could have been, the combined corps of Chrzanowski, Muhlberg, and Jankowski, could have acted upon all the corps of the enemy, which might be found between the Wieprz, the Swider, and the Liwiec. As those corps were quite distant from their main army, which was now upon the right of the Narew, and as they were even without a free communication with each other, they could have each been beaten in detail, by a prompt action on our part. I leave to the reader to decide, whether, after we should have obtained such successes over these detached corps, we could not have acted with certain success against the Russian main army.

The corps of General Rudiger, which thus escaped its fate, left for the environs of Lukow, whither it was followed by General Chrzanowski. The corps of General Jankowski returned in the direction of Macieowiec and Laskarzew, and the division of General Muhlberg returned to Minsk. The Commander-in-Chief deprived Generals Jankowski and Bukowski of their commands, and ordered them to be tried by a court-martial.

But other and even more affecting disasters were awaiting us. Poland, which had been so often made a sacrifice of, through her own generosity and confidence, now nourished upon her bosom the monsters who were plotting her destruction.

On the 28th of June, General Skrzynecki received information of a conspiracy which had for its object the delivering up of Warsaw into the hands of the enemy, by liberating and arming the Russian prisoners. Several generals, of whom distrust had been felt, and who had been deprived of their commands when the revolution broke out, having been known as the vile instruments of the former government, were at the bottom of this plot. Of this painful intelligence, General Skrzynecki immediately apprized the National Government, who, relying on his report, caused to be arrested General Hurtig, former commander of the fortress of Zamosc, and a base instrument of Constantine, General Salacki, Colonel Slupecki, the Russian chamberlain Fenshawe, a Mr. Lessel, and a Busscan lady, named Bazanow. Generals Jankowski and Bukovvski were also implicated in the conspiracy. This band of traitors intended to get possession of the arsenal, to arm the Russian prisoners, and to destroy the bridges (in order to cut off all communication with the army, which was then on the right bank of the Vistula) and the Russian army, advertised of this movement, was then to pass to the left bank of the Vistula, at Plock or Dobzyn, and take possession of Warsaw. Those traitors succeeded in setting at large a great number of Russian prisoners at Czeustochow. What a terror must poor Poland have been to the Russian Cabinet, which did not find it enough to have deluged her with their immense forces, and to have engaged all the neighboring cabinets to aid them against her, but must go further, and by the employment of such vile means, attempt to kindle hostilities in her interior, and to subject her at the same time to a civil and an external war! They had good cause for these desperate attempts; from the earliest stage of the conflict, they had seen that the Poles, nerved by the consciousness of the justice of their cause, were capable of crushing the force which they had sent to execute the will of the despot. Unable to meet us in the open field, they must invent some new method, no matter how base, to accomplish their end. It was through the instrumentality of their intrigues that the Dictatorship was prolonged. It was by such intrigues, that the apple of discord was thrown into our National Congress and even into the ranks of that handful of brave men who had sworn to sacrifice themselves in the cause of their country. They employed their vile accomplices to betray us, and they succeeded.

The discovery of this extensive treason struck the people with consternation and dismay. It drove them to a state bordering on desperation. When Poland had sent, and was sending her sons, and even her daughters, to the field of death, when she was sacrificing everything to achieve her deliverance, and was awaiting the fruits of such sacrifices, sure, if not to conquer, at least to fall with honor, - she sees that all is in vain—that her holy purposes are mocked at, and that all her noble efforts are thwarted! Can we be surprised, then, at the state of the popular mind which ensued ?

The state of feeling which these events caused was aggravated by the reflection, that the surveillance of certain individuals, of whom distrust had been already entertained, had been more than once demanded; and that from an early period it was urged upon the government, that the Russian prisoners, particularly those of distinction, should be carefully watched, and prevented from holding free communication together, or with others.   So far, however, from such care having been taken, the very Jews were permitted to communicate with them constantly, and to bring them intelligence of the events of the war. Can it be wondered then, that the neglect of these repeated warnings, and the tremendous consequences which had well nigh followed this neglect, should have weighed upon the minds of the people, and have even brought the National Government itself into suspicion? It was, in fact, from this moment, that the nation began first to look with dissatisfaction and distrust upon that government, upon Prince Czartoriski its head, and even upon the Commander-in-Chief himself. The melancholy news of the treason of Jankowski filled the minds of the patriots with bitter anticipations; they naturally foreboded, that if such treasons could be perpetrated in the Grand Army, under the very eyes of the Commander-in-Chief, the danger might be still greater in the more distant corps. Their forebodings were but too well justified by the events which took place in Lithuania, the intelligence of which was soon received at Warsaw.

CHAPTER XXIII.

General Chlapowski arrives at Keydany, having ordered General Dembinski to withdraw to Willcomierz. - The position of the two forces and their line of operations. - Examination of these arrangements. - Neglect of the important position of Kowno. - General Chlapowski, at Keydany, proposes to form a Provisional Government, and obtain a levy of troops. - Dispositions of the Lithuanians, as effected by the mismanagement of our leaden. - Advantages offered to the enemy by the delay at Keydany. - Brave defense of Kowno, by the small force left there. - Skirmish at Willcomien. - The opportunity of concentrating all the forces at Keydany, and repassing the Niemen, is neglected - The enemy presses his pursuit - Battle of Rosseyny. - Attack on Schawla. - Loss of the ammunition and baggage of the corps. - The corps retreats in order to Kurszany, protected by a rearguard of cavalry and light artillery. At Kurszany the corps is subdivided into three parts. - Destination and strength of each. - Examination of this plan.

GENERAL CHLAPOWSKI, whom we shall hereafter name as having the chief command of the Lithuanian force, arrived on the night of the 22nd of June at Keydany, having sent orders to General Dembinski to withdraw with his corps, and to march to Willcomierz. (10) [Plan XXXIV.] The corps of General Dembinski arrived, on the 21st, at Szerwinty, and on the 22nd, at Willcomierz. On quitting Podbrzeze, General Dembinski left a small detachment in the environs of Myszegola, to act as partisans.

The position of our corps was then as follows: The larger force was at Keydany (2). The corps of Dembinski was at Willcomierz, and a small corps (c) under the command of General Szymanowski was in the environs of Szawla. Our line of operations was on the River Swienta (S) and along the Wilyia (W), for a short distance below the junction of the former river with it. To defend the passage of those rivers against the enemy, the following detachments were designated: Kowno (11) was occupied by two battalions of Lithuanian infantry, recently levied, under the command of Colonel Kikiernicki, and a squadron of the 11th Lancer Regiment, also Lithuanian, and recently formed.

At Janow (12) was a battalion of infantry and a squadron of the 11th lancers, under the command of Colonel Piwecki. At Wieprz were three squadrons of the 10th lancers.

This separation of our forces in Lithuania, and, above all, this designation of the most recently organized troops for the defense of the passage of the two rivers, with a full knowledge of the great strength of the enemy, was a gross error. To leave the defense of Kowno, a place of so much importance, to three battalions of infantry and a squadron of cavalry, all of them newly formed troops, and that, too, without ammunition (for they had barely three rounds each), was a course perfectly inexplicable. Besides all this, the River Swienta was so shallow as to be fordable by both infantry and cavalry, and in some places even by artillery. Why then was that river defended? It was owing, in fact, to good fortune that all these detachments were not cut off.

On the arrival of the two corps at Keydany and Willcomierz, the organization of a Provisional Government for the province was commenced. Diets were convoked at these two places, to organize an administration, and to procure levies of forces. Although these arrangements were all proper in themselves, yet it was a late hour to undertake them, and no place could have been so well adapted for them as Wilna. Had the corps of Sacken been pursued and broken up, Wilna would have been ours; and all such arrangements could have been made there under the most favorable circumstances. In that event, the brave Lithuanians would have come in from all sides and crowded our ranks, without waiting for any appeal to be made to them. But at present, a new crisis had arrived. We had fought the battle of Wilna with a disastrous result. The enemy had become acquainted with the inferiority of our forces, and had begun to understand the efforts of our commander, and was prepared to take advantage of them. In fine, the Lithuanians themselves, witnessing all this gross mismanagement, became disgusted, and after having once so cheerfully tendered their cooperation, began, at length, to discover that they were sacrificing themselves in vain, and that the fate of the inhabitants of Wilna would await them. This people, as we have already stated, had commenced their insurrection two months before they had hopes of any assistance from our forces, and badly armed as they were, they had maintained a partisan warfare during this period with uniform success. We can, therefore, have no reason to reproach them, if after the misconduct which was exhibited before their eyes, they began to be reluctant to join their forces to our own, and chose to reserve the sacrifice of their exertions and their lives for some other occasion, when there might be some hope of useful results.

The six or seven days which we passed thus at Keydany and Willcomierz, seemed as if designed to invite the enemy to pursue his advantages, and to lead him to the idea of surrounding our forces. The enemy, fortunately for us, did not improve the opportunity which we presented him, but remained inactive. This inactivity, whether it arose from the imbecility of his commanders, or whatever other cause, afforded us an opportunity of changing our plans, and of extricating ourselves from the dangerous position in which we were placed. But instead of this, we awaited his attack. On the 29th, the enemy commenced an attack upon every point, at Willcomierz, Wieprz, Janov, and Kowno, with his whole force.

A corps of 4,000 Russians, with 16 cannon, commenced the attack on Kowno, defended, as we have said, by 2,000 new troops. From morning until night, the defense was sustained with great courage. The contest was for the first half of the day in the town itself, and the rest of the day was spent in disputing the passage of the bridge over the Wilyia. The Russians occupying all the houses upon the banks of the river, and the neighboring heights, commenced a terrible fire of artillery and musketry upon the bridge, which was defended by a body of infantry almost without ammunition. At nightfall, Colonel Eikiernicki, seeing that the Russian cavalry had found means of fording the river, ordered a retreat, but remained, himself, at the head of a single company, defending the bridge, until he learnt that the rest of the corps had passed the town of Sloboda, and had gained the heights which are behind the town. Upon that bridge fell the captain of this company, Zabiello, a Lithuanian. He was shot in the act of cutting away the bridge with his own hands. This company, after having thus sustained their post at the bridge with the greatest bravery, commenced their retreat. The Russian cavalry, having succeeded in fording the river, had already commenced acting in their rear. At the same time, the Russian columns of infantry were debouching upon the bridge. Colonel Kikiernicki, perceiving his situation, animated his little corps to make the desperate effort of breaking through the Russian cavalry, and of gaining Sloboda. His spirit was seconded by his brave followers, and this company of one hundred men, raising the hurrah, forced a passage through the enemy's cavalry, gained Sloboda, and, under cover of night, succeeded in joining their comrades.[78] In this effort, Colonel Kikiernicki fell wounded, and was made prisoner by the enemy.

The detachment, having lost one half of their numbers in the sanguinary attack to which the mismanagement of our general had exposed them, took the road to Janov. In this manner ended the attack on Kowno, and the Russians took pos-session of that important post, which might be regarded as the key to all our communications with Poland.

There can be no excuse for not having fortified Kowno. It is a town containing ten or twelve thousand inhabitants, of which one half, perhaps, were Jews, but they could have been employed in the construction of the works. It was also most favorably situated for defense, being surrounded by heights on every side.

On the same day, sanguinary skirmishes took place at Janov, Wieprz, and Willcomierz. The two first towns were abandoned. In the attack on Willcomierz, which was successfully repelled, an action took place, in which the Pozman Lancers and Plock threw themselves upon the flank of Russian cavalry, and, after causing severe loss, took about eighty prisoners, consisting of Circassians. General Dembinski, on the night of the 29th, learning that our positions of Janow and Wieprz were abandoned, quitted Willcomierz on the next day, and took the road to Schavla [Plan XXXIV. (13)]. Although the occupation, by the enemy, of the town of Kowno, and the interruption of our whole line of operations on the Swienta and Wilyia, made our situation very perilous; yet it was still possible to avoid the disasters which followed, and to effect a return to Poland. By concentrating all our forces at Keydany, we could have affected a passage of the Niemen, in the same manner as we had already done in the direction of Gielgudiski, which would have left the enemy in our rear; while on the other side of the Niemen, the enemy was not in force enough to prevent our passage. But, instead of doing this, as if to insure our ruin, a small detachment, consisting of four squadrons of cavalry, and the sappers, under the command of Colonel Koss, were sent to make a bridge over the Niemen! This measure is perfectly inexplicable. Scarcely had this detachment arrived at the river, and commenced the erection of the bridge, when they were attacked on two sides by the cuirassiers and the artillery of the enemy. They were saved only by the judicious conduct of Colonel Koss, who threw himself into the protection of the neighboring forest, and succeeded in rejoining the corps. The loss that we incurred by this expedition, of all our implements for the construction of bridges, was irreparable.

From this time, the enemy did not for a moment lose sight of us; and throwing his superior forces upon the great road which leads from Keydany, through Rosseyny (14), to Schavla, forced us to take that direction which was the most dangerous for us, as the field of operation for our forces was continually becoming more and more contracted.

COMBAT OF ROSSEYNY.

The cause of this action, which it would have been most desirable to have avoided, was a strong attack by the enemy upon the rearguard of General Chlapowski which was marching on the road to Schavla. To avoid exposing the rearguard to a great loss, or even to the chance of it, the command was given, to take position, and the corps was placed in order of battle. The battle of Rosseyny, which lasted scarcely four hours), was very sanguinary, and highly honorable to the Polish arms. The object of the enemy on this occasion was to surround our left wing. As soon as he perceived that our corps had taken position and was arranged in order of battle, the enemy brought forward his artillery, consisting of 24 pieces of cannon, and commenced a heavy fire upon our centre. This fire did not cause a great loss, for, our position being elevated, the shot struck too low to be effective. A few moments after this fire of artillery was commenced, a strong column of Russian cavalry showed itself on our right wing. This column had with it a body of light artillery, which commenced fire also. On our left wing, which was supported upon a marsh, and, for that reason, little expectation of an attack, but a small force was collected. This wing was composed of a battalion of infantry and the 1st Lancer Regiment. These troops had been placed on this wing to repose from the combats and fatigues of the day and night preceding, in which they had acted as rearguard. The brave lancers, however, at the first sight of the enemy, demanded of the general to be permitted to make a charge. This permission being given, at the first discharge of the Russian artillery, our soldiers threw themselves with impetuosity upon both the cavalry and the artillery of the enemy. The capture of sixty prisoners and the spiking of three cannon were the fruits of this brilliant attack. It was the last charge of that brave regiment.

Our centre was not less fortunate than our left wing. Our artillery being better placed than that of the enemy, several of his pieces were dismounted, and his fire began to slacken. For some hours, a light fire of tirailleurs was continued on both sides, when our generals, seeing that the enemy did not renew the attack, gave orders to evacuate the position, and to resume the march for Schavla.

On the same night, the corps arrived at Cytowiany. There our forces were joined by the corps of General Rohland, which had had a bloody skirmish at Beysagola, [Plan XXXIV. (15)], on the same day, on which General Dembinski was also attacked at Poniewieze. The corps of General Chlapowski left the next day for the attack of Schavla, which was occupied by a Russian garrison. The corps of General Dembinski, which as we have already stated, was marching by another route upon Schavla, arrived there at mid-day on the 7th. That general, considering the smallness of the Russian garrison in this town, consisting only of four battalions of infantry, and six pieces of cannon, after waiting a short time for the arrival of the corps of General Chlapowski, concluded to send a summons, by Colonel Miroszewski, to the Russian commandant, proposing to him to surrender, and save a useless effusion of blood. The Russian Colonel Kurow would not accept of these friendly propositions, and compelled General Dembinski to order an attack; a very moderate one, however, as he was in hopes that the arrival of our superior forces would soon convince the Russian commander that a defense would be useless. In fact, the corps of General Chlapowski arrived at about 5 P. M. at a village about four miles from Schavla, where he was met by an officer, sent by General Dembinski, with a report of the circumstances which had taken place. Indeed, the sound of the cannon and musketry ought already to have satisfied General Chlapowski that General Dembinski was engaged in the attack; but instead of hastening to his assistance he went into camp, and thus remained until two hours past midnight. At two o'clock then, of the morning of the 8th, the corps took up the march, and arrived by daybreak before Schavla.

ATTACK ON SCHAVLA.

On examining the plan of this battle, and considering the smallness of the Russian garrison in Schavla, we cannot but be satisfied that the tows ought to have been taken at the first assault, and it will seem almost incredible that after having occupied four hours in an unsuccessful attack, we should have at last quitted our position.

On arriving on the plain before Schavla, the two corps were placed in order of battle. The force of General Dembinski changed its position, and formed our left wing. We commenced a fire of artillery from the right wing and the centre, at the same time throwing forward our skirmishers. The enemy had made an entrenchment round the whole town, behind which his infantry was concealed; and upon the right of the town he had constructed a redoubt. On the sides of the town against which the right wing and centre were posted, a general fire of musketry and artillery was commenced, under the cover of which our light troops endeavored to take possession of the ramparts.

General Szymanowski and Colonel Fientka, who were the only general officers who were actively engaged in this battle, seeing that this attack of the light troops upon the Russian infantry, thus safely entrenched, was very destructive to us, and would prolong the attack, ordered two battalions of infantry, under Colonel Jeroma and Piwecki, to make an assault, protected by two pieces of cannon and a squadron of the 3rd Lancer Regiment. This order was executed with the greatest determination. Our artillery, having fired two rounds of grape, the two battalions of infantry entered the city at the charge, and regardless of the terrible fire from the windows of the houses, they reached the marketplace of the town.[79] The enemy was in consternation, and the taking of an hundred prisoners by us, showed the disorder into which he had already fallen. If but two other battalions had been sent to support those which had entered the town, the attack would have ended here. But this was neglected, and the latter were remaining in their dangerous situation, while the rest of our forces were uselessly engaged, and received no orders. The bold idea of the brave Colonel Pientka, of forcing the attack, was nowhere seconded. The corps of General Dembinski remained wholly inactive, although officers were occasionally sent by him to General Chlapowski for orders. By this fault, the battalions who had entered the city were exposed to the superior forces of the enemy, who, falling upon them from all sides, forced them to quit the city, leaving among their dead the brave Colonels Jeroma and Piwecki, and nearly one half of their whole number.[80] With the retreat of these brave battalions, all our forces commenced evacuating their position, we cannot tell for what reason. The enemy did not attack us; on the contrary, he was well satisfied with the cessation of hostilities on our part. At 9 o'clock our corps recommenced its march.

These are the details of the battle, or rather the attack, of Schavla, which town we. quitted, after investing it for nearly five hours, and after having sustained a severe loss in men and officers, a sacrifice which was owing to our most defective and ill-judged arrangements.

On this same day, we were again unfortunate, in the loss of all our baggage and several wagons of ammunition, which were sent forward by a road on our right, and fell into the hands of the light Circassian cavalry of the enemy.

This battle discovered an extreme negligence in our Commander-in-Chief. With the knowledge that the enemy was pursuing us in the rear, and on each side, we remained uselessly encamped during the night of the 7th, which we ought to have employed in the attack. The true course should have been to have set fire to the place, which would have required only the agency of a few bold men. This town, indeed, deserved no better fate; for it was inhabited almost exclusively by hostile Jews. When the general welfare is at risk, there should be no hesitation in sacrificing the convenience of individuals. If we compare the consequences of having burnt this town, and of having attacked it, we shall see that, by the former course, we should have compelled the Jews to fly with their effects, and the Russian garrison to surrender, without any effusion of blood, while, by attacking it, we lost nearly one thousand men, without any advantage whatever.

In regard to the attack, the surrounding of the town was a great fault; for neither the fire of the artillery nor of the light troops could be effective, as the Russian artillery was in a dominant position, and was concealed within the city, as their infantry was behind their entrenchments. The skirmishers, in approaching the city, fell, without having harmed the enemy. The plan of Colonel Pientka, of masking the attack on one side, and forcing the attack upon the other, at a single point, was well conceived, but failed, as we have seen, by the want of support.

At about ten o'clock the flanking parties of the Russian cavalry began to show themselves on each side of us, upon the road to Willcomierz, and on that of Cytowiany. Our corps was already on the march for Kurszany. The 1st Lancer Regiment and the light artillery were designated as a rearguard. This rearguard, taking advantage of a small defile, which presented a favorable position, took post there, and sustained themselves for some hours against an attack from the Russian advanced guard; thus protecting the march of our main body, which was executed with the greatest order. The lancers and light artillery then evacuated their position, by a retreat at full speed, which, by taking advantage of the windings of the road, and the vicinity of the forests, they were able to effect with inconsiderable loss. On the evening of the same day, we arrived at Eurszany. On the next day we remained some hours in that place, to hold a council of war. General Chlapowski proposed to divide our forces into three corps, each to act independently. This arrangement was carried into effect, and our forces were thus distributed.

The 1st Corps, under General Chlapowski, with which General Gielgud remained, consisted of five battalions of infantry, amounting to 1,500 men; four squadrons of the 1st Lancer Regiment, and two squadrons of Kaliszian cavalry; in all, 460 horse, and an artillery consisting of 13 pieces of cannon.

This corps received the destination, to march for Rosseyny, leaving the enemy on the right, and from thence directly for Kowno, and, by this unsuspected march, to surprise the last important position. By that means, the communication between us and Poland would be re-opened; and to protect this communication was to be the principal employment of that corps.

The 2nd Corps, under the command of Generals Rohland and Szymanowski, was composed of eight battalions of infantry, amounting to about 3,000 men; all the cavalry which was recently formed in Lithuania, consisting of nearly 1,000 horse; and an artillery, commanded by the brave Colonel Pientka, consisting of 12 pieces of cannon.

This corps was directed to march upon Polonga, a port on the Baltic. It had been rumored that two French vessels with arms, funds, and ammunition, together with a small body of volunteers, were cruising near that port. After they should have received these expected supplies, the corps was directed to inarch towards the Dwina and, by following along the banks of that river, to observe and interrupt the communications between the forces of the enemy in Lithuania, and the Province of Courland.

The 3rd Corps, under General Dembinski, was composed of three battalions of infantry of the 18th Regiment, recently formed, consisting of about 1,000 men; two squadrons of the Pozman Lancers, two squadrons of the lancers of Plock and one squadron of the 3rd Regiment of Uhlans, in all, about 600 cavalry; and seven pieces of artillery. This corps received orders to march for the environs of Schavla, traversing the forests, and leaving the enemy on the right; from thence to take a direction to Willcomierz, and thence to the envi-rons of Wilna, and to attack that city, if circumstances might allow of it; and then to maneuver in the Department of Minsk, and in the forests of Bialostok, acting there in support of the insurrection, and collecting the forces of the insurgents. An important object of this corps was to support a communication with the corps of General Chlapowski. This plan, the reader will observe, was, in many of its points, the same as that suggested by Colonel Valentin.

A proper reflection upon all these arrangements would convince anyone that much more loss than advantage was to be anticipated from them. This subdivision of the force was, in fact, a visionary scheme. Many officers openly declared their opinions to this effect, and urged that in our critical situation, almost surrounded as we were by a hostile force, so superior to our own, we ought not to form any new projects, but, profiting by the concentration of our forces, to redouble the rapidity of our march, and, taking advantage of the forests and covered roads, to reach Poland as soon as possible. This would, indeed, be attended with difficulties; but it would still be much easier of execution, and much more proper to be attempted, than the plan which we have detailed. Such views, however, were not regarded. The project was highly colored, and the most brilliant successes were promised to follow it. The separation of the corps was accordingly ordered, and our fate was sealed.

NOTES

78. With this company was the Countess Plater, and her aide-de-camp M'lle Rasynowiecz.

79. The Jewish inhabitants of the city even fired its upon our soldiers. Many of them were taken with pistols in their hands, and afterwards were executed.

80. In this affair we ought to make particular mention of the estimable Laga, a priest, who was at the head of the squadron in this attack, having the cross in one hand and the saber in the other.

CHAPTER XXIV.

The three subdivisions of the Lithuanian Corps take their respective destinations - Details of the operations of that of General Rohland. - He meets alone the attack of the whole Russian force. - Battle of Powendnny and Worna. - General Rohland, on his way to Polonga, learns that General Chlapowski had marched towards the Prussian frontier. - He presses his march to overtake and form a junction with him. - The greater part of the corps of Gielgud and Chlapowski were found to have passed the frontier, when that of Rohland came in sight - Indignation of the soldiery. - Death of General Gielgud. - General Rohland, joined by a portion of the corps of Gielgud which nad not yet passed the frontier, continues his inarch to Nowe-Miasto. - He declines a proposition from General Kreutz, to surrender. - Successful skirmish with the enemy's cavalry. - General Rohland takes a position at Nowo-Miasto, and awaits the enemy. - The Russian forces, however, do not continue their pur suit, but go into camp. - Propositions to pass the frontier are sent to General Rohland by the Prussian authorities. - They are submitted to the corps, and accepted.

ON the 9th of July, at about 10 A. M., each of the three subdivisions of the corps took the road designated for it. From this moment commences a new epoch in our operations in Lithuania, and we shall give a separate detail of the proceedings of each of these corps, commencing with that of General Rohland, which was in the line of the enemy's pursuit, and was followed by his whole force. This corps, quitting Kurszany, took the road for Telze. On the night of the 10th, it arrived at Powenduny and the Lake of Worna. Upon the road, it was joined by Colonel Koss, who had been sent, as we have said, with his detachment, from Keydany, to construct a bridge over the Niemen, and who had extricated himself from the exposed situation in which this attempt had placed him. As the position was advantageous, and as our soldiers had need of repose after their fatiguing march, we remained there the whole night. On the next day, at sunrise, our camp was alarmed by the approach of the Circassian cavalry of the enemy. Our generals decided to await the enemy's attack in their eligible position, and that day was one of most brilliant success. We will present to the reader full details of the events of that day, for they were of an extremely interesting character. The maneuvers of all our forces were admirable; but those of the cavalry were indeed extraordinary. The reader will be astonished to find how much was done by a cavalry, fatigued, their accoutrements in disorder, and almost without ammunition, against a cavalry like that of the enemy, well mounted, with fresh horses, and in every respect in perfect order.

COMBAT OF POWENDUNY AND WORNA.

The battle commenced at sunrise, as we have already mentioned, with an attack from two squadrons of Circassian cavalry. Those squadrons turned our outer guard, and came in contact with our tirailleurs, who received them with a warm and unexpected fire. These tirailleurs were concealed in the forest and brushwood. The Circassians faltered, and commenced a fire of carbines in return. Our fire could not but be attended with great loss to the enemy, and they were forced to retire. In this retreat, our own cavalry, which was at Powenduny, and which had debouched by a covered road, and taken position, entirely surrounded these two squadrons, and, attacking them on all sides, causing a severe loss and, taking forty prisoners. An hour after, the Russians renewed the attack. Strong columns of infantry and cavalry passed through a little village which is on the road from Kurszany to Powenduny. The Russian artillery took positions upon the declivity of the heights adjoining that village, and commenced a fire upon our cavalry. At the same time, several columns of the Russian infantry threw themselves into the brushwood on the right of our position, while a strong detachment, composed of infantry, artillery, and cavalry, was pushed forward upon our right wing, with the design to turn our flank, and, by surrounding us, to cut off our communications with Worna. This detachment, after losing several hours in attempting to act upon us, under the obstacles which were presented by the marshy nature of the ground, returned without having affected anything. Our generals, seeing the superior force of the enemy, ordered our cavalry to retire, and to place themselves in the rear of our artillery, which occupied heights commanding the whole vicinity, and arrested by an incessant fire, for more than four hours, the advance of the enemy. After our cavalry had retired, the tirailleurs began to evacuate the wood, and concentrating themselves upon the toad to Powenduny, retired also, after having destroyed the bridge which crosses a small marshy stream, intersecting the road, and burnt a suburb which adjoins Powenduny, and was near this bridge. Such was the state of things when, at about ten o'clock, a flag was announced from the Russian commander. It was brought by an aide-de-camp of General Delinghausen. The proposition borne by this flag was, that we should surrender, on the ground that we were engaged with the whole of the Russian force, amounting to nearly 20,000 men, and that forces had already occupied the road to Worna, the only communication which remained to us. This proposition was fol-lowed by the usual considerations, the wish to prevent the needless effusion of blood, &c. It was declined, and the aide-de-camp returned to the Russian headquarters, but in a short time appeared again with a renewal of the proposition. General Szymanowski, who received the aide-de-camp, persisted in his refusal, adding, that he knew the duties of a soldier - duties which were doubly obligatory upon one who is fighting in the cause of liberty, and in the defense of the country of his ancestors." After the departure of the aide-de-camp, the order was given to the artillery and infantry to re-commence their fire. At the same time, arrangements were made for the continuation of our march to Worna. At about mid-day, our columns of infantry, and a part of the cavalry and artillery, quitted their position, and took up the march for Worna. After a short time, there remained but one battalion of infantry, and three squadrons of cavalry. The cavalry was employed to mask the withdrawing of the remaining artillery. After our corps had, by a march, arranged in the manner we have described, reached a point sufficiently distant from our first position, the battalion of light infantry which remained in that position was ordered to withdraw as far as certain mills, keeping up a retreating fire. After passing those mills, the tirailleurs received orders to run at full speed to rejoin the corps, and to occupy the adjoining forests, while the cavalry were ordered to take post at the mills, to cover this movement, and afterwards to retire slowly, pass a small village which was on the road, and on the opposite side of that village to await the approach of the enemy. This maneuver was well executed by both the infantry and cavalry, the latter placing themselves on rather an open space behind the village, to await the enemy. After some time, six squadrons of the light Russian cavalry, consisting of hussars and Circassians, passed through the village, and seeing the small number of our cavalry, gave the hurrah, and threw themselves upon them. Our cavalry, expecting this attack, received orders to quit their position with promptness, in order to lead the Russian cavalry upon the fire of our infantry, who were concealed in the woods. The Russian cavalry, presuming that this was a disorderly retreat, followed with impetuosity, while our cavalry threw themselves on one side, to pass a ford, which had been designated for that object, and thus left the enemy exposed in a mass to the fire of our tirailleurs. This maneuver cost the Russians two hundred men, by the acknowledgment of officers who were made prisoners. After having caused this severe loss to the enemy, our infantry and cavalry retired slowly, to occupy their third position, and the enemy did not follow.

A short time after we quitted our second position, the Russian cavalry showed themselves again. General Szymanowski remained, with two companies of the 7th Regiment of the Line, to defend the passage of the third village against the enemy, and to give time for our cavalry to take a third position. This general, for nearly an hour, resisted the attack of a strong force of cavalry, but commenced evacuating the position on the approach of considerable bodies of the Russian infantry, withdrawing through the forests. The Russian cavalry, seeing that the village was abandoned by our infantry, began to debouch through it. It was as act of the greatest imprudence for the Russian cavalry, unsupported by either infantry or artillery, to advance thus upon a plain, surrounded by forests, in which they might have supposed infantry, and even cavalry, to be concealed. Two squadrons of our cavalry commenced a fire in order to harass them, and draw them onto the middle of the plain-Afterwards, those two squadrons wheeling about, laid open the Russian cavalry to the fire of our artillery, which was posted on a little elevation and concealed by brushwood. This fire of our artillery was effective. The enemy's cavalry began to waver. General Szywanowski observing this, ordered an immediate attack by our whole cavalry, consisting of twelve squadrons. This attack was made with great impetuosity. Sixteen hussars, with two officers, were taken prisoners, and forty or fifty were left, killed or wounded, on the field. After this, the corps recommenced its march to Worna, leaving two battalions of the 7th Infantry Regiment, as a rearguard, in the forests which border on that road.

The successes which we had thus obtained in our three first positions were over the advanced guard of the enemy; but in the fourth position, arranged by the brave and skillful Colonel Koss, and in which our successes were even greater, we had to encounter the whole body of the Russian forces in Lithuania, which, according to some of our pris-oners, were to be estimated at 18,000, and by others at 25,000 men, with 36 pieces of artillery, under the command of the several Russian generals, Kreutz, Tolstoy, Szyrman, Delinghausen, and Sacken. The town of Worna is surrounded by two large lakes, in such a manner that the only communication with that town to the west is by a neck of land, separating the extremities of those two lakes. The town is situated upon an elevated ground, which overlooks the whole vicinity. On our left wing was a forest that reached one of the lakes. This forest was occupied by two battalions of infantry. Our right wing leaned upon the other lake. All our artillery remained in the centre, and occupied the heights near Worna.

When our arrangements were completed, we heard the fire of the two battalions composing our rearguard, who were engaged, while withdrawing, with the Russian infantry. Strong columns of the enemy's infantry, which were following these battalions, began to debouch from the forest, and to deploy upon the plains before Worna. Those col-umns were followed by the enemy's artillery, 12 pieces of which took post on the side of the road, and immediately opened a fire upon our centre. At the same time, a warm fire of skirmishers was commenced on each side. Our artillery, which was very advantageously placed, without replying to that of the enemy, opened a fire upon the col-umns of the enemy's infantry. Before night, the whole Russian forces had deployed upon the plain, and a powerful attack on their side was expected; but instead of this we were astonished to find that their fire began to slacken, perhaps owing to a heavy rain, which had just begun to fall. Our commander, with the view to profit by this rain and the approach of darkness, after an interval of not more than ten minutes, ordered the two battalions which remained in the forests on our left, to make a sudden charge with the bayonet upon the right wing of the enemy. These battalions, under the command of the brave Colonel Michalowski, performed prodigies of valor in this charge, and bore down all before them. Colonel Koss at the same time taking the command of the cavalry, and addressing a few exciting words to them, led them upon the centre of the enemy at the charge. The consternation of the Russians was extreme. A great part of their cavalry was found dismounted, for they had not the least expectation of an attack; their artillery fled, and abandoned their cannon; the utmost disorder followed, and a vast number of the enemy fell upon the field. According to the testimony of prisoners, the consternation was at such a height that we might have put their whole corps to rout. Our forces, however, could not follow up these advantages, for the obscurity of the night and our own weakness made it impossible. We were content with having reduced the strength of the enemy by the great losses we had occasioned; and we continued our route towards the seaport of Polonga, agreeably to our orders, where we were looking for reinforcements, and where our generals believed that the corps of General Chlapowski would join, and act with us upon some new plan. On the morning of the 12th we arrived at Retov.

The battle of Powenduny and Worna, in which we had beaten the Russians in four positions, and which cost the enemy more than a thousand men, including prisoners and wounded, renewed our hopes. We were expecting, as we have said, new accessions of strength at Polonga; and we were not without hope that our other corps under Dembinski and Chlapowski, who could not have been far distant, finding that we had been thus engaged and so successfully with the whole force of the enemy, would change their plan of operations, and attack him in his rear or his flank. To this end, in fact, on the very morning of that battle, after our first successes, we sent two officers in the direction of Deiribinski and Chlapowski, to apprize them of the circumstances in which we were placed, and especially to inform them of the important fact that the whole force of the enemy was before us. With these hopes awakened in our minds, our disappointment may be imagined on learning, at Retov, that the corps of General Chlapowski had passed through that place on the day before, in a tepid march towards the Prussian frontier. During the battle of Powenduny, therefore, the corps of General Chlapowski was at the distance of only four miles from us. He heard our fire during the whole day, but instead of marching to our support, which, as we afterwards learnt, his officers and even his soldiers loudly called upon him to do, he declined doing it, answering their appeals in the following terms: "What do you ask of me, gentlemen? I can assure you that the corps of General Rohland, on whom the whole force of the enemy has fallen, is destroyed. The baggage of his officers had passed through Retow.[81] All is lost, and, surrounded as we are on all sides by the enemy, it only remains for us to seek at once the frontiers of Prussia, and to throw ourselves upon the protection of that power."

Generals Rohland and Szymanowski, on receiving the unwelcome intelligence of the course which General Chlapowski had adopted, concluded to change their plan of operations, and instead of going to Polonga, to follow the march of General Chlapowski, to endeavor to join him as soon as possible, and by exhibiting to him the unimpaired strength of our corps, which he had believed to be annihilated, to induce him to abandon the project of crossing the Prussian frontier, and to make some further attempts in junction with us.

With this view, after resting a few hours at Retov, we left, by a forced march, for Gorzdy, a small town near the Prussian frontier, at which we hoped to overtake the corps of General Chlapowski, and at which we arrived on the next day (13th) at noon. But it was already too late. The greater part of the corps of Chlapowski and Gielgud had passed the frontier at the village of Czarna, about a half league from the former place, and an inconsiderable part only of the corps, which had not yet passed over, could unite with us. The other part was already advanced a considerable distance within the Prussian territory, and having been disarmed, were placed under a guard of Prussian sentinels.

Such was the end of the corps of Generals Chlapowski and Gielgud, composed of our best troops, and which had performed such feats of valor in so many battles. Those brave soldiers were led, against their will, into the territory of a foreign nation, to seek a protection of which they themselves had not even dreamed.

This step, which every historian of our revolution will record with horror, when it was seen how totally without justification it was, awakened the disgust and indignation of all. The part of the corps of General Chlapowski which was already in the Prussian territory, when they saw the corps of General Rohland, which they had been made to believe was destroyed, continuing its march in an entire state, and even with nearly 200 Russian prisoners in its train, and hearing too the animating shouts which naturally burst from their comrades, as they came in view of them, and who called on them to rejoin them, fell into a state of the utmost exasperation. A great number rushed forward, and, breaking through the PRussian Guard, unarmed as they were, reached our side of the frontier. The brave commander of the light artillery, who was already on the Prussian territory with his battery, profiting by the circumstance that his horses were not yet unharnessed, returned, and joined our corps, with five pieces of cannon. Both officers and soldiers surrounded General Gielgud, and loudly demanded some explanation of this state of things. That general betrayed the utmost confusion, and seemed wholly at a loss to satisfy these demands; his manner, indeed, was such as to encourage the suspicions of treason, which his previous conduct had but too well justified. At this moment, one of his officers, in a frenzy of patriotic indignation, advanced towards him, drew a pistol from his side, and exclaiming, "This is the reward of a traitor," shot him through the heart. After this sad event, General Chlapowski was sought after and the same fate would have probably awaited him, had he not succeeded in concealing himself. A scene of great confusion then took place throughout the corps. General Rohland and the other officers exerted themselves to tranquillize the soldiers, reminding them that our situation was critical, and that the Russians were pressing upon us. These appeals had the effect of restoring quiet; and at about 4 o'clock the corps of General Rohland, joined by a part of that of Chlapowski, took up the march in the direction of Yurburg, in order to pass the Niemen there, and attempt to reach Poland. At night, we arrived at Wierzbna. After having marched four miles from the spot where the Prussian frontier was passed by General Chlapowski, we were met by an aide-de-camp of General Kreutz, sent with a flag of truce, and bearing a letter to General Rohland, which was read aloud, containing propo-sitions to surrender, and setting forth the circumstances under which we were placed. In declining the proposition, General Rohland, among other expressions, used the following: "The strength of your forces is well known to us; we have seen them at Powenduny and Worna. If Providence protected us there, it will still protect us; and turning towards the officers of his suite, he added, "Gentlemen, look on my grey hairs; I they have become blanched in a service of thirty years under the Polish eagles, and during that whole period I have endeavored to keep the path of honor and duty. Permit me in my old age to continue in that path." The answer having been communicated to the corps, the cry of "Long life to Rohland," burst forth on every side. The aide-de-camp departed, and we continued our route.

Having passed the night at Wierzbna, we arrived on the noon of the next day (the 14th), at Nowe-Miasto, at which place we put to flight a squadron of Russian cavalry posted there. Before reaching that town, and at the distance of about a half league from it, our cavalry had a small skirmish with four squadrons of the Russian light cavalry. This cavalry fell upon a small detachment of our sappers, which had been detailed for the object of destroying a bridge upon a branch of the main road, at the distance of about a mile from it. The sappers, in withdrawing, kept up a fire, and thus drew the enemy on, till our cavalry falling upon them, dispersed them, causing a considerable loss, and taking several prisoners.[82]

On arriving at Nowe-Miasto, our commander sent a reconnoitering party in the direction of Yurburg, in order to ascertain if any of the enemy's forces were there, and considering the strong position of Nowe-Miasto, he decided to remain there, and to await the result of this reconnaissance. Our forces were placed in order of battle, to await the enemy, in case he should choose to make an attack. Remaining for two hours in this position, we were astonished that the enemy did not show himself; and a platoon of cavalry, sent in the direction of the enemy to observe him, returned with the intelligence that he was *encamped* at the distance of two miles from us.

Four hours had thus passed, when the arrival of a Prussian officer upon the frontier was announced, who requested an interview with our general. General Rohland, accompanied with a party of officers, went to receive him. The Prussian officer was an aide-de-camp of the commandant general of the forces on this part of the frontier, (General Kraft, we believe). The officer, after some complimentary language, presented a letter from his commander, which was filled with expressions of respect and goodwill, and in which it was proposed that, in consideration of our position, surrounded as we were by a force so much superior to our own, and in a state of destitution in respect to arms and ammunition, we should accept the offer which the PRussian Government had authorized him to make, in order to save the useless effusion of the "blood of so many brave men, and throw ourselves upon the protection of its territory, where we would be convinced of the cordial disposition of that government towards us, - adding, that our sojourn there would be short, and that we should soon be allowed to return to our firesides, as was the case with the Russian soldiers who had sought the same protection. We have already mentioned that several detachments of Russian soldiers, who had before sought the protection of Prussia, had been allowed to return with their arms and ammunition. Our generals, on being thus apprized of the liberal intentions of the PRussian Government, which were confirmed by the personal representations of the officer who brought the letter, reflecting on the deplorable state of our soldiers, fatigued and weakened by so many forced marches; the greater part of the infantry being without covering to their feet, which were lacerated with wounds; the greater part of the cavalry, almost without horses (for their animals were so broken down, and chafed by unremitted use, as to be unfit for service); both artillery and infantry nearly destitute of ammunition, a great quantity of which had been thrown into the river by the orders of Generals Gielgud and Chlapowski, on passing the frontier;—considering also the assurance which had been made that we could return to our country, and hoping therefore to be able to renew their services to that country at some more favorable period, presented these circumstances to the whole corps, and solicited the opinion of the soldiers upon the question of acceding to the propositions of the PRussian Government. The soldiers,

251

manifesting their entire confidence in the judgment and the honor of their officers, signified their assent to the acceptance of the propositions, influenced strongly by the assurance of being allowed to return to their country. In consequence of this assent, a protocol was prepared that night, and signed by our generals, and by several Prussian officers on the other part, who came over for that object. On the morning of the next day, we passed the frontier and marched into the Prussian territory, and by that act the operations of the Lithuanian Corps were ended.

NOTES

81. It might have been the case that a few wagons with some of the baggage of the corps, were sent in advance in the direction of Pologna, merely as a precautionary arrangement.

82. In this affair Major, the Prince Giedrovc distinguished himself at the head of his regiment, the 6th Chasseurs, and killed with his own hand the commander of the enemy's cavalry, an officer of the rank of general.

CHAPTER XXV.

Effect of the news of the Lithuanian disasters on the minds of the people. - Distrust of the National Government - The Russian army resumes the offensive under General Paskewicz - He decides to pass the Vistula. - Examination of the merits of this plan. - Plan of General Skrzynecki to act on the different detached corps of the enemy. - Advantages of General Chrzanowski over the corps of Rudiger. - The Russian forces execute the passage of the Vistula. - General Skrzynecki crosses the Vistula at Warsaw to operate against the enemy on the left bank. - An inquiry into the conduct of General Skrzynecki, and the appointment of a Council of War is demanded by the nation. - Arrival of the corps of General Dembinski at Warsaw.

WHILE the nation was afflicted by the treasons at Warsaw, their hopes had been still kept alive by looking towards Lithuania. What, then, can express the disheartening effect produced by the intelligence that the Lithuanian Corps existed no longer; - that that pillar, so essential to the support of the fabric we had been rearing, had fallen; and that this disaster had been brought on by the gross negligence, if not the treason, of those to whom that all-important expedition had been entrusted? They felt that this was an almost mortal blow. They saw a horrible future opening upon them, prepared by parricidal hands. After such renewed outrages, the people fell into the greatest exasperation. That people, whose confidence had been so basely abused, whose holiest purposes had been so shamelessly sported with, seemed at last to have changed their nature. So often betrayed, they lost confidence in all, and seemed to see in everyone a traitor. If, in the frenzy of indignation, which such an experience had justified, they allowed themselves to be carried away by their feelings, and to be guilty of acts of severity, it can scarcely be wondered at.

Immediately after the arrival of the sad news from Lithuania, the nation demanded explanations of the Generalissimo. They demanded to know how he could have given the command of so important an expedition to a man like Gielgud, one who had never been esteemed by the nation or the army, and who had not even the reputation of a general of talent. How could an expedition which demanded the very highest talents, and the most undoubted patriotism, have been confided to a man like him? With him had been associated General Chlapowski, who was the brother-in-law of the Grand Duke Constantine. That circumstance alone, they justly considered, should have been enough to suggest suspicion, and to have at least indicated the expediency of keeping him near the eye of the Commander-in-Chief, and subject to his constant observation. Such were the complaints of the people, and they went to the heart of the Commander-in-Chief, and the president of the National Government; for they were conscious, but too late, of their justice.[83] The Russian army, the command of which, on the death of General Diebitsch, was taken by General Count Paskewicz, and the main body of which remained in a state of inaction at Ostrolenka, having no longer any apprehensions from Lithuania, could now act with freedom, and the offensive was recommenced under the command of its new chief, who decided to pass the Vistula, and to act upon the left bank.

I may be allowed to detain the attention of the reader a moment upon this passage of the Vistula by Paskewicz, a maneuver of which so much boast has been made, and to consider whether it is really to be regarded as a great and bold step, or one of necessity. What was the state of the Russian army after the battle of Ostrolenka? A month had passed, and that army had not made a single movement, but was kept there merely to be fed by Prussia. Was not this inactivity an infallible evidence of weakness? Does it not show that, alarmed by the prospects in Lithuania, it was in a state of hesitation, not daring to advance into the kingdom, and holding itself in readiness to evacuate it on an occasion of necessity, which indeed seemed near at hand? In this period of hesitation, the new general arrives from the regions of the Caucasus. He must do something. The question presents itself to him, - what course is best to be taken? His army, now reinforced by the corps which had been in Lithuania, amounted to perhaps near one hundred and fifty thousand men. Although this force was considerable, yet to attack the fortifications of Praga, which, as is known to the reader, had been augmented, and which the Russian army in their primitive and unimpaired strength had never had the temerity to attack, was out of the question. What other course could he take, unless he could submit to continue in this state of inactivity, but to pass the Vistula, and under the assistance of Prussia, to make his attempts against Warsaw on the other side, a step, however, which he never would have dared to have taken without that assistance? This is the natural explanation of that boasted plan, in which we can see nothing but an almost necessary movement, encouraged by a reliance on Prussia.

In the first days of the month of June the Russian army began to approach the Vistula, in order to execute the passage. Their march was in three principal columns, and was arranged in the following manner: General Witt, commanding the columns of the left wing, took the direction of Sochoczyn. The centre, under marshal Paskewicz, left for Sonk and Luberacz, passing the River Wkra at Maluszyn. The column of the right, consisting of the Imperial Guard, under the command of the grand duke Michael, marched from Makov, by Ciechanow and Racionz. General Pahlen commanded the advanced guard. A considerable train of ammunition, with provisions for twenty days, and a park of artillery of reserve, formed the fourth column, and followed the Imperial Guard. Detached posts towards Modlin and Serock, covered this march on the left. One regiment of dragoons remained at Pultusk. This combined force consisted of 80,000 men and three hundred pieces of cannon. Besides these forces, there were in the kingdom, the corps of General Rudiger at Klutzy, and that of General Rott at Zamosc. Those two corps might now number about 20,000 men, and some thirty pieces of cannon. Opposed to these forces, we had an army of 40,000 men, a hundred and twenty pieces of cannon, not counting the national guard of Warsaw, and the garrisons of the two fortresses of Modlin and Zamosc.

The plan of our Generalissimo was to throw himself upon the detached corps of the enemy, under Rott and Rudiger, and afterwards to act upon his main body. For this end an attack was ordered upon the corps of Rudiger, which was beaten in the environs of Minsk by the corps of General Chrzanowski, in successive actions, on the 14th, 15th, and 16th of July. A third part of his corps being destroyed, a thousand prisoners, four pieces of cannon and all his baggage taken, he was forced to retire behind Kaluszyn. After these new advantages, the Commander-in-Chief prepared to act upon the rear of the Russian main army, and to attack them while engaged in the passage of the Vistula, which he supposed they would attempt either at Plock, or between Plock and Modlin. But as he was afterwards apprized that the Russians were to attempt the passage at a much more distant point from Warsaw, and beyond his reach while on the right bank, be thought it most expedient to pass the Vistula at Warsaw, and to operate against the enemy on the other side. The Russian army thus passed the Vistula without being intercepted, between the 12th and the 20th of July. Having reached the left bank, the enemy took the direction of Lowicz, where, on the 27th, the headquarters of General Paskewicz were established, and whither our army marched to meet him.

At this important moment, when the operations of the enemy had taken a new face, and seemed, in the eyes of the people, by his near approach to Warsaw, to menace the utmost danger – made more threatening in their imaginations by the recent discovery of the conspiracy of Jankowski and the news of the misfortunes in Lithuania;—at this anxious moment, the nation demanded a council of war, and called on the National Government to make an inquisition into the conduct of the Commander-in-Chief, to demand of him full explanations of his purposes, and a submission of all his plans of operation to the examination of such a council. Such a council of war was instituted by the government and directed to be attached to the person of the general, and to be initiated into all his designs, in order to be enabled to tranquillize and re-assure the minds of the nation, which had so naturally become distrustful and suspicious, after the events which had taken place.

The council having been organized, and having taken an oath of secrecy, General Skrzynecki laid before them all the plans of operation that he had hitherto followed, as well as those which he had in contemplation, and gave a full exposition of the reasons for each. This council then published to the nation an address, announcing their entire confidence in the patriotic intentions of the Commander-in-Chief, and assuring them that the crisis was by no means as dangerous as they apprehended. By these proceedings, the minds of the people were much tranquillized, and this tranquility was increased by the arrival of the corps of General Dembinski from Lithuania after its glorious retreat; which arrival not only cheered them by the addition which it brought to our forces, but by the more encouraging accounts than had before been received, which it gave of the state of Lithuania, authorizing some hope of a renewal of the insurrection in that province at a more propitious hour.

NOTES

83. A few details of the history of the two generals who were the cause of these fatal disasters, may gratify the curiosity of the reader. General Gielgud was born in Lithuania, at Gielgudiski, (the place at which he crossed the Niemen in 1831). Passing over his early life, which presents nothing noticeable, he commenced his military career in 1812, when Napoleon entered Lithuania. In a moment of patriotic fervor, he formed a small detachment at his own expense, and joined the ranks of the supposed deliverer of Poland; and this perhaps was the most praiseworthy act of his life. During the campaigns of 1812, 13, and 14, he was in no way distinguished either for good or bad conduct. At the end of the Russian campaign, in 1815, ha was made Colonel. As during that year, Poland came under the Russian Government, our army was subjected to a change of organization, and as many officers of high rank, who were in independent circumstances, gave up their commands, Gielgud then obtained the rank of general, at about the age of thirty. This rapid advancement, as was natural to a man of weak character, inspired him with an extreme of arrogance and pretension; qualities which were encouraged in his intercourse with the Russian generals, with whom he was much associated. It was this arrogance which uniformly lost him the esteem of those under his command.

When the revolution broke out, General Gielgud was at the town of Radom, and his life was in great danger from the suspicions of which he was naturally the object, but he was protected by some of the patriots, on the assurances which he gave of his patriotic dispositions. Still, however, the military demanded his removal from his post, and, in fact, for some weeks he was without command. The Dictator, Chlopicki, whose modes of action were, as the reader knows, too often inexplicable, restored him to his command, persuading himself that he was one of the best of patriots, and that if his exterior was offensive, he was right at heart. In the war, having first commanded a brigade, and afterwards a division, - while he was attached to the Grand Army, his conduct was not marked by any very great faults; indeed, in the battle of Minsk he performed his part well. It was such occasional exhibitions of good conduct which kept him in some consideration.

After having taken command of the corps of Lithuania, and when he was removed from the observation of the army, he exhibited himself in his true character. He was giddy with the distinction, and feeling himself the absolute master of his own conduct, he gave himself up to all the suggestions of his vanity.

His first act of folly was to surround himself with a numerous suite (it was in number four times that of the Commander-in-Chief), in 'which suite those individuals were held in greatest esteem, who were most fertile in resources for amusement. It was to this love of personal gratification that we can attribute those delays which were sacrificing the cause of the country. At Gielgudiski the general gave a party to his officers; and it is not impossible that it was a motive of mere personal ostentation which induced him to make the passage of the Niemen, at that place, by which two days march were given to the retreating enemy, time was allowed him to concentrate his forces in Wilna, and that capital was lost to us!

This general was never seen to share the privations, fatigues, and exposure of his subalterns. In his personal deportment, he neglected the true means of gaining the confidence and attachment of his troops. On the eve of a battle, in moments of danger and anxiety, it is cheering to the soldier to see the face of his commander, and to hear from him a few words of encouragement. These are apparent trifles, but they are in reality of most serious consequence. They are the secret keys by which everything can be obtained from the soldier. The personal attachment of the soldier to his commander is worth more than the finest com-binations in strategy and tactics. The commander, who succeeds in gaining the affection of the soldier, inspires him with a new impulse for exertion. To his other motives is added the dread of forfeiting the confidence and esteem of a friend; and perhaps, with the mass of an army, such a motive would yield to no other in efficiency. To the modes of conduct which would have secured this result, General Gielgud was an entire stranger. Instead of freely approaching the soldier and endeavoring to gain his attachment, he treated him with uniform coldness and reserve. It is on the whole a matter of just surprise, that a man with such glaring faults of character should have been appointed to so responsible a trust.

General Chlapowski commenced his military career also in 1812, In the Russian war he advanced to the rank of officer and was made aide-de-camp of Prince Poniatowski. While in this situation he advanced to the rank of a staff officer, in which rank he left the army in 1815, and retired to his estates in the Grand Duchy of Pozen, where he married the sister of the Princess of Lowicz, the wife of the Grand Duke Constantine. The entrance of this general into the revolutionary ranks excited considerable surprise. But as he joined himself to the squadrons of Pozen, which were formed of the bravest and most patriotic materials, there was no distrust felt of him. His successes in traversing the Department of Bialostok, entitled him to the highest praise. It was this fine expedition which gained him the confidence of the Lithuanian Corps, and after the battle of Wilna, they were unanimous in inviting him to take the chief command. The nominal command, as we have related, he declined, but took a post which gave him the superintendence of all the operations. While he was thus in the direction of affairs, the greatest faults, as we have seen, were committed, for which no adequate explanation can be given. We will recapitulate some of them. - They were, 1. The sending of the sappers to build the bridge over the Niemen. 2. The ill-arranged attack on Schavla. 3. His not succoring General Rohland in the combat of Powenduny. 4. The inexplicable secrecy which he kept upon his intention of passing the Prussian frontier; having left Kurszany for that object, whilst all his officers were given to understand that the separation of the corps at that place was with the view of marching to act in the environs of Kowno. These are points upon which this officer has yet to answer at the bar of his country. Chlapowski was a more dangerous person even than Gielgud, for Gielgud was a man of such undisguised arrogance, that he repelled the confidence of others; but Chlapowski, with all the faults of Gielgud, had an exterior of dissimulation which won insensibly upon those who had not thoroughly studied his character. But none who had observed and known him well, could ever yield him their esteem.

CHAPTER XXVI.

Operation of General Dembinski's corps. - He traverses the country between Schavla and the Niemen without being observed by the enemy. - Attacks and disperses a brigade of Russian infantry. - Passes the Niemen and throws himself into the forest of Bialostok. - After leaving that forest, is joined by the corps of General Rozychi. - Reaches Warsaw. - His reception at Warsaw. - View of the exposed situation of Paskewicz after his passage of the Vistula. - Examination of the plan of operations of the Polish commander. - Morbid state of the public mind at Warsaw. - Skrzynecki and Czartoriski deprived of their trust. - Capture of the city. - Documents showing the influence exercised by the cabinets in discouraging active operations. - Conclusion.

THE corps of General Dembinski had been more fortunate than those of Chlapowski and Rohland. That general, quitting Kurszany on the 9th of July, returned, in obedience to the orders which we have detailed, by means of the forests, to the environs of Schavla, leaving the enemy upon the right, and without being observed by him; having advanced with his whole force in the direction of Worna, under the belief that our undivided forces were in that position. This corps traversed the country between Schavla and Rosseyny, and arrived during the night of the 15th at Janow, where they dispersed a squadron of the enemy's cavalry and took fifty prisoners, and passed there the Wilyia River without interruption. From thence they left for the environs of Kowno, where, not far from Rumszyski, on the 16th, they met a brigade of Russian infantry, which was on the march from Wilna to the frontier of Poland.

General Dembinski attacked this brigade with such impetuosity, that they were thrown into the greatest consternation. Two cannons and several prisoners were taken. The great forests, by which the Russians were able to effect their escape, alone saved this brigade from entire destruction. Having thus opened their road, they took the direction of the town of Lida, passing the Niemen not far from that place. Afterwards they threw themselves into the forests of Bialostok, and in these forests the corps was reinforced by a considerable number of Lithuanian insurgent cavalry, which had been acting with great advantages over the enemy, by cutting off his transports of ammunition and other modes of harassing him, during the whole of our campaign. This force was under the command of Colonel B***. General Dembinski quitted the forests in the environs of Orla, and leaving the town of Bielsk on his right, passed through the town of Bocki, near which he surprised and dis-persed a Cossack regiment, and took several prisoners, among them a number of officers. In the environs of Siemiatycze, where the corps arrived on the 20th of June, they were arrested by the sudden appearance of a large body of troops. General Dembinski halted and placed his forces in order of battle, sending his flankers in advance. On the other side the same movement was made. The flanking parties of the opposite forces approached each other, but. what was the astonishment of the two corps at seeing the tirailleurs, in place of firing upon each other, rushing into each other's arms, and rending the air with patriotic exclamations. The corps which was thus met by that of General Dembinski, was the corps of General Rozychi, which had been sent from our Grand Army to reinforce the corps of General Gielgud. The reader will now call to mind the plan of operations proposed by Colonel Valentin after the battle of Wilna; and the arrival of this reinforcement at the very spot which was to have been the point of concentration aggravates the regret that his plans were not adopted. Nothing could exceed the satisfaction of the two corps at thus meeting. General Rozychi, learning the disastrous circumstances which had occurred, changed this plan of operation, and decided to unite himself with the corps of General Dembinski, and to return with it to the Grand Army. The junction of these two corps had scarcely taken place, when a cloud of dust, in the direction of Bielsk, announced the march of another body of troops. A small reconnaissance, sent in that direction, returned with the intelligence that it was the Russian corps under Golowkin. Our generals, considering all circumstances, determined not to engage with them, and continued their march towards Poland, passing at night the Bug River. They then took the direction of Wengrow and Kaluszyn, and by that route arrived at Warsaw, toward the end of the month of July.

The corps of General Dembinski, which had traversed more than four hundred miles in about twenty days from its departure from Kurszany, in the midst of detachments of the enemy, was received by the nation with the greatest enthusiasm. The president of the Senate, Prince Adam Czartoriski, the Generalissimo Skrzynecki, with all the officers of the government, followed by an immense body of citizens, met him at the distance of a half league from the city; and he was greeted with an address expressive of the thanks of the nation for his courageous and persevering exertions. It ended in the following terms: "Dear General, and brethren-in-arms, you will be a living reproach to those who, forgetting their sacred duties, have, by their misconduct, forced their countrymen to lay down their arms, and seek the protection of another nation."

To commemorate the brave exertions of this corps, and to transmit these events to posterity, the address above referred to was ordered to be enregistered in the volumes of the public laws. A printed copy was also given to each soldier of the corps. At the same time a commission was appointed to inquire into the conduct of Generals Gielgud and Chlapowski.

When we consider the manner in which the Russian army, after their passage of the Vistula, passed the interval between the 27th of July (the day of their arrival at Lowicz) and the 15th of August, we shall be at a loss to account for their inaction. If General Paskewicz was in a condition to take Warsaw, he could gain nothing by this repose. Nay, every moment of delay might increase the difficulties he would have to overcome. Why then all this delay? What could have prevented us from reinforcing our ranks, strengthening the fortifications of Warsaw, and even sending another corps, however small, into Lithuania, to support a new insurrection? Such a corps could have easily made its way even in the midst of the Russian detached corps remaining on the other side of the Vistula, and indeed those corps, so imprudently left there, could have been beaten in detail by our forces. If these circumstances are well considered, the reader will be satisfied that this maneuver of passing the Vistula, though in appearance so threatening to us, was in reality a most imprudent step on the enemy's part, and exposed him to the most imminent danger. Many detailed considerations might be given upon this point, but as they would occupy much space, and would withdraw us too far from the purpose of this narrative, we must leave them to abler pens. The general view, however, which we have taken of the position of the enemy, will be enough to awaken the astonishment of the reader that the event of the contest should have arrived so suddenly and so fatally to us. We are, therefore, led to present some reflections upon what seems to us to have been the true causes of the disastrous issue of the struggle.

We may, in the first place, be permitted to remark that the removal of our army from Warsaw to Lowicz to meet the enemy there, does not appear to have been a fortunate disposition. By it, some twenty days were spent in indecisive maneuvers against a superior force. If, during that interval, in place of marching to meet the enemy, the army had been concentrated in the environs of Warsaw, and employed in constructing fortifica-tions upon the great roads leading to Warsaw, from Blonia, Nadarzyn, Piaseczna, and Kalwaryia, as a first line of defense, and in strengthening the great fortifications of Warsaw: then, leaving half of our force to defend these fortifications, we might have crossed the Vistula with the other half, and acted upon all the detached corps of the enemy on the right bank, and have, besides, intercepted all the reinforcements for the main army of Paskewicz. Our communications, also, with the provinces, being thus opened, and their territory freed from the presence of the enemy, we should have again been enabled to avail ourselves of their co-operation. I cannot but think that if such a plan of operation had been adopted, for which, in fact, there was ample time in the interval above named, an altogether different turn would have been given to our affairs.

If the objection should be made that the delay which actually occurred could not have been reasonably anticipated, and that Paskewicz might have immediately advanced to the attack of Warsaw, still, without entering for the present into more detailed considerations in support of my opinion, it will be enough to answer, that if twenty-four hours merely were to be had, those twenty-four hours should have been employed in fortification rather than maneuvering, for it was not at Lowicz, but under the walls of Warsaw, that the enemy were to be fought. As it was at Warsaw, then that the decisive encounter must inevitably have taken place, would it not have been the most judicious course, to have confined our operations on the left bank of the Vistula, to the strengthening of the defenses of Warsaw; to have in fact adopted in regard to the enemy, who had now transferred his strength to the left bank of the Vistula, the same course of operations which we had hitherto pursued against him while he was in occupation of the right; in short, to have made of Warsaw another Praga. Our course of operations should in fact have been just reversed, to correspond with the change which the enemy's passage of the Vistula had made in our relative positions. While he was on the right bank, the region on the left of the river was open to us, and there were our resources; but now that he was acting with his main army on the left bank, it should have been our aim, by annihilating his detached corps, to have opened to our operations the whole region of the right, which was far more extensive than the other, and which, besides, had the advantage to us of being contiguous to the insurrectionary provinces. In case of an attack on Warsaw, which of course could not be an affair of a few days only, that part of our forces operating on the right bank could be withdrawn in ample season to present our whole strength to the enemy in its defense.

Since I have allowed myself to make the above remarks in regard to the plans of the Commander-in-Chief, I must also be permitted to add that, at that period of inquietude and distrust, the presence of the Commander-in-Chief and of the President of the National Government, at Warsaw, was of the utmost importance. That presence was continually needed to act on the minds of the people, to preserve union and tranquility, and to discover and bring to exemplary punishment the traitors who had been plotting the ruin of their country; in short, to encourage the patriotic and to alarm the treacherous. If those two individuals so deservedly beloved and honored by the nation had been present, we doubt whether those melancholy scenes at Warsaw, on the 14th, 15th, and 16th of August, when some forty persons who were under conviction of treason, perished by the hands of the people, would ever have taken place. Revolting as those scenes were, we must yet consider whether the circumstances of the moment will not afford some palliation for them. Deserted by those who had been the objects of their profoundest attachment and confidence, haunted by the recollections of' the terrible disasters which had been incurred, and which they could attribute to nothing short of treason, seeing twenty days again sacri-ficed, during which the Russian corps from Lithuania were permitted to pass the Vistula (that of Kreutz at Plock, and that of Rudiger at Pulawa) and join their main army; in fine, seeing this immense Russian force approaching the capital, from which perhaps they were expecting a repetition of all the atrocities of Suvarov, remembering the thousands of victims which these traitors had already sacrificed, and reflecting on the thousands whom they had plotted to sacrifice; can it be wondered that, in those moments of despair, that people should have yielded to their impulses of indignation and have chosen rather to sacrifice at once those convicted traitors, than permit them to live, and perhaps be the instruments of the vengeance of the conqueror. Abandoned thus by those who should have been near to tranquillize them, the people took that justice into their own hands which the government had neglected to execute, and with their suspicions operated upon by this accumulation of disasters, they went to the degree of demanding the removal from their posts of Prince Czartoriski and the Commander-in-Chief. Such are, I think, the true explanations of those acts, so serious in their consequences, and which have created so much surprise. The removal of Skrzynecki from the chief command was certainly one of the most deplorable results of this disordered state of the minds of the people; for who could so well meet the exigencies of the time as he, familiar with every detail, engaged in the midst of events, and possessing the entire confidence of the army? It was in this period of distrust and suspicion that the Russian army, which seemed to have been waiting only for such a moment, received the intelligence from some traitors, yet undiscovered, within the walls of Warsaw, that the time had arrived for their attack. It was undoubtedly directed by such intelligence, that they made their attack on Warsaw, at the moment when the greater part of our army had been sent by its new commander, Prondzynski, to act on the right bank of the Vistula against the corps of Golowkin, which was menacing Praga. The city thus defended by the National Guard and a small part of the army alone, and distracted by the divisions which Russian intrigues had fomented, fell, after a bloody defense,[84] and the fate of Poland was decided.

We have stated our belief that the fatal events which hastened the catastrophe might have been prevented by the mere presence, at the capital, of the heads of the army and the National Government, at those trying moments which brought on that disordered state of the public mind. Of this error, we cannot readily acquit them, upright and patriotic as we know their intentions to have been. But upon the other point—that mysterious inaction of our forces, for so considerable a period, there is an important light thrown, in the following extracts from the correspondence of the Prince Czartoriski with the French Minister of the Exterior, read in the Chamber of Deputies, on the 19th of September, by the venerable General Lafayette, and in the extracts from his remarks, and those of General Lamarque, made on that occasion, and which have probably before met the eye of the reader.

EXTRACT PROM THE LETTER OF PRINCE CZARTORYSKI.

"But we relied upon the magnanimity and the wisdom of the cabinets; trusting to them, we have not availed ourselves of all the resources which were at our command, both exterior and interior. To secure the approbation of the cabinets, to deserve their confidence, and to obtain their support, we have never departed from the strictest moderation; by which moderation, indeed, we have paralyzed many of the efforts which might have saved us in those latter days. But for the promises of the cabinets, *we should have been able to strike a blow, which perhaps would have been decisive.* We thought that it was necessary to temporize, to leave nothing to chance - and we have at last seen the certainty, at the present moment, that there is nothing but chance that can save us."

General Lafayette: "If it be said that the promises here referred to might have been only an affair of the gazettes, - answer, that I have demanded explanations of the Polish legation, and here is the reply which I have obtained:

"In answer to the letter which we have received from you, General, we hasten to assure you -

"1. That it was the Minister of Foreign Affairs who engaged us on the 7th of July, to send a messenger to Warsaw, whose traveling expenses were advanced by the Minister: that the object of this messenger was, as his Excellency the Count Sebastiani told us, to induce our government to wait two months longer, for that was the time necessary for the negotiations.

"2. That the circular of our Minister of Foreign Affairs, dated the 15th of August, signed by the Minister ad interim, Audne Horodyski, and also another circular of the

24th of the same month, signed by the new Minister of Foreign Affairs, Theodore Morawski, came to our hands by the post of the 14th current; that they are the same circulars which we at first officially communicated to the Count Sebastiani, on the 15th of September, and which we immediately after addressed to the journals, where they appeared on the 17th and 18th, and that those two circulars in fact explain the effect which the mission of the above envoy produced at Warsaw.

"GEN. KNIAZEWIECZ—L: PLATER."

Paris, the 20th November, 1831.

Gen. Lamarque: "Poland! Can it be true that this heroic nation, who offered her bosom to the lance of the Tartars only to serve as a buckler for us, is to fall because she has followed the counsels which France and England have given her. Thus then is to be explained the inaction of her army at the moment when it ought to have taken a decisive step. Thus, is to be explained the irresolution of the Generalissimo, who from the first moment had showed so much audacity and skill. We may now know why he did not profit by the passage of the Vistula, which divided the army of the enemy, to give him battle either on one bank or the other. The Minister rejects with indignation this imputation of complicity. He declares formally that he had made no promise, that he had given no hope, that he had fixed no date. Honorable Poles, whom I have seen this morning, affirm the contrary. Our colleague, M. Lafayette, will give you details, almost official, on this subject."

SESSION OF THE 13th SEPTEMBER.

Gen. Lafayette: "I will ask this, without the least expectation of receiving a reply, but only to render a just homage to the conduct of the Poles, and of their government,—I will ask, if it is true that the Poles were urged by the French Government, by the English ministers, and by the French ambassador at London, to use moderation, and not to risk a battle, because the measures 'which those powers were to take in behalf of Poland would not be delayed but for two months, and that in two months Poland would enter into the great family of nations. - Those two months have expired; and I state this here to render justice to the conduct of the Polish Government, the Polish Army, and its chief, who may have thought that on his giving a general battle, to prevent the passage of the Vistula, they could thwart the good intention of the French and English governments in this respect. I think that this will be considered a fair procedure towards Messieurs the Ministers, to whom the questions shall be addressed on Monday, to apprize them that this is one of those which will be then submitted to them."

These documents will be for the present age and for posterity an explanation of the true causes of the ruin of Poland. She fell not by the enormous forces of her enemy, but by his perfidious intrigues. We cannot accuse France or England, and indeed no Pole does accuse them; for, although we may have some enemies in those countries, yet we cannot conceive of the existence of any causes of hostility towards us, by which those nations can be actuated:[85] They were blinded by the promises of Russia - by the solemn assurances[86] which she gave, that she would soon arrange everything in the most favorable manner for Poland. In this web of intrigue were those cabinets entangled, who would else have followed the common dictates of humanity in succoring Poland. While she was thus deceiving the cabinets, Russia was doing her utmost to sow distrust and disunion among our people. It was her intrigues, through the instrumentality of the traitors whom she had gained for her accomplices, that caused the estrangement of the nation from Skrzynecki, who, having a true Polish heart, had repelled all her vile attempts to shake his integrity, and who, by his talent and energy, had so often defeated and might still defeat the enormous masses which she had sent against us. Those intrigues succeeded, and Russia gained her end in overwhelming Poland with misery; not reflecting that by so doing she was bringing misfortunes upon her own head. Russia, by a liberal concession to Poland of her national rights, could have been truly great. Not to speak of the influence of the Polish institutions upon the happiness of her own people; her true stability and strength could in no way be so well secured as by the independent existence of Poland. They who have labored for our destruction were not then true Russians; they were the enemies of their country and of humanity — heartless calculators, acting with a single view to their own personal aggrandizement — men, in fact, who have no country but self. Equally the enemies of the monarch and of the people, they make the one a tyrant, and sport with the misery of the other.

NOTES

84. As the author was attached to the Lithuanian Corps, and as he was actually in a Prussian prison at the time of the capture of Warsaw, he cannot undertake to give any details upon so important an event with the limited information at present at his command.

85. Appendix No. III, IV.

86. Appendix No. IV.

APPENDIX

No. I.

HISTORICAL VIEW OF LITHUANIA

IF, notwithstanding the many good works recently published upon Poland, the history of that country is still but imperfectly known to the rest of the world it may be said that the history of Lithuania is almost absolutely unknown to the people of the West. It is generally thought that it has always composed an integral part of the Russian Empire, and that it was only occasionally that it has held relations with ancient Poland —a false impression, and one which the public journals have but too frequently assisted in propagating. The truth is, that for 500 years, Lithuania has voluntarily associated herself with the destinies of ancient Poland, and it is only with shame and reluctance that she has borne the Russian yoke. But that which is of great importance at present to consider, is, the ancient sympathy which has constantly united the two people. There is a common spirit of nationality, which, notwithstanding the studiously contrived disintegration of their territory, has always animated the Lithuanians and the Poles; - a most important fact, for it is on this fraternity of feeling and community of opinion between the ancient Polish provinces, that the salvation of modern Poland essentially depends. We will endeavor, by presenting to the reader the following extracts from the work of Leonard Chodzko, to throw some light upon the political history of this interesting portion of the Slavic race.

" For a long time a distinct power, and governed by its Grand Dukes, united for the first time with Poland in the year 1586, and making, in 1569, an integral part of the Republic of Poland, Lithuania, from that epoch, to that of 1795, formed, in the political state, the third province of Poland; being composed of the palatinates of Wilna, of Troki, the duchies of Starostia, and Samogitia, of Nowogrodek, of Brzsclitewski, of Minsk, of Polock, of Witepsk, Mscislaw and of Smolensk. This Grand Duchy was bounded on the north by Courland, Semigallia, Polish Livonia, and the province of Great Nowogorod; on the east by Moscovy; on the south by the Ukraine, Volhynia, and the country of Chelme; on the west, by the Baltic Sea, the duchy of Prussia, and the palatinates of Podlasia and Lublin. Its arms were a cavalier at full speed, with a saber raised over his head. This cavalier of Lithu-ania, joined with the white eagle of Poland, figured inseparably upon the arms of the Republic, upon the national standards, the public edifices and the coins, up to the moment when foreign force and domestic treason struck a liberticide blow at that union which ages had consecrated. In 1813, for a moment, those fraternal arms were united; but separated again, they once

271

more floated upon every banner after the memorable date of the 29th of November. According to ancient traditions, towards the year 900, there landed on the coast of Samogitia, between Memel, Polonga, and Libau, a colony of Italians who introduced into that country a certain degree of civilization, and from thence came that multitude of Latin words which are to be remarked in the Lithuanian language. From these Italian families arose several sovereign dynasties, which governed Lithuania and Samogitia. Of this origin were, without doubt, the Gerules or Hercules, who formerly governed Lithuania. This people is the same which in the fifth century invaded Italy, with Odacre, and returning on their steps, spread themselves upon the shores of the Baltic, which embrace, at the present day, Oriental Prussia, Lithuania, Samogitia, and Courland.

"The Lithuanians, though subjugated first by the Russians, did not fail to make their strength soon felt by their invaders. In the 13th century, when the Tartars ravaged on one side the Russian States, the Lithuanians on the other side took possession of Grodno, Brzesc, and Drohyczyn, and did not stop till they reached the banks of the Prypec and the town of Mozyr. In the north their victorious arms were pushed as far as the Dwina, and the city of Polock. In the year 1220, the Russians, under Mscislaw-Romanowicz, declared war upon Lithuania, but they were beaten near the Tasiolda River, and the Lithuanians augmented their possessions by the occupation of Pinsk and Turow. Ringold was the first who took the title of Grand Duke of Lithuania, in Mindowe or Mendog, having promised the Pope to embrace the Christian religion, was crowned King of Lithuania in 1259, at Nowogrodek; but this did not continue long, for Mindowe, finding himself deceived, returned to paganism, and died in 1263. From 1280 to 1315, the dukes Latuwer and Witenes reigned over this country; but the greatest power of Lithuania dates from the fourteenth century, when Gedymin seized the reins of government. Impatient to crush the Russian power, which had distressed Lithuania, this prince defeated the enemy in 1320, upon the Pirna River, made himself master of Volhynia, of Kiiovie, of Sewerie, of Czerniechovia, and extended his boundaries as far as Putiwel upon the Diesna. In 1340, when Gldymin perished upon the field of battle by the hands of the Teutonic Knights, the Tartaro-Russian power commenced ravaging Polodia, but Olgerd, successor of Gedymin, came to the succor of his nephews, Koryatowicz, who were in possession of that province, defeated the Tzars of the Tartars in a pitched battle, and extended the territory of Lithuania as far as the banks of the Don and the Black Sea. To form an idea of the extent of the Lithuanian provinces, it is sufficient to point out here the partition between the sons of Gedymin: Monwid possessed Kiernow and Slonim; Narymond— Pinsk, Mozyr, and a part of Volhynia; Olgerd—Krewo, the ancient capital of the duchy, and all the country as far as the Berezina; Kieystat— Samogitia, Troki, and Podlachia: Koryat—Nowogrodek and Wolkowysk: Lubar—Wlodgimierz, with the rest of Volhynia: Jawnat—Wilna, Osmiana, Willkomierz, Braslaw. The last succeeded first to his father, but after his death it was Olgerd who took the reins of government.

"Olgerd was the most powerful of the sovereigns of Lithuania. The Republic of Pskov, in 1346, and that of Novogorod, in 1349, acknowledged him for their master. In 1363, the Tartars of Perikop (Crimea) became his vassals. On the east, embracing the cause of the Duke of Tver, he came three times, in 1363, 1370, 1373, to break his lance against the ramparts of the city of Moscow; of that city where at a later day the great generals of Po-land and of Lithuania, and at last, in 1812, the Gallo-Polono-Lithuanian lances were crossed in front of the superb Kremlin! Kiegstut powerfully seconded his brother in his conquests. It was under such auspices that Olgerd, descending to the tomb, left his brilliant inheritance to Jagellon, one of his thirteen sons. Jagellon, who ascended the grand-ducal throne in 1381, ceded it to his cousin Witold, in 1386, when he went to place upon i the crown of the Piasts, to unite his hand to that of Hedwige, and to cement forever the glorious junction of Lithuania and Poland. In 1389, he gave the government of the Duchy of Severie-Novogorodian and the Republic of Novogorod-the-Great to his two brothers, while on the other side, his cousin Witold, being attacked in his new conquests by the Tartars, beat them, chased a part of them beyond the Don, and transported those who fell into his hands into the different countries of Lithuania, where, instead of reducing them to slavery, he gave them possessions, with the liberty of freely exercising their religious rights; he was the descendants of those Tartars who showed themselves such worthy children of their adopted country, at the epoch of the war of independence, in 1794, and in the campaign of 1812. In this manner Witold acquired the possession, not only of the Russian territories, delivered from the yoke of the Tartars by his grandfather and his uncle, but those which were held by the other small Trans-Borysthenian Tzars. Turning then his victorious army to the north, he forced the northern republics, whose fidelity he suspected, to humble themselves before him, and recognize his unqualified supremacy. In fine, Poland and Lithuania arrived, at that epoch, to such a degree of power, that the dukes of Mazovia and Russia, the Tzars of Moscow, Basile, that of Twer Borys, that of Riezan, Olegh, the little Tzars of Perikop and Volga, the Teutonic masters, the Prussians and Livonians, in fine, the Emperor of Germany, Sigismond himself, accompanied by his wife, and several princes, Erik, Kings of Denmark and Sweden, as well as the ambassadors of the Emperor of the East, Paleogogns, presented themselves to Vladislas-Jagellon at Luck, in Votkynia, and held there a general congress in 1428 in which they deliberated upon the war against the Ottomans; and at which the Emperor of Germany attempted in vain, by means of intrigues, to throw some seeds of dissension between Jagallo and Witold. Witold died in 1430. Kasimir the Jagellon, successor of Vladislas, was reigning still with brilliance; when the moment approached, at which from one side the Ottomans began to take possession of the Tavride, while a new Muscovite power, subjugating the Russians from the north and east, were soon to contract the frontiers of Lithuania.

"All this, however, could have no effect upon the union of the two nations, which daily acquired new strength; for, subsequently to the first union of 1386, a Diet, in 1413, held in the bourg of Horoldo, having declared the Lithuanians to be on an equal footing with the Poles in regard to taxes and laws, many Lithuanian families allied themselves with Polish families; in fine, the arms of the two nations were united. It was then determined that the Lithuanians should receive their grand duke from the hands of the King of Poland, and that, when the latter should die without children or descendants worthy to succeed him, the Poles should elect their new king conjointly with the Lithuanians. The alliance concluded in 1413, was renewed in 1499; and it was added, explicitly, that the Lithuanians should not elect their grand duke without the concurrence of the Poles, nor the Poles their king, without that of the Lithuanians. In 1561, the knights militant submitted themselves, and the part of Livonia which, remained with them, to the domination of the King of Poland, as Grand Duke of Lithuania; the new Duke of Courland became also his feudatory, v In fine, in 1569, under Sigismond-Augustus, the Poles and Lithuanians held a Diet at Lublin, in which the grand duchy was limited to the Kingdom of Poland, so that they thereafter formed but one body, subject to one prince, who was conjointly elected by the two nations, under the double title of king of Poland and Grand Duke of Lithuania. It was agreed, also, that the Diet should be always held at Warsaw, that the two people should have the same senate, the same chamber of deputies; that their coins should be of the same designation that, in fine, their alliances, their auxiliary troops, and everything, should be in common. The campaigns of Moscow under Sigismond III., Vladislas IV., and Etienne Batory, amply proved that the Lithuanians were worthy of calling the Poles brethren; for they were found ready for every sacrifice, when the general good of the country was in question, by the laws of 1673, 1677, and 1685, it was ruled that each third Diet should be held in Lithuania at Grodno; the Diets of convocation, and of election and coronation were excepted, however, from this rule. In 1697, the Polish and Lithuanian laws received an equal force and authority.

"At the epoch of the regeneration of Poland, the Lithuanians gave the most convincing proofs of their devotedness to the Polish cause, in the last years of the existence of Poland. In effect, when they became satisfied that, for the common interest, and to give more consistency to the new form of government which it was proposed to establish, at the Diet of 1788, it was necessary to strengthen still more the relations between Lithuania and the crown; that is to say, between Little and Great Poland, so as to form out of the three provinces a single powerful state, and to obliterate totally all the distinctions which had before existed between the Poles and the Lithuanians, they made a voluntary sacrifice of the privileges which they had held with great pertinacity, and renounced, without hesitation, that of having a separate army and treasury, consenting to unite themselves under a single administration with the two other provinces.

"The whole world was witness to the heroism which the Lithuanians displayed in the glorious confederation of Bar, from 1768 to 1772; in the campaigns of 1792 and 1794, against foreign rapacity, when Kosciuszko, a Lithuanian by birth; covered with im-perishable laurels the chains of Poland. The Lithuanians fell, but they fell with the whole of Poland, and were buried in the common ruin. How nobly have not the Lithuanians been seen to figure among the brave Polish patriots, who sought in France, in Italy, and in Turkey, some chances of restoration for a country which had been the victim of foreign ambition! And how many of them have not been found under the banners of Dombrowski, in Italy, and under those of Kniaziewiez, upon the Danube? Have we not seen, in the years 1806 and 1809, twelve thousand Lithuanians, united with their brethren, the Volhynians, the Podolians, and the Ukranians, hastening to range themselves under the banners of the army of the Grand Duchy of Warsaw? In 1812, their joy was extreme, when they thought that their political existence was, at last, about to be renewed. Then was seen the cavalier of Lithuania, united with the white eagle, decorating the flags planted on the walls of Wilna. But the disastrous retreat of the French army struck a mortal blow to the destinies of those countries. The' Kingdom of Poland was proclaimed in 1815; the Diets of Warsaw, of 1818, 1820, and 1825, preserved silence respecting the lot of the Grand Duchy of Lithuania. A look full of hope from all Lithuania was turned once more towards Warsaw, upon the 94th of May, 1829, the day of coronation of Nicholas the 1st, but the reunion of Lithuania was not even made a question of."

[*Tableau de la Pologne, ancienne et moderne, par Malte Brum, edition refondue et augmentée par Leonard Chodsko Paris*, 1851. pp. 988—995. Tom. I.]

No. II.

ADDRESS OF THE NATIONAL GOVERNMENT OF POLAND TO THE INHABITANTS OF LITHUANIA, VOLHYN1A, PODOLIA, AND UKRAINE.[87]

Brethren, and Fellow Citizens

The National Government of regenerated Poland, happy on being able at last to address you in the name of the bond of brotherhood and liberty, is anxious to lay before you the present state of our country, and to show you our wants, our dangers, and our hopes.

The wall which separated us is broken down—your wishes and ours realized. The Polish eagle flies over our territory. United as we are, hand and heart, we will henceforth proceed in concert to accomplish the difficult, perilous, but just and sacred work—the restoration of our country.

The Manifesto of the Diet, in explaining the cause of our rising, gave an account of our sentiments as well as yours. Scarcely had we risen in arms, provided with but few means, and uncertain what course to pursue, before we showed to the world and to the Emperor Nicholas- that the same spirit animated us, and that we were desirous to become, as we had formerly been, but one and the same nation. The Emperor Nicholas did not wish to conse-crate the tomb of his brother by a monument, which, during the life time of Alexander, would have sealed the glory of his reign.

He did not wish to regard us as Poles, bowed down with injuries—as citizens of a free and independent country — and would treat with us only as slaves who had rebelled against Russia. We have arrested—we have driven back the threatening phalanxes of his different corps. Of the forces of which our army was composed, some fought here against the main body of the enemy; others penetrated into your provinces to call forth our brethren to range themselves under the national banner. You did not wait for this appeal.

At the very commencement of the insurrection, many of your citizens explained their sentiments and their wishes in the National Assembly, and some raised regiments; dignified by the names of your provinces; in fine, whole districts of Lithuania and Volhynia rose *en masse*.

The partition of Poland has been denominated a crime by the unanimous voice of Europe, and who at this day will revoke such a decision? Who will venture to come forward as the champion against it? Undoubtedly none! And we have the well-grounded hope that Europe will hasten to recognize our independence, as soon as we have proved by our courage, our perseverance, our union, our moderate and noble conduct, that we deserve to be a free nation. This revolution is only a consequence of our oppression and our misfortunes. It was the wish of our hearts, and arises from the nature of our history, which displays our determination from the very beginning, and proves that our rising was not of foreign prompting. It is not civil war—it is not tainted with the blood of our brethren—we have not overturned social institutions in order to raise up new ones at hazard —it is a war of independence, the most just of wars. This is the character of our revolution, which is at once mild, but firm—which with one arm conquers the enemy, and with the other raises and ennobles the needy peasant.

We admire England and France - we wish to be, like them, a civilized nation, but without ceasing to be Poles! Nations cannot and ought not to change the elements of their existence. Each has its climate, industry, religion, manners, character, education, and history. From these different elements spring the feelings or passions which display themselves in revolutions, and the circumstances proper to be adopted in their future conduct.

Individuality strongly expressed, forms the power of a people. We have preserved ours in the midst of slavery. Love of country, prepared to make every sacrifice—courage, piety, noble-mindedness, and gentleness, formed the character of our forefathers. These qualities also are ours.

The patriots of Warsaw triumphed without chiefs and without law; yet with what crime can they be charged? An army of 80,000 men, and, in short, the whole kingdom, rose as if by enchantment; and how did they conduct themselves towards the Grand Duke Constantine? That prince, who for fifteen years had shown himself destitute of regard or pity for our feelings and liberties, was in our power; but he knew the nation, and, just to it for once only, he entrusted his person and his army to our honor! At the moment of alarm, we did not listen to the voice of public vengeance, but respected the Prince and his troops, without taking advantage of our superiority. Our battalions, which had awaited with a firm determination all the forces of Russia, allowed to pass through their ranks the fallen enemy, whose safety was guaranteed by the national honor.

The generosity of the nation has been proved by many isolated facts, and Europe admires our moderation as much as our valor. Brethren, fellow-citizens, equal admiration still awaits us. Without delay, then, come forward with the whole of your force simultaneously, and act as one man in peace and in war; it is the people who are the source of all power. To the people, then, direct your views and your affections. Children, worthy of your fathers, you will act like them; you will break the odious bonds, and you will cement a holy alliance by reciprocal benefits and by gratitude. In other countries it is by force, and force alone, that the people recover their liberties—here those liberties are received as the gift of their brethren. A generous, just, and necessary deed will become the act only of your own choice, and you will proclaim to the people their independence, and the return of the Polish eagles to their native soil. Our fields will lose nothing in cultivation and value when they are tilled by the industry of brave men. You will be ennobled in the eyes of civilized Europe, and your country will gain millions of fellow-citizens, who, like our brave peasants, will fly to the defense of their liberty, and drive back a power whose character is that only of slavery. Do not forget, brethren and fellow citizens, that the Greek religion is professed by a great part of the people. Toleration is one of the qualities of civilization. The clergy, the churches, and religion, shall be placed under the protection of the government, and will lend you their assistance in carrying this measure of justice into effect.

[The address goes onto enlarge upon the respect paid by Polish noblemen to religious rites and feelings, and calls on the people on this occasion to follow their example; also to send deputies from the different provinces to the National Congress. It then goes onto describe the vast power of Russia, and the difficulties to be encountered, much in the same manner as the proclamation of Skrzynecki, and concludes thus:

God hath already wrought prodigies for us. God, and, not the Emperor of Russia, will be our judge! He will decide.

He will decide who hath committed perjury, who has been the victim of oppression, and who ought to obtain the victory. We have already fought with success in the name of the God of our fathers; and we will fight till at length we have accomplished the ends of justice. All the nations of Europe possessed of the feelings of humanity tremble for our fate, and exult with joy at our successes. They only wait your general rising to hail you as members of the free and independent nations of Europe.

Brethren and fellow-citizens! when we shall have finished this terrible and unequal contest, we will invite the Powers of Europe to form themselves into a tribunal of justice; we will appear before them covered with our blood, lay open the book of our annals, unroll the chart of Europe, and say, "Behold our cause and yours! The injustice done to Poland is known to you: you behold her despair; for her courage and generosity appears to her enemies!"

Brethren! let us hope in God. He will inspire the breast of our judges, who, obeying the dictates of eternal justice, will say, "Long live Poland! free and independent!"

The President of the National Government,

(Signed) The PRINCE CZATORYSKI

Warsaw, May l3, 1831.

NOTES

87. Not having a copy of this address in the original, we make use of a rather unsatisfactory translation, which we find in the journals of the day.

No. III.

There is a rich consolation for the sufferings of a just cause, in the demonstrations of sympathy which my countrymen have uniformly met with on the part of the people among whom they have been thrown in their exile. I cannot refuse myself the satisfaction of inserting here one among the many notices which have appeared in the journals of the day, exhibiting the warm interest with which they have been regarded by the people of France.

[From the *N. Y. Courier* of the United States, 7th April.]

"The *Journal of Saône and Loire* publishes full details of the arrival of the Poles at Maçon. The reception given to the third detachment, which has passed through that city, was even still more marked, affectionate, and touching than that of the preceding. All the inhabitants of the country quitted their labors, to go out to meet the exiles. The National Guard and the troops of the line paid them the honors of the place. Salvoes of artillery announced their arrival and their departure. It was a triumphal march. The director of the packet boats gratuitously transported the Poles from Chalôns to Lyons. At Macon, just as the packet bout pushed off, a Polish captain threw his sword upon the bank, exclaiming, "Brave Maçonnois, I give you the dearest possession I have in the world; preserve it as a token of our gratitude." The sword was carried in triumph to the *Hotel de Viile*, of Maçon, where it was deposited, and a subscription was opened to make a present to the brave stranger of a sword of honor.

"The arrival of this column at Lyons was celebrated with great solemnity. An idea of it may be formed from the recital which is given in the *Precurseur de Lyon*.

"Since the triumphal passage of the Veteran of Liberty, Lyons has seen nothing so magnificent as the great movement of which the arrival of the Poles was the signal. From eighty to a hundred thousand souls marched before the column, upon the road of Bresse, and from far beyond the suburbs. Having reached the entrance of the city, escorted by the elite of its inhabitants, the Poles found themselves in the midst of an immense crowd, who made the air ring with their cries of enthusiasm and sympathy. From thence to the Place de Terreaux, the column experienced extreme difficulty in advancing through the throngs of the delirious multitude. Words would fail to give the brilliant colors of this truly sublime picture.

"Maledictions against the infamous policy of the Cabinets, mingled with the cries of 'Vive la Pologne!' The accents of generous indignation were united with those of a deep and heart-felt pity for those remnants of an exiled people.

"A banquet was prepared at the Brotteaux. One of the committee ascended a carriage to conduct thither that young heroine [the Countess Plater], we presume, who follows to a land of exile her noble companions in arms, as she had followed them upon the field of battle. The people had scarcely recognized her, when they precipitated themselves towards her, unharnessed the horses, and dragged the carriage in triumph to the place of the assemblage.

"The banquet was attended by more than 500 persons, and the committee had been forced to refuse a great number of subscribers, on account of the smallness of the accommodations.

"The first toast, given by the President, M. Galibert, was, 'To immortal Poland!' This toast, enlarged upon with an eloquence full of warmth and pathos, excited an universal enthusiasm. The French embraced their noble guests, and it was a touching spectacle—this assembly, electrified by the purest emotions of the soul, and in which tears flowed from every eye.

"It was affecting to see the physiognomies of the brave Poles during this solemnity. Many of them understood the French language, and tears flowed down their cheeks at each of the allusions which the orators made to their absent country, their crushed revolution. The young heroine, seated by the side of the President, and who excited a profound and general interest, could hardly suppress the sobs which oppressed her.

"The most perfect order reigned through the whole fete. Not a gendarme was present, and no excess of the slightest kind occurred. This countless multitude was calm, notwithstanding the violence of its emotions. The people proved how little their masters understand them."

No. IV.

The following extract from the *London Courier* of April 9th, 1832, in reference to the recent Imperial Manifesto which converts Poland into a province of Russia, may serve to confirm the remarks which we have made in the text, on the system of deception practiced by the Emperor Nicholas towards the cabinets both of England and France, on the subject of Poland.

"We perceive that the Manifesto of the Emperor of Russia, relative to Poland, which we gave on Saturday, has excited general indignation in France, as well as in this country. Perhaps, as the Poles are not of a character to be awed into submission by the power of their oppressors, whilst the slightest chance of emancipation is open to them, it is better for the cause of humanity that they should be tied hand and foot in the bonds of slavery, than that any opportunity should be afforded them of again saturating the soil of Poland with the blood of its best and bravest patriots. If life with disgrace be better than death without dishonor, the destruction of the nationality of Poland may not be so great an evil as the world at large imagine. If the utter impossibility of successful revolt be clearly shown, the Poles may at length wear their fetters without resorting to vain attempts to shake them off; and the monarch who has enslaved them, may gradually witness the extinction of mind, in proportion as he coerces and binds the body. But what a sad disgrace it is upon the government and people of this country to have neglected, in proper season, the means of securing to the brave and unfortunate people of Poland a nationality which would have given to them the form and substance of liberty, without involving the necessity of a rupture with the power which has conquered them. Is it not true, that, at a time when the warm-hearted and generous portion of the people of this country were calling upon the Government to exercise the influence and power of the British Crown on behalf of the Poles, the reply was, "We cannot go to war with the Emperor of Russia for foreign interests—we cannot insist upon his evacuating Poland, and leaving the country in a state of complete independence; but we will use our good offices towards obtaining favorable terms for the insurgents; and we have already the satisfaction of knowing that the Emperor Nicholas has declared that the nationality of Poland shall in no case be forfeited, and that in all other respects the world shall be astonished at the extent of his generosity towards the vanquished."

"Is there a member of the Government, or any other person, who will tell us that such language as this was not made publicly and privately, in Parliament and out of Parliament, in the newspapers and out of the newspapers, and that the sole excuse for non-intervention was not the real or pretended belief that the nationality of Poland would be respected, and the conduct of the Emperor Nicholas be full of generosity and magnanimity? Gracious God! And are we come to such a pass that the sovereign of a semi-barbarous country can laugh at the honor and dignity of the British name? Is all the respect that he can show to the good offices of the British Government, in behalf of a great-minded people, to be found in empty professions and unmeaning declarations; and are we to put up tamely with one of the greatest insults that ever was inflicted upon the Government of the country? Was it for this that we conciliated the Autocrat of the North on the Belgian question? And is all the return of our concessions a bold and naked defiance of our power, and a determination to convince the world that the days of British influence are passed forever? Perhaps we shall be told, even now, of the magnanimous intentions of the Emperor of Russia; but the cheat is too stale. Everybody knows not only that we have truckled to Russia in vain, but that to deception she has added insult, and that at this moment there is a Russian Ambassador in town, with instructions to cajole the Government on the Belgian question, and to withhold the ratification of the treaty until after the passing or rejecting of the Reform Bill, when the Emperor may be enabled by a change of government to dispense with it altogether. But we are tired of the subject; the more we look at it, the more we feel disgraced. We blame not this or that minister; for the intentions of the government towards Poland, we firmly believe, were kind in the extreme; but we blush for the country at large in having purchased the chance of peace at the sacrifice of honor."

No. V.

The following is the Imperial Manifesto referred to in the preceding article, as it appears in the *Berlin State Gazette*, under the head of Warsaw, March 25th, 1832:

"By the grace of God, Nicholas I, Emperor of Russia, King of Poland, etc. When, by Our Manifesto of Jan. 2, last year, We announced to Our faithful subjects the march of Our troops into the Kingdom of Poland, which was momentarily snatched from the lawful authority, We at the same time informed them of Our intention to the future fate of this country on a durable basis, muted to its wants, and calculated to promote the welfare of Our whole empire. Now that an end has been put by force of arms to the rebellion in Poland, and that the nation, led away by agitators, has returned to its duty, and is restored to tranquillity, We deem it right to carry into execution Our plan with regard to the introduction of the new order of things, whereby the tranquility and onion of the two nations, which Providence has entrusted to Our care, may be forever guarded against new attempts. Poland, conquered in the year 1815 by the victorious arms of Russia, obtained by the magnanimity of Our illustrious predecessor, the Emperor Alexander, not only its national existence, but also special laws sanctioned by a Constitutional Charter. These favors, however, would not satisfy the eternal enemies of order and lawful power. Obsti-nately persevering in their culpable projects, they ceased not one moment to dream of a separation between the two nations subject to Our scepter, and in their presumption, they dared to abase the favors of the restorer of their country, by employing for the destruction of his noble, work the very laws and liberties which his mighty arm had generously granted them. Bloodshed was the consequence of this crime. The tranquility and happiness which the Kingdom of Poland had enjoyed to a degree till then unknown, vanished in the midst of civil war and a general devastation. AM these evils are how passed. The Kingdom of Poland, again subject to Our scepter, will regain tranquility, and again flourish in the bosom of peace, restored to it under the auspices of a vigilant government. Hence, We consider it one of Our most sacred duties to watch with paternal care over the welfare of Our faithful subjects, and to use every means in Our power to prevent the recurrence of similar catastrophes, by taking from the ill-disposed the power of disturbing public tranquility. As it is, moreover, Our wish to secure to the inhabitants of Poland the continuance of all the essential requisites for the happiness of individuals, and of the country in general, namely, security of persons and property, liberty of conscience, and all the laws, and privileges of towns and communes, so that the Kingdom of Poland, with a separate administration adapted to its wants, may not cease to form an integral part of Our empire, and that the inhabitants of this country may henceforward constitute a nation united with the Russians by sympathy and fraternal sentiments, We have, according to these principles, ordained and resolved this day, by a new organic statute, to introduce a new form and order in the administration of Our Kingdom of Poland.

" St. Petersburg, February 26,1832.

"NICHOLAS.

" The Secretary of State, COUNT STEPHEN GRABOWSJCI."

After this Manifesto, the organic statutes of Poland are given, the principal of which are as follows:

"By the grace of God, we, Nicholas I., Emperor and Autocrat of all the Russias, King of Poland, &c. &c.

"In Our constant solicitude for the happiness of the nations which Providence has confided to Our government, We are occupied in fixing the basis for the future organization of the Kingdom of Poland, having regard to the true interests and positions of the country, and to the local wants and manners of the inhabitants,

GENERAL DISPOSITIONS

"Art. 1. The Kingdom of Poland is forever to be reunited to the Russian Empire, and form an inseparable part of that empire. h ahsil have a particular administration conformably to its local necessities, as well as a civil and military code. The statutes and the laws of cities and towns remain in full vigor.

"Art 2. The Crown of the Kingdom of Poland is hereditary in Our person and in Our heirs and successors, agreeably to the order of succession to the throne prescribed by all the Russias.

"Art. 3. The Coronation of the Emperors of all the Russias and Kings of Poland shall be one and the same ceremonial, which shall take place at Moscow, in the presence of a deputation from the Kingdom of Poland, which shall assist at that solemnity with the deputies from the other parts of the Empire.

"Art. 4. In the possible event of a regency in Russia, the power of the regent or regentess of the Empire will extend over the Kingdom of Poland.

"Art. 5. The freedom of worship is guarantied; everyone is at liberty to exercise his religion openly, under the protection of Government; and the difference of Christian faiths shall never prove a pretext for the violation of the rights and privileges which are allowed to all the inhabitants. The Roman Catholic religion, being that of the majority of Our Polish subjects, shall be the object of especial protection of the Government.

"Art. 6. The funds which the Roman Catholic clergy possess, and those of the Greek church united, shall be considered as the common and inviolable property of the hierarchy of each of those creeds.

"Art. 7. The protection of the laws is assured to all the inhabitants without distinction of rank or class. Each shall be empowered to assume dignities or to exercise public functions, according to his personal merits or talents.

"Art. 8. Individual liberty is guarantied and protected by the existing laws. No one shall be deprived of his liberty, or called to justice, if he be not a transgressor of the I a win all the forms prescribed. Everyone detained shall be apprised of the motive of arrest.

"Art. 9. Each person arrested must submit to a delay of three days to be heard and judged of, according to the forms of law, before competent tribunals: if he be found innocent, he will instantly obtain his liberty. He will be equally restored to liberty who shall furnish a sufficient surety.

"Art 10. The form of judicial inquests directed against the superior functionaries of the kingdom, and against persons accused of high treason, shall be determined by a particular law, the foundation of which shall be accordant with the other laws of Our empire.

"Art. 11. The right of property of individuals, and of corporations, is declared sacred and inviolable, inasmuch as it wiH be conformable to the existing Jaws. All the subjects of the Kingdom of Poland are perfectly free to quit the country, and to carry away their goods, provided they conform to the regulations published to that effect.

"Art. 12. The penalty of confiscation shall not be enforced but against state crimes of the first class, as may be hereafter determined by particular laws.

"Art. 13. Publication of sentiments, by means of the press, shall be subjected to restrictions which will protect religion, the inviolability of superior authority, the interests of morals, and personal considerations. Particular regulations, to this effect, will be published according to the principles which serve as a basis to this object in the other parts of Our empire.

"Art. 14. The Kingdom of Poland shall proportionally contribute to the general expenditure and to the wants of the Empire. The proportion of taxes will be stated hereafter.

"Art. 15. All contributions and all taxes which existed in November, 1880, shall be levied after the manner formerly settled till the new fixing of taxes.

"Art. 16. The treasury of the Kingdom of Poland, and all the other branches of the administration, shall be separated from the administration of the other parts of the kingdom.

"Art. 17. The public debt of Poland, acknowledged by us, shall be guarantied as formerly, by the government, and indemnified by the receipts of the kingdom.

"Art. 18. The bank of the Kingdom of Poland, and the laws respecting credit, shall continue under the protection of Government.

"Art. 19. The mode of commercial transactions between the Russian Empire and the Kingdom of Poland shall be regulated according to the respective interests of the two countries.

"Art. 20. Our army in the Empire and in the kingdom, shall compose one in common, without distinction of Russian or Polish troops. We shall reserve to Ourselves a future decision of this, by an especial law, by what arrangement, and upon what basis, the Kingdom of Poland shall participate with Our army. The number of troops which shall serve as the military defense of the kingdom will be also ultimately determined upon by a law.

"Art 21. Those of Our subjects of the Empire of Russia, who are established in the Kingdom of Poland, who possess or shall possess, real property in that country, shall enjoy all the rights of natives. It shall be the same with those of Our subjects of the Kingdom of Poland, who shall establish themselves, and shall possess property, in the other provinces of the Empire. We reserve to Ourselves to grant hereafter letters of naturalization to other persons, as well to strangers as to Russians, who are not yet es-tablished there. Those of Our subjects of the Russian Empire who may reside for a certain time in Poland, and those of Our subjects of the Kingdom of Poland who may sojourn in the other parts of the Empire, are subject to the laws of the country where they reside.

"Art. 22. The superior administration of the Kingdom of Poland is confided to a council of administration, which shall govern the kingdom in Our name, under the presidency of the governor of the kingdom.

"Art. 23. The council of administration is composed of the governor of the kingdom, of superior directors, who superintend the commissions, and among whom are divided the interests of the administration, of comptroller, presiding over the Supreme Chamber of Finance, and of other members, whom We shall appoint by special orders."

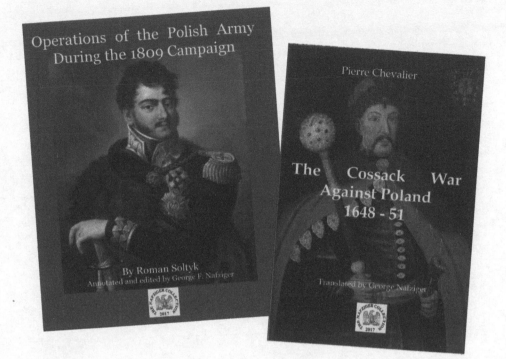

For more information please feel free to contact us at:

The Nafziger Collection, Inc.
PO Box 1522
West Chester, OH 45069-1522
www.nafzigercollection.com

Winged Hussar Publishing, LLC
1525 Hulse Road, Unit 1
Point Pleasant, NJ 08742
wingedhussarpublishing.com
732-714-7000